JACOB GOLOMB

NIETZSCHE'S ENTICING PSYCHOLOGY OF POWER

NIETZSCHE'S ENTICING PSYCHOLOGY OF POWER

by

JACOB GOLOMB

IOWA STATE UNIVERSITY PRESS, AMES
THE MAGNES PRESS, THE HEBREW UNIVERSITY, JERUSALEM

Jacob Golomb is a professor in the Department of Philosophy at The Hebrew University, Jerusalem.

© The Magnes Press, The Hebrew University, Jerusalem 1987

Published in the United States and Canada
by Iowa State University Press, Ames, Iowa 50010

Printed in Israel

First Hebrew edition, 1987
First revised English edition, 1989

Library of Congress Cataloging-in-Publication Data
Golomb, Jacob, 1947-
   Nietzsche's enticing psychology of power.
   Bibliography: p. 333-343
   Includes index.
   1. Psychology.   2. Nietzsche, Friedrich Wilhelm, 1844-1900.
3. Power (Philosophy)   4. Psychoanalysis and Philosophy.   5. Freud,
Sigmund, 1856-1939.   I. Title.
BF41.G65   1989   150.19   87-35363
ISBN 0-8138-1122-8

For Barbara, my mother
and in memory of my
father, Elijah

ACKNOWLEDGMENTS

This book first appeared in 1987 in Hebrew at The Magnes press, Jerusalem.

Professor Alan Montefiore, of Oxford, convinced me that the revised English version needed editing and referred me to Alison E. Denham of Balliol College, who made a Herculean effort to turn it into readable English.

The S.H. Bergman Center for Philosophical Studies at the Hebrew University of Jerusalem assisted me with a grant to carry out this project.

Professor Yirmiyahu Yovel supervised my dissertation at the Hebrew University and encouraged me to reshape it into book form.

Professor Reuven Yaron, the Academic Director of The Magnes Press, contributed valuable time to save me from some mistakes.

I wish to express my gratitude to those, and many others, who have helped along the way.

Jacob Golomb
Jerusalem 1988

CONTENTS

PART TWO:

PSYCHOLOGY OF POWER

Key to Abbreviations

A note on Nietzsche's and Freud's texts may be found in the Bibliography.

The abbreviated titles of Nietzsche's works are according to those established by the editors of *Nietzsche-Studien* 3 (1974): 213–215, and by the editors of *Nietzsche Werke: Kritische Gesamtausgabe*, ed. Giorgio Colli and Mazzino Montinari, 30 vols. (Berlin, de Gruyter, 1967–1978).

GT — Die Geburt der Tragödie

UB — Unzeitgemässe Betrachtungen

DS — D. Strauss, der Bekenner und Schriftsteller

GD — Götzen-Dämmerung

HL — Vom Nutzen und Nachteil der Historie für das Leben

SaE— Schopenhauer als Erzieher

WB — R. Wagner in Bayreuth

MA — Menschliches, Allzumenschliches (I und II)

M — Morgenröte

FW — Die fröhliche Wissenschaft

Z — Also sprach Zarathustra

JGB — Jenseits von Gut und Böse

GM — Zur Genealogie der Moral

EH — Ecce Homo

AC — Der Antichrist

NW — Nietzsche contra Wagner

WM — Die Nachlass-Kompilation, "Der Wille Macht"

BA — Über die Zukunft Unserer Bildungsanstalten

Thus, for example: GM V-2; KSA 5: 248 refers to *Genealogy of Morals, Vorrede* (Preface), section 2; found also in *Kritische Studienausgabe*, Vol. 5, p. 248.

PREFACE

> That a psychologist without equal speaks from my writings,
> is perhaps the first insight reached by a good reader — a
> reader as I deserve him...[1]

Nietzsche referred to himself as the first great and *"new
psychologist"* of the West.[2] It is not surprising, then, that he
complained in 1888 that no one had so far characterized him "als
Psychologe".[3]

Almost one hundred years have passed since, and yet (as
Kaufmann rightly points out[4]) most philosophers and Nietzsche
interpreters have disregarded his wish to be recognized as a
psychologist, and have failed to come to grips with the essential
psychological aspects of his thought.[5] This conspicuous lacuna

1. EH III 5; KSA 6: 305.
2. JGB 12; KSA 5: 27. Cf. also: GT-V 2; MA I-V8; FW-V2; JGB 45; GM I-1; GM
   II-11; GM III-9, 19, and 20; GD-V; GD I-35; GD X-3 and 4; AC 24, 28 and 29;
   NW-V; EH-V3; EH I-8; and: "Who among philosophers was a *psychologist* at
   all before me, and not rather the opposite ...? There was no psychology at
   all before me. To be the first here may be a curse; it is at any rate a destiny ..."
   (EH IV-6; KSA 6: 371). See also a letter where Nietzsche describes himself
   proudly : *"Ich bin ein Psychologe"*. (To August Strindberg, 7th December
   1888 — FNW, IV, p. 930.)
3. Letter to Carl Fuchs, 29th July 1888 — FNW IV, p. 900.
4. Walter Kaufmann, "Nietzsche als der Erste Grosse Psychologe",
   Nietzsche-Studien 7 (1978): 261–275.
5. Kaufmann, in his otherwise comprehensive work *Nietzsche: Philosopher,
   Psychologist, Antichrist* (Princeton, 1968), suggests rightly that the
   psychological aspect of Nietzsche's thought is no less significant than the
   philosophical and atheistic. However his book does not adequately

in scholarship hinders any comprehensive understanding of his philosophy and its primary aims. The principal assumption underlying the present study is that one of the best ways to explore Nietzsche's aphoristic labyrinth is to take his psychological perspective as a guide. Psychology thus becomes the key to Nietzsche's philosophy, leading to a reconstitution of his positive theses. In particular, it can illuminate his thesis of the morality of Power, a thesis which has been largely ignored by many commentators who have tended to over-emphasize Nietzsche's "nihilistic" overtones. The interpretive framework proposed here is not, however, a reductive framework; I do not intend to reduce Nietzsche's philosophy to a psychological theory. Moreover, I do not claim an exclusive priority for the perspective here adopted, important though it may be. To be faithful to Nietzsche one must regard *all* perspectives as legitimate as long as they abjure any such claims.

Many Nietzsche scholars have complained that he did not develop an explicit methodology and theory of knowledge. Yet one should not infer from the absence of explicit method that Nietzsche has no method at all. In the First Part of this study I shall suggest that Nietzsche repeatedly uses a specific method of psychologizing, which I shall term *psychologization*. This method exposes and "puts on ice" values, ideals and current ideologies. This Nietzschean tactic of "freezing" has been largely overlooked despite its significance and central position in his philosophy. The ultimate objective and praxis of Nietzsche's method of psychologization is not the refutation of man's

---

elucidate Nietzsche's positive psychology. The reader asks himself, therefore, why Kaufmann found it necessary to call Nietzsche a "psychologist", when apart from several insights and lengthy aphorisms (without any commentary — e.g. pp. 181–182) little is offered to justify the word in the title. The more so since Nietzsche's "psychological inquiries" are presented by Kaufmann as side effects and temporary digressions (p. 122) from the main issues of values and happiness.

intellectual constructions (such as metaphysics), but the freezing and transforming of his emotional constitution.

However, when we try to explicate the nature and content of his freezing psychologization it will become evident (in the Second Part) that Nietzsche's "unmasking psychology" itself unmasks a psychology: through its application to various cultural objects such as art, science, religion, philosophy and morality the psychologistic method is developed into a positive psychology of power manifesting some of the most original and far-reaching elements in his thought.

One of the central purposes of this exposition and reconstruction is to elucidate and justify Nietzsche's rather enigmatic claim that "all psychology so far has ... not dared to descend into the depths", and that in his thought the *new* psychology "is now again the path to the fundamental problems"[6] — these being the problems of morality. The present interpretation thus appeals to Nietzsche's own approach to any "great philosophy", proposing that "the moral (or immoral) intentions constituted the real germ of life from which the whole plant had grown".[7]

The "real germ" of Nietzsche's philosophy is — as the Third Part will argue — the morality of positive power.[8] In attempting to construct this morality, Nietzsche needed a special type of psychology (quite unlike contemporary empirical psychology) which would *entice* his readers into discovering in themselves and for themselves the genuine roots of their creative powers. This part of the study offers a detailed examination of certain of Nietzsche's key concepts, locating them within the development of his psychology: positive enticement (*Versuchung*) as against

6. JGB 23; KSA 5: 39.
7. JGB 6: KSA 5: 19–20.
8. Thus I wholeheartedly agree with Bernard Williams' contention that "Nietzsche was the greatest moral philosopher of the past century", "Nietzsche's Centaur", *London Review of Books* (Vol. 3, 1981), p. 17.

negative seduction (*Verführung*) and the concept of mental power (*Macht*) as against physical force (*Kraft*). These concepts have been almost entirely ignored by Nietzsche's commentators.

The study is thus divided into three parts: *Part One* describes Nietzschean psychologization as a method affecting people's attitudes towards their values and beliefs. In the first three chapters we shall see how Nietzsche applies this method in order to "freeze" our beliefs in pseudo-ideals, especially in Chauvinist Nationalism, Historicism, Scientism, and Transcendentalism. It will be shown that Nietzsche's psychologization functions in two main ways: first, as a way of regarding and analyzing psychological issues, and second, as a tactic of psychological transformation. I shall attempt to isolate the initial, implicit transition from the psychologizing method towards a positive and comprehensive psychological doctrine.

Part Two examines this transition in text and context, leading from the psychologization of the "Human-All-Too-Human" to a positive psychology of power. I shall analyze the psychological meanings of the principle of power (*Macht*), and attempt to show how it derives from Nietzsche's generalization of findings which resulted from the application of his psychologizing method. We will thus see how his method and his positive psychology sustain each other and why both are vital to the final development of his moral philosophy.

Part Three deals with Nietzsche's philosophy and morality of power, elucidating the negative and positive cultural manifestations of power — its two diametrically opposed vectors and patterns. The function of Nietzsche's psychology is not only to make perspicuous the reasons (as opposed to justifications) for adopting his morality of positive power: its other important role is as an enticing, persuasive tool designed to help us recognize our power and use it creatively in authentic patterns of life — which I shall refer to as *the pathos of positive power*. This (mainly philosophical) section examines both (i) how "the doctrine of the development of the will to power"[9] (which Nietzsche identifies with psychology) is established, and (ii) how the concept of *Macht* becomes the central, systematizing, axis of Nietzsche's entire thought. Nietzsche claims *Macht* is the "common root", "the fundamental will of knowledge" out of which grew his whole philosophical "tree". His moral theory of power may thus be understood as the centerpoint around which his earlier and later views "became ... more and more firmly attached to one another, ... entwined and interlaced with one another".[10]

A psychological interpretation of Nietzsche's thought may prove particularly fruitful by inviting commentary which makes more coherent many of his thousands of seemingly disparate aphorisms and fragments, and providing them with a developmental context. The positive elements of his moral philosophy may be explicated in terms of certain psychological concepts (e.g., sublimation, repression, the unconscious and the super-ego). These concepts clearly anticipate the psychoanalytic "discoveries" of Freud, who was deeply impressed by Nietzsche's psychological teaching.

A secondary aim of the present study is to fill a significant lacuna in the history of ideas in respect of the relation between Freud and Nietzsche.[11] I will synchronically analyze various parallels

---

9. JGB 23; KSA 5: 38.
10. GM V-2; KSA 5: 248.
11. This gap still exists notwithstanding the impressively long list of comparative studies dedicated to both thinkers. Cf. for example: Mitchell Ginsberg, "Nietzschean Psychiatry", in *Nietzsche*, ed. Robert, C. Solomon (New York, 1973), pp. 293–315; Richard, Waugman, "The Intellectual Relationship between Nietzsche and Freud", *Psychiatry* 36 (1973): 458–467; R. Bilz, "Der Verdrängungsschutz — Eine Untersuchung über das Paradigma der Verdrängung bei Nietzsche und bei Freud", *Der Nervenarzt*

PREFACE

between their thought, and this comparison will shed new light on Nietzsche's philosophy. The resemblance between them is based not only on features internal to Freud's writings, but also on the Nietzschean views that often stimulated it.[12] An analysis of these views with reference to Freud provides a new prism

29 (1958): 145–148; Rudolf J. Brandt, "Freud and Nietzsche: A Comparison", *Revue de l'Université d'Ottawa* 25 (1955): 225–234; Christo Dimitrov and Assen Jablenski, "Nietzsche und Freud", *Zeitschrift für Psychosomatische Medizin und Psychoanalyse* 13 (1967): 282–298; Bruce Mazlish, "Freud and Nietzsche", *The Psychoanalyic Review* 55 (1968): 360–375; Friedrich Tramer, "Friedrich Nietzsche und Sigmund Freud", *Jahrbuch für Psychologie, Psychotherapie und Anthropologie* 7 (1960): 325–350; Richard Schmitt, "Nietzsche's Psychological Theory", *Journal of Existential Psychiatry* 2 (1961): 71–92; Edouard Gaède, "Nietzsche précurseur de Freud?", in *Nietzsche Aujourd'hui* (Paris, 1973), Vol. 2, pp. 87–118; Jean Granier, "Le statut de la philosophie selon Nietzsche et Freud", *Revue de Métaphysique et de Morale* 86 (1981): 88–102; and last but not least the Lacan-oriented comparison by Paul-Laurent Assoun, *Freud et Nietzsche* (Paris, 1980). The main weakness of most of these comparisons between Nietzsche and Freud lies in their tendency to excerpt various ideas out of the wider philosophical context of Nietzsche's general thought, and to compare them, in their "nakedness", to parallel Freudian concepts — notwithstanding the fact that Nietzsche's ideas are interrelated and intelligible only when set against his wider philosophy.

12.   In this context it is crucial to note that Freud has already begun to quote from Nietzsche's writings as early as 1875. In a letter to his friend Silberstein (Vienna, 13th March 1875) Freud quotes from Nietzsche's essay on David Strauss as follows: *"So Leben wir, so wandeln wir beglückt"*.

Apart from the fact that Nietzsche actually wrote his "David Strauss, the confessor and the writer" (the first essay of *Untimely Meditations*) in 1873 and not in 1875, as Freud stated, the quotation is exact and comes from section four of the essay. Hollingdale translates this sentence, which Nietzsche quoted from Strauss's book *Der alte und neue Glaube* (1872), as: "Thus we live and go our way rejoicing" (p. 18).

That Freud correctly quotes from this relatively unimportant essay of Nietzsche only two years after its first publication testifies to the intensive interest with which he followed Nietzsche's writings during his university days, probably the most impressionable days of his life — as he himself indicated in his letters to Silberstein.

As various other sources show, Nietzsche attracted an intensely loyal following among the students of Vienna. They read and discussed his earliest works shortly after they were published, and Freud was by no means the only notable example. See also Chapter One, fn. 75.

through which one may filter Nietzsche's so-called "unsystematic" aphorisms, and presents a new interpretation of Nietzsche's psychological thought which helps to resolve several problems and alleged contradictions occurring in his writings. The analogy with Freud will clarify certain elements of this thought which may remain obscure if considered in isolation from the later psychological notions which they initiated or influenced. These elements include Nietzsche's preference for the process of *Sublimierung* to that of *Verinnerlichung*, his explanation of how and why the "slaves" have overcome the "masters" in Western culture, his vehement attacks on *"ressentiment"* and asceticism, and his distinction between the negative and positive expression of *Macht*.

The comparison with Freud will bring into focus the psychologist in Nietzsche and balance certain one-sided interpretations of his philosophy, e.g.: the Heideggerian view[13] which presents him as the last great metaphysician of the West; Danto's approach,[14] treating Nietzsche as a forerunner of analytical philosophy; and Jaspers' interpretation[15] which portrays Nietzsche's deliberate and inadvertent contradictions as a mirror of the inherent ambiguities of *Existenz*. The analytic comparisons between Nietzsche and Freud will reveal that the theoretical core of psychoanalysis is already part and parcel of Nietzsche's philosophy, insofar as it is founded on concepts which are present in (and developed by) it — concepts such as the unconscious, repression, sublimation, the *id*, the super-ego, the secondary gains of illness, the primary and secondary processes, and the interpretation of dreams. It may also be

---

13. See particularly his *Nietzsche*, 2 vols. (Pfullingen, 1961); *Vorträge und Aufsätze* (Pfullingen, 1954); and *Holzwege* (Frankfurt am Main, 1950).
14. Arthur C. Danto, *Nietzsche as Philosopher* (New York, 1965).
15. Karl Jaspers, *Nietzsche: Einführung in das Verständnis seines Philo-sophierens* (Berlin, 1950).

suggested that the theoretical bond between the two thinkers reflects a formative Nietzschean influence on Freud's meta-psychology; but such a possibility is bound to remain historically conjectural.

★ ★
★

If theoretical psychoanalytic doctrine becomes a heuristic and didactic tool for a deeper understanding of Nietzsche's psychological teaching, then psychoanalytic therapy itself (even more than the doctrine) may provide a primary model for the explication of Nietzsche's psychology and of its unique role in his overall philosophy. The ultimate goal of Nietzsche's psychology, like that of psychoanalytic therapy, is the positive enticement of the reader (the patient) into certain modes of life. Both the psychology and the therapy aim to re-activate and use creatively the individual's suppressed power. Nietzschean psychology is not merely developed as an instrument of pure philosophical inquiry; it is also intended as an operative and existential vehicle of positive power. It is an "experiment" (*Versuchung*) — a speculative hypothesis and a temporary perspective — but it offers an enticement as well in terms of the influence it exerts on both its writer and readers: Nietzsche's psychology is an hypothesis intended to redirect man to his positive power and to examine the extent to which he is actually capable of attaining and maintaining it. This psychology is designed to cultivate the powerful and creative life-pathos of a vital, developing temperament. Yet every healthy process of creative and organic growth involves the inevitable destruction or removal of the unhealthy elements. Likewise, all positive power requires the overcoming of the repressive and counter-productive manifestations of negative power. Nietzsche's enticing psychology is presented as an aid in this process of overcoming, and in this respect psychoanalytic therapy provides a concrete, heuristic model for understanding its special function.

The object of psychoanalytic therapy is to develop the healthy power still present in the neurotic personality. By helping the patient to overcome the defence mechanisms that repress his vitality and inhibit his ability to function freely and creatively, psychoanalysis aims at realizing his potential as an autonomous agent. Psychoanalytic sessions engage the patient in an explicative process intended to remove his defensive masks and to expose the illusionary super-structures on which he relies. The success of this process is judged by the same criterion as is the power of the *Übermensch*: how much truth one can bear without retreating into mental defences and illusions — into Nietzsche's 'Apollonian fictions'. In this respect Nietzschean philosophy and Freudian psychoanalysis share a similar aim: self-overcoming, self-education and the self-formation of an authentic and creative personality.

The penultimate proposition of Wittgenstein's *Tractatus Logico-Philosophicus* instructs the reader to "throw away the ladder ... after he has climbed it";[16] in other words, he is asked to discard the metaphysical discourse of that very book. I feel Nietzsche also might have found this metaphor appropriate for elucidating the real aim of his unique psychology. His own 'ladder' consists of four distinct steps:

1. Psychologization (especially in *Untimely Meditations* and *Human, All Too Human*

2. A positive psychology of Power (especially in *Daybreak* and *The Gay Science*)

16. Ludwig Wittgenstein, *Tractatus Logico-Philosophicus* (London, 1961), Proposition 6.54.

3. Explication of Power (in *Beyond Good and Evil*)

4. Genealogy of Power (in *On the Genealogy of Morals*)

One must bear in mind, however, that Nietzsche's ladder is not constructed of separate and distinct steps. These four components of his psychology are all mutually supportive and are intertwined in a complex structure. A primary aim of this study is to reveal the methodical order inherent in this ostensible psychological chaos. To this end, I have found it useful to reconstruct Nietzsche's thought through a diachronic analysis of his writings. This procedure brings to light the consistent development of his psychology and of its requisite trans-formations.

Nietzsche's psychology poses the problem of a possibly vicious circle obtaining in the relation between its positive doctrine and the sceptical ramifications of his theory of perspectivism, This difficulty may be resolved by discussion of the psychology from a therapeutic vantage point: by elaborating the concept of enticement, one may conclude that his psychology does not contradict any criterion of 'objective truth', for any commitment to such truth is already 'frozen' by Nietzsche in his preliminary discussions. For this reason, I have come to the conclusion that there is no purely *intellectual* justification for rejecting his enticing psychology. My study does not attempt to deal directly with Nietzsche's epistemology and perspectivism,[17] and thus does not pursue the question of a circularity between his

17. Dealt with extensively by Rüdiger H. Grimm, *Nietzsche's Theory of Knowledge* (Berlin, 1977; "Monographien und Texte zur Nietzsche Forschung", Vol. 4); John T. Wilcox, *Truth and Value in Nietzsche* (Ann Arbor, 1974); Jean Granier, *Le Problème de la Vérité dans la Philosophie de Nietzsche* (Paris, 1966); Alexander Nehamas, *Nietzsche: Life as Literature* (Cambridge, Mass., 1985).

anthropology and his theory of knowledge. I believe, nonetheless, that the matter will be somewhat clarified if one regards his scepticism as a crucial step in his therapeutic efforts to reveal and activate the positive powers of man and his culture. Viewed in this way, then, the truth of Nietzsche's psychology is irrelevant *vis a vis* its enticing and healthy effect for human existence. The present discussion also attempts to counter the accusation of 'psychologism' and 'reductionism', and argues that his moral theory contains no 'esoteric' values; it is not, in fact, a prescriptive doctrine, but a descriptive and explicative theory.

If one considers Nietzsche's thought as a didactic means of enticing the reader, it is easier to understand the provocative and poetic form in which it is presented. The sharp and polished aphorisms, the ruthless style, the figurative language, the use of myths, labels and bold slogans — all of these techniques are intended to shock the reader and incite an emotional response which assists the process of his 'transfiguration'.

This method of philosophizing leaves little scope for the commentator to assume an 'objective' stance. He too is often forced to respond to the texts with a certain emotional intensity (at times against his wishes), whether the response is one of unqualified rejection or of unreserved acceptance. For this reason, among others, very few of Nietzsche's interpreters have managed to remain neutral or indifferent. His method of philosophizing demands a personal reaction, and this can often make it difficult to satisfy the requirements of a measured and balanced philosophical critique.

Indeed, the present study occasionally exhibits a certain enthusiasm and pathos in both expression and attitude. This notwithstanding, the author hopes that he has enjoyed a degree of success in his attempt to remain sufficiently disinterested and has at least avoided an unconditional surrender to the enticing allure of Nietzsche — the *seducer*.

Part One:

NIETZSCHE'S METHOD
OF PSYCHOLOGIZATION

CHAPTER ONE

THE BIRTH OF PSYCHOLOGY
OUT OF TRAGEDY

Introduction

Revolutionary ideas characteristically exhibit a certain disorder in their composition, and the advent of Nietzsche's new psychology was no exception. His youthful predilection for Schopenhauerian metaphysics and enthusiastic devotion to the romantic music of Wagner at first precluded Nietzsche from understanding the genuine character of his own work. His vision became clearer, however, as he overcame his hasty enchantment with Schopenhauer and Wagner.

In the critical and sober introduction to the second edition of *The Birth of Tragedy* ("Attempt at a Self-Criticism", 1886) Nietzsche declares that the central problem of the book is: "What is Dionysian?"[1] In other words, what is instinct? And how, out of the various transformations of nature, is a culture born and developed? These questions constitute the psychological problem *par excellence* as Nietzsche defines it.

In hindsight, then, Nietzsche perceives his first work as a psychological treatise, and views its problems as psychological in nature — problems which he treated in specifically psychological language (although this language is not yet as

1. GT "Attempt" — 3; KSA 1:15

distinctive, as unmistakable, as it is to become in his later writings). The sort of Schopenhauerian metaphysics which considerably influences this work also manages to obscure its innovations. Moreover, it is here that Nietzsche mobilizes all his early philosophical acumen in defence of Richard Wagner, to whom he looked (unrealistically) for cultural salvation.

Early misconstrual of the real intention underlying *The Birth of Tragedy*, together with the book's lack of clarity, led Nietzsche's commentators astray. They did not perceive the novel psychological insights behind the Wagnerian-Schopenhauerian facade; neither did they give sufficient weight to Nietzsche's later comments regarding the true character of his treatise. In particular, commentators have typically understood the distinction between the Dionysian and Apollonian principles to be identical with Schopenhauer's distinction between the world as Will and the world as Representation.[2] Yet as we shall see, this early dualism eventually disappears; the Dionysian takes on new meaning and becomes a symbol of the "will to power", and of vital creative life, as opposed to Christianity and ascetic morality. Thus we find him later speaking of "Dionysus

---

2. See, e.g., Walter Kaufmann, *Nietzsche* (Princeton, 1968), p. 128n. This tendency of some of Nietzsche's commentators to revert to the "blind will" and the supposedly dominant influence of Schopenhauer disregards passages written some five years before GT, where it becomes clear that from the outset Nietzsche had many reservations concerning Schopenhauer. Thus, for example, in 1867 he writes of him: "...the mistakes of pre-eminent people are much admired because they are more productive than the truths of less significant people..." *Musarion Ausgabe*, Vol.I, p. 393 (my translation). A notable exception is perhaps Martin Heidegger, who holds that at the time of GT the opposition between the Apollonian and the Dionysian "is still thought in the sense of Schopenhauerian metaphysics, although — rather, because — it is part of a confrontation with such metaphysics; by way of contrast" (*Nietzsche*, Vol.I: "The Will to Power as Art", New York, 1979, p. 102). See also Richard Schacht, *Nietzsche* (London, 1983), pp. 485–486. Notice that I prefer to use the term "Apollonian" rather than Silk and Stern's "Apolline" in their *Nietzsche on Tragedy*, (Cambridge, 1981).

versus Jesus", instead of "Dionysus versus Apollo"; the earlier duality is subsumed under a new concept of the Dionysian. According to Nietzsche, the Apollonian principle is itself a drive which struggles as an equal power with the Dionysian instinct, and at times defeats it. Hence one cannot speak of the ontological primacy of the Dionysian principle, as some have done, speaking about "the derivative status of Apollo".[3] In Schopenhauer, by contrast, Representation is an inadequate reflection of Will, which is always ontologically primary.[4] Representation cannot struggle with Will since it is secondary to and derived from the latter.

If we examine the introduction to the 1886 edition of *The Birth of Tragedy*, we can see that the problems with which Nietzsche was struggling in this book are already couched in unmistakably psychological language. One such problem is the origin of the phenomenon of pessimism. Pessimism, he maintains, is not exclusively intellectual; rather it is to be conceived of as an emotional pattern of "instincts" and "strength".[5] The diagnosis of superficial optimism as a cultural phenomenon is based on psychological analysis, an analysis formulated in terms of a reservoir of instinctual energy in man. It is a source of energy which is undermined by the repressive weight of Socratic rationalism. This latter is described as a means of protection or, in Freudian terms, as a "defence mechanism". In the light of his psychological genealogy of the art of tragedy it becomes clear to

---

3. Jerry S. Clegg, "Nietzsche's Gods in The Birth of Tragedy", *Jrnl. of the History of Philosophy* l0 (1972): 431–438; and see also Charles M. Barrack, who claims that "Apollo, powerful on the level of phenomena, is a mere manifestation of the Dionysian *Ding an sich*, the reality beneath all appearance" in "Nietzsche's Dionysus and Apollo: Gods in Transition", *Nietzsche-Studien* 3 (1974): 115–129.
4. Arthur Schopenhauer, *Die Welt als Wille und Vorstellung* (Wiesbaden, 1966): Erster Band, Zweites Buch, and esp. Zweiter Band, Kap.19, "Vom Primat des Willens...".
5. GT "Attempt" — 1; KSA 1:12

Nietzsche that pessimism is actually a positive expression of superabundant spiritual power, and that optimism is no more than a degenerate defence mechanism offering refuge from that power when the spirit is too weak to bear it. This radical re-evaluation of the phenomena of pessimism and optimism illustrates the depth and originality of Nietzsche's psychological thought.

It is a re-evaluation which becomes possible only through a penetrating psychological study. Here for the first time appears the significant link (later to be strengthened) between Nietzsche's psychology and the central expression of his thought — *"Umwertung aller Werte"* (Revaluation of all Values). From this new perspective he reformulates the book's primary task: *"to look at science from the perspective of the artist, but at art from that of life".*[6] By this formula Nietzsche does not intend the reduction of the values of truth and falsehood to the aesthetic values of beauty and ugliness; it is in "life" — at any rate in its healthy powerful patterns — that Nietzsche perceives the basic principle upon which the entire cultural superstructure stands. And of all the many meanings which Nietzsche attributes to the term "life", the psychological is paramount. Psychological criteria, therefore, form the basis for his "re-evaluation of all values".

The central status of psychology in Nietzsche's thought is exhibited by his search for the psychological genesis of art, creation, and culture. It is this genesis, he says, which presents "such a difficult psychological question".[7] This is a "question for psychiatrists";[8] their task is to uncover the origin of Greek tragedy in such psychological phenomena as "Dionysian madness" and "neuroses of health". This context necessarily

---

6. GT "Attempt" — 2; KSA 1:14
7. GT "Attempt" — 4; KSA 1:15
8. GT "Attempt" — 4; KSA 1:16

broadens the scope of the Nietzschean discussion, which does not in fact deal with art *per se*, and certainly not with tragedy alone. Rather, its preoccupations are with individual experience and with the "urge" of "the Greek soul".[9]

The analysis of Greek culture constitutes for Nietzsche a paradigm and historical model, but behind his discussion of the psychology of classical Greek culture looms the fundamental question of the psychological sources of human culture in general. Since one of the central constituents of culture is art, it is in this domain that he commences his study. Nietzsche, however, never engages in a deliberate study of some spiritual realm simply for its own sake; consequently we shall not find any development of a pure philosophy of art as such. The emphasis rather is on *"Artisten-Metaphysik"* or, more accurately, the psychology of the artistic personality, and the psychological sources and processes of creativity — from which Nietzsche generalized to all cultural creations, regarding them as by-products of basic human psychological needs. The psychologistic genealogy which is Nietzsche's method of analysis in this treatise obliges him to go beyond the investigation of creation as a finished product back to a study of the creator himself, and of those creative processes which motivate aesthetic praxis.[10] In this way Nietzsche discovers the particular psychological mechanism which constitutes and shapes human culture — the mechanism of *sublimation*. It is through sublimation that the artist creates nature anew by imposing order and harmony on amorphous raw materials; in this way he overcomes his inner

---

9. *Loc. cit.* This perspective deeply influenced Nietzsche's fellow student and colleague, the well-known classical philologist Erwin Rohde in his *Psyche*, trans. W.B. Hillis (London, l925).
10. Therefore I agree with Heidegger's observation that "Nietzsche speaks only of the 'artist phenomenon', not about art", and that "art must be grasped in terms of creators and producers", *Nietzsche*, Vol.I, "The Will to Power as Art" (New York, 1979), p. 70.

mental conflict, and "frees himself from the *distress* of fullness and *overfullness* and from the *affliction* of the contradictions compressed in his soul".[11] This revelation of the psychological process of sublimation at work within the foundation of human culture is one of Nietzsche's seminal insights, a *sine qua non* for understanding his philosophical psychology as a whole.

Once sublimation, this intensifying life mechanism, has been presented, Nietzsche abandons his preoccupation with art and embarks on the genealogical study of other cultural phenomena — science, religion, and, most important of all, morality. In these other cases the mental defence mechanisms take on an entirely different character, that of a violent and destructive repression. Nietzsche had already begun to deal with these in *The Birth of Tragedy*, where he articulated the psychological-aesthetic perspective from which to evaluate the Socratic tradition. His attitude to rationalism is psychological too, as he himself notes in a retrospective passage; there he states that his insight regarding Socrates' "decadence" was for him an unequivocal sign of the sureness of his "psychological grasp".[12] In this context it should be noted that the further Nietzsche removes himself from the ambiance of the days in which he wrote his first book, the more soberly he regards the specifically psychological aspects of his philosophy. When he finally becomes certain as to what he is,[13] he identifies himself as a psychologist who in *The Birth of Tragedy* was already dealing with a new psychological issue: the "psychology of tragedy", and the "psychology of the artist".[14]

---

11. GT "Attempt" — 5; KSA 1:17.
12. EH — GT 2; KSA 6:311
13. EH — GT 3; KSA 6:312
14. GD 9–8; KSA 6:116

I. The "Dionysian Barbarian" and the Freudian "Id"

Nietzsche's early philosophy formed itself around the distinction between the Apollonian and Dionysian principles. This is in essence a psychological distinction, and, in all its various incarnations, constitutes one of the unifying motifs of his entire thought. Accordingly, to discuss Nietzschean psychology, the meaning and significance of this fundamental distinction must be clearly understood.

Its significance is revealed in the first chapter of *The Birth of Tragedy* where Nietzsche presents the dualism in clear psychological terms and speaks of the Dionysian and the Apollonian as *"so verschiedene Triebe"*, ("such different drives or instincts" and not just, as Kaufmann translates, "tendencies"). It follows from this description that the Apollonian, as well as the Dionysian principle, is a drive attesting to instinctual and psychological processes in humankind. This emerges explicitly from Nietzsche's own definition, and is also implicit in his description of a perpetual "striving"; for drive and will can struggle in a battle of equals only against another drive and instinct. Drive cannot fight against reason (or vice versa) unless there is an instinctual-energetic element in reason which can be mobilized against the impulse aspiring to destroy it. Nietzsche understands this very well and speaks of Apollo as an instinctual artistic power, a driving force struggling fiercely in the creative human soul against a different and "dangerous force" until it succeeds in effecting the "reconciliation ...taking the destructive weapons from the hands of his powerful antagonist".[15] All this occurs within the context of a balance of power, and an energetic *status quo*.

Here we find a description of two instincts within the single psychological framework of the "Hellenic will", or simply the

15. GT 2; KSA 1:32

human will. In fact Nietzsche depicts a "will" as comprised of two antithetical elements, and it is their struggles and varying power relationships which ultimately produce art, science, religion, and morality — the cornerstones of culture.

This interpretation is reinforced by the analogy which Nietzsche draws between these two principles and the two *"physiologischen Erscheinungen"* of "dreams and rapture" (*der Rausch*).[16] Now, it is important to stress that dreaming and rapture are, *qua* psychophysical phenomena, on the same ontological level. Therefore their psychological analogues — Apollonianism and Dionysianism — must also be on a par ontologically. One cannot say that either of them is more primordial.

Rapture, an expression of "the Dionysian barbarian", opposes the principle of individualization. Rapture is an escape from individual distinctiveness to the chaotic amorphism of the instincts. In rapture the ego escapes from itself: in the dream it escapes from the external world and the principle of reality. And even though Nietzsche employs the typically Schopenhauerian concept *"principium individuationis"*,[17] Schopenhauer's metaphysics is not required to understand this dimension of his thinking, or to unravel the original aspects of his approach.[18]

16. GT 1; KSA 1:28. I prefer to render *"Rausch"* as "rapture" and not "intoxication" (as Kaufmann's translation) because of the erotic connotation intended by Nietzsche: see GD 9–8. It should also be noticed that whenever Nietzsche mentions "Physiology" he means to emphasize the bodily state; but the latter is in itself already something psychic, and therefore also a matter for "psychology". cf. Heidegger, *Nietzsche*, Vol.I, *op.cit.* p. 96.
17. GT 1; KSA 1:28
18. Thus my perspective attempts to counterbalance the metaphysically oriented interpretations of Nietzsche's aesthetics as suggested, for example, by Leon Rosenstein, "Metaphysical Foundations of the Theories of Tragedy in Hegel and Nietzsche", *Journal of Aesthetics and Art Criticism* 28 (1970): 521–533, and by Richard Schacht, "Nietzsche on Art in *The Birth of Tragedy*" in G. Dickie and R.J. Sclafani (eds.), *Aesthetics: A Critical Anthology* (New York, 1977), pp. 269–313.

To illuminate the novelty of his psychological ideas it is far more fruitful to look forward in time and consider Nietzsche's concepts from the perspective of Freud, who was influenced by these concepts and developed them into a comprehensive meta-psychological theory. It then becomes clear that Nietzsche's concept of "the Dionysian barbarian" anticipates the Freudian idea of *"das Es"*, the unformed unconscious *id*. The *id* consists of the chaotic instincts which by their very nature negate distinctiveness and individual character; likewise Nietzsche's barbarian and ecstatic Dionysian is an elemental amorphous *per se*, in which the principle of individuation disintegrates.

There is little doubt that Freud had read Nietzsche's *The Birth of Tragedy*, or that at least he had read its poetic paraphrase in Lindsay's book *Dionysos*, presented to him by its author and still to be found in his library at the Freud Museum in London.[19] While Freud does not refer directly to the Dionysian concept, it is clear that the later Nietzschean term of *"das Es"*, (which appears, e.g., in JGB 17), derives from the concept of the Dionysian

19. Jack Lindsay, *Dionysos: Nietzsche Contra Nietzsche*, An Essay in Lyrical Philosophy (The Fanfrolico Press, London, 1929). Freud, however, said that when he first used the term *id* in his psychoanalytic doctrine (SE, *19*:23), he borrowed it indirectly from Nietzsche, through Groddeck. Nonetheless, in a later series of lectures, *An Introduction to Psychoanalysis* (1932), he acknowledged that he borrowed the term directly from Nietzsche (SE, *22*:72). This is confirmed by Freud's faithful assistant, who writes: "We decided for linguistic reasons to use the Latin *Id* to translate the German *Es* (=It) ... It is a term that had been extensively employed by Nietzsche, and recently popularized by Groddeck" (Ernest Jones, *Sigmund Freud: Life and Work*, London 1957, Vol.3, p. 303). See also Freud's letter to Groddeck where he states: "I think you got the It (in a literary, not an associative way) from Nietzsche". In George Groddeck, *The Meaning of Illness* (New York, 1977), p. 76.

Freud's student, Carl Jung, was profoundly influenced by Nietzsche's distinction between the Dionysian and the Apollonian, and used it in his own typology: the introverted type is dominated by the Apollonian principle of individualization, and the extroverted type by extroverted Dionysianism which overflows the boundaries of the individual Ego. See, e.g., Carl G. Jung, *Psychological Types* (Princeton, 1971), pp. 136–146, 506–507.

barbarian. If any doubt exists concerning the nature of Nietzsche's influence on Freud, in this one central issue at least there is no room for uncertainty. The close link between them in this is not only linguistic, but evidently conceptual. In the treatise, "The Ego and the Id" (1923), where he borrows the Nietzschean concept, Freud assumes the division of the personality into the *id*, the ego and the super-ego. Thus he arrives at a stage beyond psychological speculations, incorporating ideas on culture that go beyond the analysis of an individual personality. Here too, one can discern the influence of Nietzsche on psychological thought.

In Freud's doctrine the *id* represents the natural domain of man, a domain of unrestrained impulses. It is the beast in man, the river bed where the turbulent current of the primordial being of nature and sexual-aggressive impulses surges, often overflowing its banks. In the *id* there is no foothold for culture, which restrains and moulds the drives into accepted patterns, into rational cognition, and into consciousness.

Nietzsche's "Dionysian barbarian" appears in various manifestations, one of which is the satyr of the Dionysian rite: "Nature, as yet unchanged by knowledge, with the bolts of culture still unbroken ... a symbol of the sexual omnipotence of nature."[20] All the characteristic attributes of the *id* are salient in this description of the satyr, symbol of the inchoate in man. Pre-cognitive and pre-conscious nature — this is both the Freudian *id* and Nietzsche's "Dionysian barbarian", outside the cultural pale, uncultivated and unadulterated in all its sexual and natural primordiality.

> In nearly every case these festivals centred in extravagant sexual licentiousness, whose waves overwhelmed all family life and its venerable traditions; the most savage natural

20.   GT 8; KSA 1:58

instincts were unleashed, including even that horrible mixture of sensuality and cruelty which has always seemed to me to be the real 'witches' brew.[21]

The Freudian *id* is not only characterized by archaism and pure impulsiveness. It is also the superabundant overflow which, free from inhibition, resists all containment. Nietzsche appropriately identifies this type of instinctual experience with *rapture*, a "mystic feeling of oneness"[22] in which the individual loses his personality and his distinctiveness.

Nietzsche is repelled by the unrestrained primordial drive and the beast in man, but he does not deny its existence. On the contrary, Nietzsche consistently opposes all cultural devices and patterns which aim to destroy that very instinct which serves as the basic raw fibre for the fabric of a creative *"Übermensch"*. The stronger the impulse, he will later argue, the more efficacious is the "will to power". The formula which then emerges is this: wherever there is drive, there is power (*Macht*); and wherever there is power there exist the conditions for cultivating the *Übermensch* and the superior culture. But while Nietzsche is well aware of the necessary function of the raw drive which is the basis of culture, he clearly considers it in a negative light, as shown in his description of the manifestation of the "Dionysian barbarian" as "the real 'witches' brew".[23]

Freud characterizes the *id* in terms of the drives and raw irrational impulses which wish to break loose and find resolution and satisfaction. It is impossible to encounter these drives directly and, moreover, impossible to manifest them at the verbal-conceptual level. They can find expression only in explosive "Dionysian" acts, lacking any differentiation, organi-

21. GT 2; KSA 1:32
22. KSA 1:31
23. *"Hexentrank"*: KSA 1:32. This notwithstanding the fact that in rapture he sees an indispensable condition for art, and see,e.g., GD 9–8.

zation or·purpose. Nietzsche's description of such acts as "rapture" or "barbarism" is an accurate picture of their primordiality, and volcanic anti-cultural character.

II. On the Apollonian Principle

Let us now consider Nietzsche's Apollonian principle as realised in the dream phenomenon. He writes:

> This joyous necessity of the dream experience has been embodied by the Greeks in their Apollo: Apollo, the god of all plastic energies ... is also ruler over the beautiful illusion of the inner world of fantasy ... this deep consciousness of nature, healing and helping in sleep and dreams, is at the same time the symbolical analogue ... of the arts generally, which make life possible and worth living.[24]

This passage anticipates some of the characteristic aspects of Freud's "primary processes".[25] These are first of all a means of expressing the imaginary content of fantasies, in opposition to the principle of rational reality which dominates in the external world. Furthermore, these means of expression are characteristic of the dream phenomenon, and they have a liberating and cathartic function which makes possible the delicate equilibrium in civilized man between the domain of the *id* and the self-restraint necessary to preserve appropriate social functioning. This equilibrium is maintained in spite of the conflict inherent in civilized life. Both Freud and Nietzsche perceive dream and fantasy as providing an escape from reality. But this is an escape *for the sake of life itself.*

In the dream, in contrast to Dionysian rapture, Apollonian form and organization are predominent, albeit on a lower (or

24. GT 1; KSA 1:31
25. See SE, *5*:597–609; *12*:218–226; *14*:186–189

paleological) cognitive level. There is also an Apollonian dimension to the revealed dream, the dream as remembered by the person on awakening. The revealed dream, according to Freud (and, as we shall see below, to Nietzsche as well), is the result of the dream being processed by the censoring restraining forces of the super-ego and ego. The dreamer is conscious only of the final reconstruction and not of the original raw content in which the uncensored and genuine desires of the *id's* drives find expression. In order that the dream should enter our consciousness and be preserved in our memory, the Apollonian ego must shape and regulate the instincts. This motif of "The Dream-Work"[26] constitutes the artistic creative facet of Apollo. He kneads unstructured material into a form; he compresses, displaces, and condenses its expressions until the final product is a new creation altogether. The dream takes on a new content which artistically transforms the primary, unprocessed text. Psychotherapy, using hermeneutics, unmasks this primary text with all its hidden primordial impulses.[27] The dream therefore represents, not the Apollonian as such, but rather the Apollonian capacity to harness the Dionysian barbarian for the purpose of preserving life.

The activity of the restraining and purposeful Apollo is most pronounced in the sphere of art. In the creative artistic process the Apollonian exploits the Dionysian drive for its own expression and externalization. The difference between the dream and the artistic act is quantitative: each principle is represented *proportionately* in the final synthesis. From the purely structural point of view, then, Nietzsche is justified in treating dreams and artworks, as expressions of the same

---

26. SE, *15*:170–183.
27. On an interesting attempt to present psychoanalysis as hermeneutics or as a "semantics of desire", see Paul Ricoeur, *De l'interprétation: essai sur Freud* (Paris, 1965).

continuous "striving" which always ends with a similar psychological result — a necessarily unstable "reconciliation" between the Dionysian barbarian and Apollonian principles (or, in Freudian terms, between the *id* and the *ego*).[28] This synthesis in the soul of man is what gives us art. Thus Wagner's words on the nature of art, cited by Nietzsche, are most fitting: "all poems and versification are but true dreams' interpretation".[29]

III. The Sublimatory "Metaphysical Comfort" of Art

The subjugation by Apollo of the unrestrained drives of the Dionysian barbarian is the source, according to Nietzsche, of art in general. Greek tragedy is a particular and ideally paradigmatic case. This synthesis does not produce an Aristotelian catharsis, but instead provides one with "the metaphysical comfort"[30] which allows man to affirm existence despite its horrors. In Freudian terms, one would speak of the sublimation of the turbulent and threatening *id*. Blocking the Dionysian forces of the *id*, diverting them into channels of illusion and creativity, and thus transforming them into forces which facilitate existence — this is the effect of sublimation and "metaphysical comfort". Moreover, by this process, through which man is purified of his cruder components, he is himself transformed into an object of art, into an artistic sublimation: "He is no longer an artist", Nietzsche tells us, "he has become a work of art".[31] This in fact is

28. Like Nietzsche, Freud also discusses the psychological nature of artistic creation and compares it to the creative processes which find expression in dreams: SE, *9*:143–153. See also SE, *12*:224, where he speaks of art as a synthesis betweeen primary and secondary processes, and SE, *16*:375–377; *19*:207–208
29. GT 1; KSA 1:26. On this reading it is hard to accept Heidegger's contention that "the Dionysian and the Apollonian are two kinds of rapture, rapture itself being the basic state", *Nietzsche*, Vol.I, pp. 97–98.
30. *"Der metaphysische Trost"*, GT 7; KSA 1:56.
31. GT 1; KSA 1:30

the later image of the authentic man who individualizes and creates himself. Only in this act of creating selfhood do creator and creation merge; the alienation between man and his created objects is overcome, for these objects are part of his psychological make-up, not merely circumstantial and external expressions of it.[32] For Nietzsche then, the work of art is a product of sublimation, displacing and transforming man's stormy drives; moreover, it is this sublimation by art which enables one to remain a man and continue to live. Art protects man from the fear of existence and the struggle with absurd reality. However, in contrast to religion, ascetic morality and science, art does not repress man's instinctual Dionysian elements. Religion, morality and science do fulfil a "protective" function, but they do so at the cost of repressing the Dionysian. In contradistinction, art allows it to be manifest by transforming the world into an "aesthetic phenomenon" in which "even the ugly and disharmonic are part of an artistic game that the will in the eternal amplitude of its pleasure plays with itself".[33] In being presented as an aesthetic phenomenon, the world is rendered enjoyable in spite of its inherent pain. Yet in *The Birth of Tragedy* a somewhat different idea is already beginning to take root, an idea which is later to become more central to Nietzsche's thought: this is the concept of "the tragic way of life" or "the

---

32. On this account I cannot accept Clegg's reservation concerning the psychological interpretation of Nietzsche's duality in GT. He objects that "the psychic state of an artist cannot identify the artifact he makes", and that "one cannot say that 'Apollonian' and 'Dionysian' denote only psychological types. They refer to specific kinds of artifacts as well" (Jerry S. Clegg, "Nietzsche's Gods", p. 43l). However, Nietzsche, who regards art mainly in terms of the artist, actually claims here that this "psychic state" of the artist is in itself an artifact, and thus he does not distinguish — as Clegg does — between the artist's psychological make-up and his artifacts. Similarly Nietzsche's theme in GT is not art *per se*, but the artistic mode of being in the world.
33. GT 24; KSA 1:152

tragic man". The first suggestion that the merely aesthetic solution for life be rejected exists already in the idea of "art for the sake of life". The life-affirming character of the later Nietzsche is achieved without any "metaphysical comfort"; rather, life is affirmed in spite of the conditions which cause man to require such comfort. This affirmation is the tragic way of *amor fati* which for Nietzsche constitutes the most exalted and powerful human response to the problems of existence.

One Apollonian principle, well expressed in the command "Know Thyself",[34] is self-awareness and self-consciousness. In psychoanalytic theory also, this is the principle of the ego and the important goal of psychoanalytic treatment. Here "Know Thyself" means knowing one's own instinctual desires, being aware of one's hidden wishes and of the instinctual nature of one's genuine, uncensored character. At the same time it recommends the possibility of coming to terms with them, and living with them in a well-functioning and healthy manner. The Nietzschean ideal likewise is to affirm life while nonetheless recognizing its absurdity and lack of meaning. The really powerful is he who possesses a positive and genuine life-power, and who, although cognizant of sickness, says "Yes to life and to health".

IV. The Dionysian and Apollonian —
Powers of Nature Enhancing Life

Thus far we have discussed Nietzsche's description of the Apollonian and Dionysian principles. We have seen that his original psychological language sufficed in itself to give a faithful account of his most fundamental intuitions. But already in Section Two of *The Birth of Tragedy* he anchors the

---

34. GT 4: KSA 1:40

psychological *cum* aesthetic values in an ontological framework. He speaks of the Apollonian and the Dionysian as "artistic energies which burst forth from nature herself, *without the mediation of the human artist* — energies in which nature's art impulses are satisfied in the most immediate and direct way".[35] (In this way Nietzsche projects and personifies nature in absolute contradiction to the later motif in *The Gay Science*, where he speaks of the death of God and his shadows.) Apollo and Dionysus now are not only human instincts and drives but natural powers which also reveal themselves as "imitations" in such psychological phenomena as dreams and artistic creation. Nature takes on a character of creative dynamism, and this constitutes the genesis of Nietzsche's artistic metapsychology which perceives nature as an artistic interplay of these universal powers.[36] Man is the meeting place where the Apollonian and Dionysian powers are merged and processed together, creating the personality with its artistic expressions. Every artist is, therefore, "an imitator"[37] of the two creative powers of nature, and gives them expression in a limited human way. In consequence, the Apollonian dream, the Dionysian rapture, and art in general all reflect the "truth" of nature, for they are a direct expression of the impulses and powers of reality itself.

The same dynamics are also present in illusion which, according to Nietzsche, has a simple psychological explanation. The Greeks, in virtue of their "overwhelming dismay in the face of the titanic powers of nature"[38] attempted to escape the Dionysian "terror". The Apollonian culture recognised in nature and in its own creations only the rational principle, and therefore

---

35. GT 2; KSA 1:30.
36. Nietzsche returns to this idea of the artification of nature in *Philosophy in the Tragic Age of the Greeks* (1875–76) in sections dealing with Heraclitus, esp. Section 7.
37. GT 2; KSA 1:30
38. GT 3; KSA 1:35

perpetuated an illusion regarding its own genuine essence. This illusion is not, however, simple deception, for it is in fact created by nature itself in the realization of its own intentions. Nonetheless, this illusion prevented the Greeks from achieving authentic existence. For this reason, Nietzsche ultimately rejects the aesthetic solution as an escapist one, and proposes instead an existence stripped of veils and self-deceptions. This attitude is characteristic of life at the higher psychological level of the *Übermensch*; it is an attitude which leads to the recognition of our Dionysian barbarian nature and the acquisition of profound self-knowledge by destroying our various rationalizations through the process of "unmasking". Such a recognition is the prerequisite for achieving the more mature Dionysian conception of life, as Nietzsche later develops it.

An essential part of the unmasking process begins with an awareness of the real nature of human knowledge. This will issue directly from the realization that the Apollonian principle, the rational drive towards individuality and organization, must be also a real, psychological power of nature. The move is later summed up in the typically Nietzschean statement that knowledge is equally a drive and that in fact there is no Kantian "pure reason" free from a partisan emotional basis. Therefore, the journey along the path of authentic, healthy life must in addition pass through a realization of the true nature of cognition.

The network of Apollonian categories, superimposed over the *id*-like Dionysian contents, also represents a powerful emotional drive. This idea is heavily emphasized in the psychological genealogy of the Olympian-Apollonian artistic culture, at whose foundation Nietzsche discovers "the same impulse that embodied itself in Apollo".[39] Here we find the recurrent question

---

39. GT 3; KSA 1:34

that constitutes a major methodological principle in Nietzsche's psychologistic investigations. It can be paraphrased as "What is the value of x?" — in other words, what is the *psychological function* of any given phenomenon, area of culture, theoretical preoccupation, etc.? The question is not concerned with a metaphysical or rational justification of any given realm, rather it seeks to expose why we are prompted to believe in the existence of such a realm, and what sort of psychological need is materialized through it.

In Section Three of the work Nietzsche asks this anthropological question concerning the function of the Greek dynamics of representation and illusion: "What dreadful need was it that could produce such an illustrious company of Olympian beings?"[40] Nietzsche feels that at the foundation of the "Olympian culture" (in which the Apollonian principle is dominant) lies some instinctual force, whose existence cannot be denied even when it produces illusory phantoms. The Apollonian is an expression of this self-interested impulse, of this undeniable need for illusion as a life-sustaining force. Illusion, through the use of images, "seduces"[41] man to survive and sustain life in spite of its horrors and absurdity.

After Nietzsche opens up "the Olympian magic mountain [and reveals] its roots to us"[42] through psychologistic analysis, a naturalistic monism emerges beyond the psychological dualism of Apollonian and Dionysian. It becomes clear that this life drive, which is the provenance of art and culture, is necessary in order to withstand a hostile meaningless world. This existential

---

40. *Loc. cit.* I translate *"ungeheures Bedürfnis"* as "dreadful need", and not as Kaufmann's colloquial "terrific need".
41. *"verführende* Ergänzung und Vollendung das Daseins", GT 3; KSA 1:36 (my italics). On the important concept of "Verführung" — as negative seduction (thus for the preservation of life but not its intensification) see Chapter Seven.
42. GT 3; KSA 1:35

principle, which speaks of *"Moira"* — of blind and absurd fate — will later become embodied in the Nietzschean idea of *"Ewigkeit Chaos"* and the *"Notwendigkeit"*.[43] Nonetheless, Nietzsche is quite far here from Schopenhauer's pessimistic metaphysical romanticism,[44] as well as from the naturalistic romanticism of Rousseau; for beyond the so-called Apollonian "natural naivete"[45] and illusionary attitude lurks another perspective which is suspicious of nature, and realizes its threat. This perspective makes no attempt to merge with nature, or to commit suicide under the spell of "the blind will", but instead tries to survive by actually overcoming nature. The idea of monistic naturalism is grounded here, in the primariness of "nature". Apollonianism, therefore, is in fact an expression *par excellence* of the impulsive and creative nature of man.

The natural quality of Apollo distances Nietzsche even further from the metaphysical framework of Schopenhauer and Kant. The system of Apollonian categories is not just a derived epiphenomenon, as in Schopenhauer, nor an *a priori* abstract universal structure as in Kant, but rather a functional, instinctual system of human nature, with an overriding biological and psychological purpose. This purpose is not the foundation of knowledge and science, but existence and the preservation of

---

43. FW 109; KSA 3:468. This reading of Nietzsche obliges me to reject George F. Sefler's interpretation — attractive though it is — distinguishing between "The Existential vs. the Absurd Aesthetics of Nietzsche and Camus", *Journal of Aesthetics and Art Criticism*, 32 (1974): 415–421. Nor can I accept his other thesis, that "Illusion is the underpinning of Nietzsche's aesthetics" (*ibid.*, p. 417).
44. Against which he emphatically declares: "Schopenhauer, the last German worth of consideration ... has interpreted *art*, heroism, genius, beauty ... as consequences of negation or of the 'will's' need to negate — the greatest psychological counterfeit in all history, not counting Christianity" (GD: "Skirmishes of an Untimely Man", 21; KSA 6:125). And see also *ibid.*, section 22.
45. Cf., e.g.,: Jerry S. Clegg, "Freud and the 'Homeric' Mind", *Inquiry* 17 (1974): 445–456.

life, the *sine qua non* for all possible knowledge. Therefore, although he consciously uses Kantian and Schopenhauerian language in describing the world of representation, Nietzsche tries — in complete contrast to Kant and Schopenhauer — to explain the specifically psychological functions of these Apollonian structures. In doing this he in fact psychologizes the Kantian categories. It should be pointed out, however, that in this first book Nietzsche himself is not entirely aware of these differences. He is still struggling with the metaphysical heritage of Kant and Schopenhauer on the one hand, and with his own intuitions and original psychological insights on the other. As a result, in the fourth section of *The Birth of Tragedy* the conservative component of his ambivalent relationship with philosophical tradition still comes to the fore, and he relies on the cosmic-metaphysical dimension of Schopenhauer to explain his distinction between the Apollonian and Dionysian principles.

V. The Epistemological and
Ethical Implications of the Distinction

From an examination of the epistemological aspect of the Apollonian/Dionysian distinction we can derive two distinct cognitive approaches to reality.[46] These are also related to Nietzsche's psychological doctrine. We saw above that the Apollonian principle exercises its drives in direct opposition to the Dionysian barbarian instincts — an opposition necessary for the preservation of life. It does this through the creation of

---

46. Since this study does not deal with Nietzsche's epistemology I cannot elaborate the complex relations between his theory of knowledge, his ethics and his aesthetics, and must confine myself to some occasional observations. For a detailed discussion of this subject consult Rüdiger H. Grimm, *Nietzsche's Theory of Knowledge*; and John T. Wilcox, *Truth and Value in Nietzsche*, esp. Ch. 5.

sophisticated images, imposition of order, and projection of an intellectual and causal network onto the world. Yet the Apollonian *per se* cannot stand aloof as an autonomous faculty of human intellectual activity. The threatening incursions of the Dionysian barbarian ensured that the Greek was brought down from his summit of "Olympian culture", back into the chaotic Dionysian abyss below:

> Despite all its beauty and moderation, [Apollo's] entire existence rested on a hidden substratum of suffering and of knowledge, *revealed* to him *by the Dionysian*. And behold: Apollo could not live without Dionysus![47]

This "revealed knowledge" is central to the cognition of the "Dionysian Greek": it includes the tragic conception of life and the serious truth, namely, the awareness of the lack of order, organization, meaning, or any objective correlation between "the truth" and empirical reality. Such revealed knowledge, as will be later argued, is at the heart of Nietzsche's later *theory of perspectives*, which was put forward to replace the classical theory of correspondence.

It is worth emphasizing the dialectical nature of the relationship which exists between the Apollonian and the Dionysian Greek, a relationship absent from the monistic Schopenhauerian picture of the "Blind Will". Apollonianism is an expression of the life drive that endeavours to overcome the "tragic truth" revealed from the Dionysian Greek perspective. It is therefore in a sense dependent on the Dionysian. Conversely, the Apollonian affords the Dionysian cognition a conceptual and representable form and content. Springing as it does from the unstructured flux of instinctual drives, the Dionysian cannot by itself find conceptual expression. Thus Apollo serves the

47.   GT 4; KSA 1:40 (my italics)

serious, tragic Dionysian intuition, and in turn is nourished by it.[48]

The life-serving Apollonian drive leads to the "self-knowledge" which encounters and subordinates the Dionysian eruptions which threaten to dissolve the individual personality. In this way, the Apollonian's "striving" assumes the character of "self-overcoming" (*Selbstüberwindung*), of self-sublimation, and of the creating and shaping of selfhood. As such, the striving embodies the clearly ethical principles of self-restraint and self-limitation — "the delimiting of the boundaries of the individual".[49] Through its conquest of the instincts for the sake of orderly cultural life (indeed of life itself) Apollo is thus not only the deity of knowledge and reason but the "ethical deity"[50] as well. We will observe later that here Nietzsche was already on the road leading to a new ethics of immanence — without God, and without absolute reason or the Kantian rational will. His search is for a non-transcendent ethics that will be based on the idea of self-creation.

As such the Nietzschean paradigm is not science — as it was for Kant — but art, which expresses and emphasizes the creative process of refining and sublimating raw instincts. The preference for psychological and aesthetic values is clearly expressed in a key sentence from The Birth of Tragedy: "for it is only as an

48. Nietzsche derives this also from his position that art manifests the synthesis between the Apollonian and Dionysian principles. As there is no art without Apollonian structure and form, so there is no knowledge without cognitive Apollonian elements (words and concepts); see GT, Section 6. However, he does not provide any detailed "Schematism" (of a Kantian kind), to explain how subsumption of the Dionysian drive under the Apollonian concepts takes place, and what makes it possible. Thus the postulated synthesis remains in the domain of psychological speculation, or as Nietzsche claims in the first sentence of GT, of the "unmittelbare Sicherheit der Anschauung" (KSA 1:25).
49. GT 4; KSA 1:40
50. *Loc. cit.*

aesthetic phenomenon that existence and the world are eternally justified".[51] What, in essence, is this justification? The existence of beauty? Of harmony? Nietzsche later abandons his search for a metaphysical (or any other) justification for life, realizing that the search itself is a symptom of weakness and of a failure to fulfill the project of overcoming. He subsequently concludes that man's value derives from the fact that he is himself an artistic creation; a personality that overcomes its anarchical instincts. One is then provided with a description of the psychological mechanisms which life uses to intensify and form itself.[52]

This approach, maintaining that existence is justified inasmuch as it is an "aesthetic phenomenon", already contains the first indication of that Dionysian conception of life (as opposed to the Christian conception) which emerges later in Nietzsche's thought. Games and art have no end or moral purpose whatsoever, but are expressions of unceasing and spontaneous activity for its own sake. Hence Nietzsche's early predilection for the "aesthetic" values: these represent an antithesis of the (essentially Hegelian) idea of a teleological or rational perspective.

VI. The Dionysian versus the Apollonian Psychological Patterns

The contrast between the Apollonian perspective, which creates illusions, and the demystifying Dionysian which deals with "tragic truth", enables Nietzsche to delineate two types of psychological patterns, each with a different function. The Apollonian pattern constructs artistic representations and

---

51. GT 5; KSA 1:47
52. This description, among other things, is what makes Nietzsche the great predecessor of Freud, who likewise portrays the mind as a kind of poetry-making faculty.

fictions for the sake of life, functioning as the source of the various kinds of metaphysical comfort. Reliance on this comfort suggests the existence of an untiring will-to-life, but nonetheless a will-to-life which requires certain metaphysical supports if it is to maintain its course. But in this resides an insurmountable difficulty: as a fictive psychological pattern, which builds masks and illusion, it is continuously imperilled, and may be condemned to collapse if penetrated by an intuition of the tragic absurdity of existence. Then "the danger to ... will is greatest"[53] and, in consequence, the danger to *life*. We see, therefore, that the second kind of psychological pattern — the Dionysian serving the Dionysian intuition, and performing the unmasking — is the more powerful of the two and fulfils a greater and more long-range function toward life-intensification. The man who adopts the Dionysian psychological pattern is "the Dionysian man", who "now sees everywhere only the horror or absurdity of existence". Indeed, in the short run, extreme danger confronts this man who has suddenly exploded all the fictions and suffers the epistemological trauma of authentic insight. The initial and natural psychological reaction to this epistemological trauma is the creation of "an ascetic, will-negating mood" — the emergence of a strong disinclination to continue and participate in a life comprised only of an absurd comedy of errors.

This is the reaction of the weak man, incapable of functioning under the Sisyphian burden, and with respect to this failure of character Nietzsche claims that "knowledge kills action", for "action requires the veils of illusion".[54] For such persons the Dionysian pattern is destructive (in contrast to the Apollonian); it undermines rather than intensifies life. They require the Apollonian artistic devices of fiction and pure illusion to come to

53. GT 7; KSA 1:57
54. *Loc. cit.*

51

their aid. Yet this solution is no longer the result of a balanced synthesis between the two principles — a synthesis which sublimates the volcanic drives of the Dionysian. It has become another sort of art altogether, one which has the purely Apollonian function of displacement and escape:

> Here, when the danger to his will is greatest, *art* approaches as a saving sorceress, expert at healing. She alone knows how to turn these nauseous thoughts about the horror or absurdity of existence into notions with which one can live.[55]

This displacement in art is no longer a productive synthesizing process but instead an escapist and mechanical measure. And it is extremely doubtful whether it will succeed as a completed project: being no longer the reconciliation with the "Dionysian barbarian", it is merely a temporary bypass of the disruptive Dionysian channels. This is the defence of the failed personality which has no sufficient inner resources to withstand Dionysian insight, and so its mechanism is eventually bound to collapse. This personality will then once again be exposed, even more dangerously, to the barbarian within itself. No defensive solution is finally adequate to shelter man from the hardships of existence.

This is the overriding theme of the new Nietzschean perspective, to be developed further in his later writings: there is no "metaphysical comfort" in the face of the "tragic truth". This truth, obstinate and clamorous, will inevitably rally against and overwhelm makeshift defensive barriers. The positive solution, according to the later Nietzsche, lies in education and character development, in reactivating positive individual power, and in overcoming mental weaknesses until one is transformed into

---

55. GT 7; KSA L:57. Compare Nietzsche here with Freud's argument on art as the outcome of psychological displacement or substitution (SE, *20*:64–65; *21*:75, 82–83).

"the Dionysian man". Relieved of the need for "metaphysical comforts" or for Apollonian fictions, the Dionysian man is less vulnerable. As soon as he is enabled to become a powerful person all these defences become meaningless and superfluous. The Dionysian pattern and perspective then enters a crucial phase in the process of shaping man into an *Übermensch* with optimum life power. It puts to test the authenticity of this life power by posing its most dangerous and exhilarating challenge: how to become strengthened by "tragic insight" rather than succumb to it.

Nietzsche's philosophical radicalism consists precisely in the fact that he creates and responds to this challenge: in doing so, he set in motion a technique of inquiry which later culminated in modern existentialism.[56] Until Nietzsche, the primary preoccupation of Western philosophy had been the formulation of a "true" doctrine — a static and metaphysical world-view accurately reflecting or explaining empirical reality as it is constituted by the categories of human knowledge. This attempt to build within theory functional, life-sustaining but — for all that — *non-authentic* fictions is, according to Nietzsche, a specifically Apollonian tendency. The purpose of Nietzsche's philosophy, in contrast, is to transcend the "Apollonian knowledge", for he did not believe in its ability to hold up under the internal pressures of Dionysian forces. He aims for attainment of the Dionysian perspective whose purpose is to unmask the fictive Apollonian basis of traditional metaphysics, and to peer under the intellectual superstructures of culture into the abyss of Dionysian intuitive truth. Traditional philosophical "truth" exists for Nietzsche *only to be overcome* once its sustaining rationalizations are unmasked. The process of exposure is characteristic

---

56. Notably, but by no means only, in Albert Camus, *The Myth of Sisyphus* (London, 1955) and in his *The Rebel* (New York, 1954).

of the tragic Dionysian man, whose positive power[57] is to be measured by how much "truth" he can overcome, and how much "serious truth" he can bear while functioning with vitality, without any metaphysical comforts. The unmasking progression towards authentic existence which begins to emerge in this, Nietzsche's first treatise, is fundamental to his psychology.

VII. Psychoanalytic Therapy as the Model for Understanding the Objective of Nietzsche's Psychology

The significance and viability of Nietzsche's new Psychology can be better appreciated by examining the form of psychological praxis which was to emerge after his death. It is in psychoanalytic therapy that we discover the workings of the Apollonian and Dionysian forces. The patient undergoing therapy is initially a non-authentic personality, characterized by self-denials, rationalizations, and other ineffective defence mechanisms. It is obvious that this personality is, for the most part, unable to function on its own, and relies on therapeutic aid and support. In the process of psychoanalytic therapy the Dionysian insights unmask the Apollonian superstructures and illusions. This is done in the course of attempting to assist the personality to function effectively without these defective neurotic mechanisms. If the therapy succeeds the Dionysian man flourishes, having become immune to the very Dionysian psychology which he and his therapist had used to unmask and free him from his Apollonian defences. The success of psychoanalytic therapy, like the power of the *Übermensch*, is measured by the same criterion, namely, how much truth one can bear without renewed escape to Apollonian fiction and a

---

57. For a discussion of this crucial concept of Nietzsche's mature philosophy, see Part Three of this study.

distorted mental defence mechanism. Seen in this way, the objectives of Nietzschean philosophy and Freudian psycho-analysis are quite similar — self-overcoming through education and the shaping of a healthy, authentic personality which will be able to function creatively in life despite its awareness of malady. This is the source of what is profound and therapeutic in Nietzsche's thought, and one reason it holds so much appeal.

We have seen that Nietzsche rejects the primordial instinct — the "Dionysian barbarian" — which is without any self-restraint in spite of being the life-sustaining instinct. In Nietzsche's eyes instinctuality *per se* in the absence of self-overcoming is worthless, because ultimately it will destroy itself. Nietzsche needs the process of psychological sublimation to restrain the life drive without, however, completely destroying it. Apollonian mystifications answer to psychological needs for self-preservation; they also constitute inner barriers against which drives struggle to erupt. Dionysian psychology opposes the Apollonian structures even though the price for destruction of these is a thorough awareness of the terror and meaninglessness of existence. So, in spite of the synthesis between them there exists a continuous struggle between the two kinds of perspective — the Apollonian and the Dionysian — or, in the terms we shall use later, a struggle between two kinds of *power* — the negative and the positive.

These grand psychological patterns, the Apollonian and the Dionysian, do not operate independently, but in a relation of *reciprocity*. The means employed by the Dionysian man, with his consciousness and self-knowledge, to unmask the Apollonian superstructures are Apollonian means *par excellence*; for only the Apollonian knows how to speak and think, and how to conceptualize the Dionysian intuitions. This is why Nietzsche regards Greek tragedy, which expresses these intuitions aesthetically, as an arena in which the necessary synthesis between the Apollonian and Dionysian takes place. There is, then, a striking similarity between Nietzsche's perception of the essence of Greek tragedy and the nature of psychoanalytic therapy, in which a synthesis must occur between the *id* and the rational organized *ego*. The *id* requires the Apollonian principle to organize and channel its erupting drives. The result is the creation of the primary processes in which the *id* expresses itself in the language of dream, free associations and neurotic symptoms. These dynamics exhibit a close affinity with the Apollonian-Dionysian synthesis in Greek tragedy.

These primary processes themselves, however, require penetrating analysis and rational interpretation. For this the psychoanalyst uses the hermeneutic-theoretical system of Freud's metapsychological doctrine in conjunction with the thoroughly rational and conceptual secondary processes. In this way he arrives, together with his patient, at a therapeutic and liberating interpretation. This is also the task of Nietzsche's philosophy which, in *The Birth of Tragedy*, employs analogous theoretical distinctions and concepts — such as those of the Dionysian and Apollonian — in order to analyse tragedy. This also has a therapeutic function as a liberation from ineffective "metaphysical comforts" (which parallel neurotic symptoms) and the construction and shaping of the tragic Dionysian *Übermensch*. The far-reaching purpose of psychoanalysis is to raise acts of human repression to the conscious level, and, through exposing them, to try to cope with them by conscious and creative overcoming — not by avoidance or escape. This is Nietzsche's aim as well, especially after *The Birth of Tragedy*. Art, as an inauthentic and "comforting" solution, makes way for the genuine unmasking perspective of the healthy and creative *Übermensch*, who no longer needs any comforting illusions.

At this point one might object to the parallel that we have drawn between the objectives of Freudian psychoanalytic therapy and those of Nietzsche's psychological philosophy by claiming that while Freud, as a practising clinician, was mainly

interested in the healthy individual in the given culture, Nietzsche
— the philosopher — was more concerned about the healthy
Übermensch in a superior culture yet to be realized.
Consequently Nietzsche, in criticizing prevalent values, would
be expressing a revolutionary tendency — in opposition to
Freud's seemingly more conservative approach, which stresses
the more limited ambition of adaptation to culture rather than its
"transfiguration".

There are two arguments, which are complementary and which
together meet this objection. The first proposes that Freud was
much more revolutionary than is generally assumed; the second,
that Nietzsche was less radical than he appears on the surface.

Taking the first argument, one may point out many passages
in which Freud criticizes the prevailing values of society, its
ethos and double standards. In these contexts he (implicitly)
recommends quite radical cultural reforms and modifications.[58]
Most of these statements are to be found in his later
metapsychological writings, dealing mainly with "civilization and
its discontents". Like Nietzsche before him, we find that Freud
stood on the side of the individual in his ineluctable fight against
social repressions. "Psychoanalysis", he wrote in 1921, "stands in
opposition to everything that is conventionally restricted, well-
established and generally accepted".[59]

Freud's Civilization and Its Discontents sets out the
irreconcilable conflict between the demands of the instincts and
the restrictions of civilization. In the first sentence of the work,
Freud expresses his almost Nietzschean suspicion of the
prevailing ethos:

It is impossible to escape the impression that people

---

58. Thus one tends to sympathize with Roazen's exclamation that "Freud
    stands out as one of history's great reformers". Paul Roazen, Freud:
    Political and Social Thought (New York, 1970), p. 252.
59. SE, 18:178

commonly use false standards of measurement ... and that they underestimate what is of true value in life.[60]

Freud did not merely aspire to accommodate the individual to a given society. He always sought the individual's happiness and self-fulfillment. His notion of health, like Nietzsche's notion of the creative *Übermensch*, was an ideal and revolutionary "ought" — not the conservative "is". He did not wish simply to accommodate the individual to society but dreamt, more ambitiously, of imposing "a therapy upon the group",[61] so that it could accommodate itself to the individual. While it may be that society provides the norm, Freud never accepted the term "normal" at face value, and was critical of its conventional, positive connotations. He notes, for example, that

> In an individual neurosis we take as our starting point the contrast that distinguishes the patient from his environment, which is assumed to be 'normal'.[62]

Freud (like Nietzsche) regarded repressive civilization as a primary cause of man's neuroses. The "fateful question" for him was "whether and to what extent [human] cultural development will succeed in mastering the disturbance of their communal life".[63] In consequence he sometimes played with the reformative idea of effecting "some particular form of civilization",[64] where the conflict between the "claim of the individual and the cultural claims of the group" would be reconciled. This conflict, described as a struggle between "Eros and Civilization", foreshadows Marcuse's revolutionary application of Freud's

---

60. SE, *21*:64
61. SE, *21*:144
62. *Loc. cit.* and cf. Philip Rieff, *Freud: The Mind of the Moralist* (New York, 1961), p. 390.
63. SE, *21*:145
64. SE, *21*:96

instinct theory, from which he derives the notion of "a non-repressive civilization".[65] Like Nietzsche's superior culture, Marcuse's civilization also revolves around the mechanisms of sublimation rather than those of repression.

The theoretical possiblity of such a reformative application of Freud's theory (and Marcuse is not the only example)[66] offers historical testimony that Freudian psychoanalysis contains a number of revolutionary elements — elements which narrow the gap between his therapeutic-clinical orientation and Nietzsche's "radical" philosophy.

From quite a different direction, Freud's psychoanalytic theory includes a principle which again allies him closely with Nietzsche: this is the well-known "Nirvana Principle", which was given currency in the West by Schopenhauer, and which Freud formulates as a tendency expressing "the effort to reduce, to keep constant or to remove internal tension due to stimuli".[67] Since Freud held no great hope of transforming the whole of civilization, but at best only some of its individual members, it was left to his cured patients to grow *equable*, and to attain a state of quietude. "Reality", he says, "is too strong for [us]",[68] recommending that we acknowledge its exigencies, and become sufficiently immunized in order to preserve our inner life from easy disturbance. This essentially conservative attitude appears also, as we shall see, in Nietzsche's notions of *amor fati* and *Nothwendigkeit*.

Both Nietzsche and Freud aspire to provide a therapeutic, philosophical cure for the sickness of our civilization. In this aim each appears to subscribe to the familiar prayer which asks that

65. Herbert Marcuse, *Eros and Civilization* (London, 1969), pp. 29, 112.
66. See other writings of the so-called "Frankfurt School": Habermas, Karl-Otto Apel, Adorno, Mitscherlich and others.
67. SE, *18*: 55–56
68. SE, *21*:81

we be endowed with three virtues: endurance — to accept the things we cannot change; courage — to overcome the things that can be overcome; and wisdom — to distinguish between the two. The quest for this wisdom, and the suggestions of rather similar techniques for its development constitute the main bond between Nietzsche and Freud.

VIII. Socrates Confronts the Dionysian-Apollonian Sublimation

We have seen that Nietzsche interprets tragedy, and art as a whole, as the product of a sublimatory synthesis which is "the expression ot two interwoven art-drives [*Kunsttriebe*], the *Apollonian* and *the Dionysian*".[69] He regarded sublimation as the psychological-aesthetic solution *par excellence* for man's primitive, Dionysian drives, restrained by rational, Apollonian structure. The danger of the Dionysian drives is eliminated by their reproduction at a higher level of creative expression; the instinctual, Dionysian content, however, remains intact and nourishes the Apollonian forms.

But with the appearance of Euripides, the Socratic rationalist, this creative synthesis was undermined; the rational, Apollonian principle began to dominate the raw Dionysian components. Moreover, the Apollonian was now displaced by Socratism, the latter aiming to completely suppress the Dionysian, to render it ineffectual and, ultimately, to dislodge it from its place in human nature. The supra-historical Socrates comes to represent the antithesis of the tragic Apollonian-Dionysian synthesis. Modified by the Socratic pressure, the aesthetic conception of truth is no longer a higher, sublimated expression of the chaotic Dionysian. It instead assumes the character of mimetic truth, a conception of truth as a precise reflection of empirical reality. Dionysian

---

69. GT 12; KSA 1:82 (my translation)

aesthetics, by contrast, does not attempt to model itself on the structures of the physical world; neither does it pretend to generate truths about it. In order to preserve spontaneous creativity, Dionysian aesthetics abjures scientific pretences and assiduously avoids any conflation of art and the scientific enterprise. The project of art is rather to shape and restrain human nature, providing an articulated form for the instinctual nature which, of itself, has no expressive capability apart from the mute eruptions, the dangerous, affective gestures of the "Dionysian barbarian". Moreover, the Apollonian perspective makes no claim to ultimate truths since, in the final analysis, it presents an *aesthetic* conception of the world.

With the emergence of Socratic rationalism, however, there arose a demand for absolute, immutable truths. This demand issues in a direct confrontation with the expressive project of Dionysian-Apollonian aesthetics. Such is the origin of Socrates' attempt, continued by Euripides, to reduce aesthetic values to clearly rational values. The motto, "To be beautiful everything must be intelligible",[70] is the motto of *"aesthetic Socratism"* under which the reduction was to be accomplished. From here it is a small step to the aesthetics of Euripides: "To be beautiful everything must be conscious". The Apollonian tendency is withdrawn, in Nietzsche's words, into "the cocoon of logical schematism".[71]

Nietzsche vehemently rejects this rational Euripidean aesthetics because it consciously aspires to undermine the Dionysian principle in the artistic synthesis that sublimates the instinctual drive. The Socratic/Euripidean attempt to "forcibly uproot" the Dionysian is, according to Nietzsche, an attempt to reduce art to a logical and conceptual abstraction, and to empty it of its nourishing and motivating principle. This uprooting of

70. GT 12; KSA 1:85
71. GT 14; KSA 1:94

the Dionysian can have only one consequence: the annihilation of a vital instinct without which there is no genuine art. With the destruction of the Dionysian, life itself is impoverished and its power is gradually eroded. For this reason, Nietzsche perceives Socratic rationalism as a profound threat to human culture. It prevents the highly developed, individually created art from evolving; it precludes the "rebirth of tragedy" which is essential to the "transfiguration of nature". It is with similar criticisms that Nietzsche later attacks science, ascetic morality and religion, and the various metaphysics which have been constructed to justify them.

But why should we consider the tragic man as a higher manifestation of human nature than the Socratic-theoretical man? To answer this question, we may turn to the psychoanalytic construal of the concepts of repression and sublimation and examine them more closely. These concepts are an ideal heuristic device for understanding the salient motifs of Nietzsche's psychological teachings. The question does pose a particularly thorny problem, because the theoretical world-view does appear, *prima facie*, to be more life-preserving than the Nietzschean perspective. Many rationalists affirm the world as good *just because* its structure is perspicuous under the light of reason — because it is in principle intelligible. Nietzsche's own world-view emphasizes the tragic and inscrutable dimensions of human existence: why should it not then be characterized as *hostile* to life?

IX. Repression : Freud and Nietzsche

The term "repression" or *"die Verdrängung"* is a key concept in Freud's psychoanalytic theory.[72] It refers to the process

---

72. On Freud's use of the term "repression" see particularly his 1915 treatise "Repression", SE *14*:146–158. On the four main meanings of this concept,

whereby a person tries to reject or confine to the unconscious those thoughts, images and memories which are bound to instinct. This process serves to displace and transform their energy and effect, and takes place when the gratification of a desire (pleasurable in itself) incurs displeasure, punishment and regret as a result of particular socio-cultural demands. Freud regarded repression as a general psychological mechanism which was fundamental to the notion of the unconscious as a separate domain of the psyche. In a broader sense, repression refers to any defensive mechanism and stands as the prototype of those defensive mental processes which are the mainsprings of much cultural creativity. Freud argues that repression is a *sine qua non* of cultural activity[73] and is particularly prominent among "saints and ascetics".[74] However, it is only a short-term defensive measure, for instinctual drives cannot be annihilated; they can only be temporarily inhibited. At best, repression constitutes a brief holding operation, after which instinct manifests itself with even greater destructive force, having been pent up within the confinement of the unconscious.

In developing the concept of repression, Freud referred directly to Nietzsche.[75] He was impressed by the latter's insight

and its relationship to other psychoanalytic concepts, see: Peter Madison, "Freud's Repressive Concept", *The International Journal of Psycho-Analysis*, 37 (1956): 75–81.

73. SE, *22*:110.
74. SE, *9*:35.
75. Freud posits that Schopenhauer "also knew of the mechanism of repression", but that he, Freud, arrived at the concept independently, and that his insights on the matter are not related to his study of Schopenhauer, for "I read Schopenhauer very late in my life. Nietzsche, another philosopher whose guesses and intuitions often agree in the most astonishing way with the laborious findings of psycho-analysis, was for a long time avoided by me ... [for] I was less concerned with the question of priority than with keeping my mind unembarrassed". SE *20*:59–60. In any event, as the still unpublished correspondence with his friend Silberstein testifies, young Freud did not avoid, in his early years at the University of Vienna, becoming an active member of a philosophical discussion group (around 1874) to

into the nature of repression and oblivion and their hidden defense mechanisms. This insight is aptly expressed by Nietzsche in terms of the relations of pride and memory.

> 'I have done that' says my memory. 'I cannot have done that' says my pride, and remains inexorable. Eventually — memory yields.[76]

This quotation from Nietzsche appears in Freud's personal album of quotations (at present in the Freud Museum in London). Looking at Freud's letter to Wilhelm Fliess, dated February 1, 1900, in which he informs his friend that he "[has] just acquired Nietzsche, in whom [he] hopes to find words for much that remains mute in [him]",[77] it seems reasonable to assume that the book in question is *Beyond Good and Evil*, where the quotations about the repression of memory appear.

In any case, Freud often emphasizes the close relationship between the phenomenon of repression on the one hand, and oblivion and its motivations on the other.[78] Although Freud is

which also belonged his other two good friends: Josef Paneth and Siegfried Lipiner. Both were very much interested in Nietzsche and eventually established a close friendship with the philosopher. Thus they brought Freud some knowledge of Nietzsche's ideas and notions (a fact admitted by Freud in his letter of 1934, published in Jones, New York, 1953–1957, Vol. III, p. 460). See also: William J. McGrath, *Freud's Discovery of Psychoanalysis* (Ithaca, 1986), Ch. 3 (esp. pp. 138–139), and mine: "Freudian Uses and Misuses of Nietzsche", *American Imago* 371–385.

I am grateful to Sigmund Freud Copyrights Ltd. of Colchester, England for giving me permission to use the relevant German letters of Freud to Silberstein for my research.

76. JGB 68; KSA 5: 86. Freud could have quoted another aphorism even more relevant to psychoanalytic doctrine, an aphorism declaring that we unconsciously repress and forget entire sections of our past out of a self-delusion that aims to idealize the ego (MA II: 1–37).

77. *The Complete Letters of Sigmund Freud to Wilhelm Fliess*, ed. Jeffrey M. Masson (Harvard University Press, 1985), p.398.

78. See, e.g., SE 6:4–7, 13–15, 19–24, 39–45. Freud's first use of the term 'repression' (in 1895) coincided with his study of oblivion in the hysterical patient (SE 2: 10).

here referring to Nietzsche's later book, in the philosopher's first treatise we already find the idea of the repression of the instincts and of representations that are linked to an instinct. In this context, Nietzsche refers to the figure of Hamlet as an exemplar of the man who is cast into the "chasm of oblivion", a chasm opened up by "true knowledge, an insight into the horrible truth".[79] Significantly Freud exemplifies his concept of "repression" — namely, an unconscious attempt to reject ideational concepts and thoughts which cause pain — using the same figure. For Freud too, Hamlet symbolised the man who represses the impulses and ideas that threaten his personality and wholeness.[80]

The idea of repression reappears with Nietzsche's introduction of the figures of Socrates and Euripides. Euripides, "uprooter of the Dionysian", and to a greater extent, Socrates, are the forerunners of a new culture, based not on the Dionysian-Apollonian synthesis, but on reason and logic alone. Nietzsche attacks the supplanting of art by science. To reject the Dionysian principle which is so essential to artistic creation is to transform artistic creation from an act of sublimation into an act which represses instinct. Science, according to Nietzsche, insofar as it aims to suppress instinct, is akin to the ascetic impulse which not only tries to suppress the instinctual, but also kills artistic creativity in consequence. It is impossible to eliminate the instinctual, Nietzsche argues, because it is in part constitutive of human psychology. However, instinct can be unduly constrained — as is evidenced by the Socratic *"logischer Trieb".*[81] Science successfully represses instinct, for it is itself a form of instinct.

In overcoming the Dionysian instinct, the drive of science and

79. GT 7; KSA 1:57.
80. SE 7:309–310.
81. GT 13; KSA 1:90.

reason may also bring about the *destruction of life itself* — an effect exemplified in the image of "the dying Socrates". Socrates defeated the life drive in overcoming the fear of his own death, and destroyed himself with his own hands: he "brought [it] about with perfect awareness and without any natural awe of death".[82] This is symptomatic of Nietzsche's account, and of his persistent opposition to any kind of battle against instincts. The attempt to annihilate them cannot produce a more powerful character; it will only weaken and ultimately destroy the personality.

Repression of the vital instincts results in a broken and chaotic personality which has lost both its coherence and authenticity. It is a process culminating in the state of "aggravated neurosis" which Freud discusses: a personality breakdown. The *Übermensch*, by constrast, possesses a unified personality, as Nietzsche so often emphasizes. Thus we have the principle which often recurs in Nietzsche's writings:

> To *have* to fight the instincts — that is the formula of decadence; as long as life is *ascending*, happiness equals instinct.[83]

Socratic rationalism and Christian asceticism both tend by nature to suppress the Dionysian instincts. The most threatening ramification of this tendency is the total confinement of artistic expression, which would block the natural course of sublimation or displacement. Instinct could then only be realized in the unrestrained form of the "Dionysian Barbarian". Its violent and indiscrimate aggression would then mark the destruction of human culture.

Repression is an integral part of the process of internalization (*"Verinnerlichung"*)[84] which consolidates the *authoritative* realm

82. GT 13; KSA 1:91.
83. GD "The Problem of Socrates" — 11; KSA 6: 73.
84. GM II — 16; KSA 5:322.

in man. Freud later interpreted this realm in terms of the super-ego, which represses instinct and thereby produces the psychological attitude of guilt — an attitude which Nietzsche vehemently criticises throughout his philosophical writings.[85] If the force of repression is manifest in cultural ideology, the attitude of guilt will dominate. But if sublimation is encouraged in its stead, a truly superior cultural expression may be possible. When repression is most prominent, such a culture can never develop. Here, then, we observe a further implication of the repressive tendency.

This repressive tendency is identified in Nietzsche's mind with the figure of Socrates and, despite his well-known admiration for the courage of *"the dying Socrates"*,[86] Nietzsche could not support the Socratic enterprise. As we shall see, Nietzsche, and Freud after him,[87] constantly argue in favour of sublimation against the processes of repression and suppression, and in order to achieve a clear understanding of why this choice was made, we shall have to examine the complexities of that key concept of both psychoanalysis and Nietzschean psychology — sublimation.

X. Sublimation: Freud and Nietzsche

According to Freud, *Sublimierung* describes an unconscious

---

85. For details see Part Three of his study. I agree with Bernard Lauret's *Schulderfahrung und Gottesfrage bei Nietzsche und Freud* (München, 1977), pp. 71–235, who argues that one of Nietzsche's concerns was the radical diminution of the guilt-feelings present in our culture. Curiously enough this author does not deal at any length with the concepts of repression, *Verinnerlichung* and *Sublimierung*.
86. GT 13; KSA 1: 91. And see Werner J. Dannhauser, *Nietzsche's View of Socrates* (Ithaca, 1974).
87. SE *11*:59–137; *16*:376; *17*:182; *21*:74–85, and Jacob Golomb, "Freud's Spinoza: A Reconstruction", *The Israel Annals of Psychiatry* 16 (1978): 275–288.

process in which the aim of an impulse is modified before it finds gratification. He postulated this process in order to account for a wide range of human activities which have no apparent connection with the instincts, but which are assumed to be motivated by them. An instinct is said to be sublimated when it meets three necessary conditions: a) it diverges from its original object and is deflected towards a new one; b) it is deflected from its original aim and is diverted towards a new one; c) its gratification by means of "civilised activity" has higher social value in a given culture than its gratification by means of the original form of expression.[88]

The term 'sublimation' was known before Freud, and he never claimed to have invented the concept. It is to be found in the works of Novalis, Goethe, Schopenhauer and particularly Nietzsche.[89] We might also include in this group Hegel, with his central notion of *Aufhebung*. This term has a clear structural affinity with *Sublimierung* since in both concepts the initial components are neutralised, preserved and sublimated. This affinity holds up despite the fact that Hegel tended to emphasise the logical-cognitive aspect of the process.

It will not be possible here to deal comprehensively with all the problems related to the psychoanalytical concept of sublimation,[90] and therefore we will concentrate exclusively on those aspects that play an important role in Nietzschean psychology.

What has already emerged in the foregoing is that the Freudian

88. SE *9*:187.
89. See Walter Kaufmann, *Nietzsche*, p. 219; Henri F. Ellenberger, *The Discovery of the Unconscious* (New York, 1970), p. 505; Norman O. Brown, *Life against Death* (Middletown, 1959), pp. 135–176.
90. See Edward Glover, "Sublimation, Substitution and Social Anxiety", *The International Journal of Psycho-Analysis* 12 (1931): 263–296; Frances Deri, "On Sublimation", *Psychoanalytic Quarterly* (1939): 325–334; Harry B. Levey, "A Critique of the Theory of Sublimation", *Psychiatry* 2 (1939): 239–270.

conception of sublimation, evident also in Nietzsche, involves the idea of transformation of value, sublimated activities being transformed into those that are held in highest esteem by society. This presupposes the existence of some mental faculty which internalises the dominant values of a given culture and is responsible for the whole process of sublimation. Freud referred to this faculty as the Super-Ego (*Über-Ich*, and its Nietzschean equivalent is the "higher self" (*das höhere Selbst*).[91] Thus a link can be made between Freud's concept and Nietzsche's as it is laid out in *The Birth of Tragedy* in virtue of the fact that during the process of sublimation the unifying characteristic of the Dionysian instincts is emphasised. Moreover, in Freud, the sublimated *Libido* instinct is transformed into *Eros* and this notion is reminiscent of Nietzsche's later view that the Dionysian is the result of the primary synthesis between the libidinous Dionysian-Barbarian and the rational Apollonian, the outcome of which is *Eros* — a dynamically creative superior culture.

Nietzsche's controversial preference for the likes of Cesare Borgia over Parsifal[92] can be better understood in the light of Freud's view that sublimation processes are especially developed in people with unusually strong instincts. This also goes some way towards explaining Nietzsche's vehement attacks on those religious ascetics who, by having eradicated the instinctual in themselves, were no longer capable of making a significant contribution to human culture. For Freud, sublimation is the only alternative to excessive repression which may deteriorate into an acute neurotic conflict. He writes:

> It is precisely in neurotics that ... the formation of an ideal heightens the demands of the ego and is met with the most powerful factor favouring repression; sublimation is a way

---

91. See below, Chapter Three.
92. EH III — 1; and AC 46; 61.

out, a way by which those demands can be met *without* involving repression.[93]

This comment accurately reflects the ideas which Nietzsche had formulated on sublimation years before Freud.

Another area of agreement between the two thinkers appears in their conceptions of art; both hold the view that art and artistic creation provide the main heuristic model for the mechanism of sublimation, and Nietzsche often reiterates the point that every enlightened culture is built upon artistic-sublimated creativity. He reached this conclusion in the light of his supra-historical investigations into the genesis of classical Greek culture and this is, no doubt, one of the reasons why he was so attracted to this period. His analysis of the cultural and psychological nature of ancient Greece was prompted by his intuition that this culture embodied and developed *certain individual patterns and dynamic psychic forces.* Nietzsche's preoccupation with the birth of Greek tragedy was in the main an attempt to isolate and define in this broad cultural context the psychology of *homo faber* — the creative individual. Thus *The Birth of Tragedy* was the seedbed of Nietzschean psychology and provided the framework for his later philosophical development.

A further aspect of Freud's conception of sublimation is his insistence that through this mechanism man becomes an autonomous subject, one who no longer depends on repressive exigencies external to himself in order to achieve his aims:

> The task here is that of shifting the instinctual aims in such a way that they cannot come up against frustration from the external world. In this, sublimation of the instincts lends its assistance. One gains the most if one can sufficiently heighten the yield of pleasure from the source

93. SE *14*:95.

of psychic and intellectual work. When that is so, fate can do little against one.[94]

If sublimation can divert the instincts from external aims and objects to products of spontaneous creativity then it should be possible for a man to determine his sublimated activities according to his aptitudes and personality. He will become self-governing, relatively free from and unconditioned by external circumstances, in contrast to the person whose actions are imposed upon him by mechanisms of repression and suppression which lead to internal conflict and transform him into a passive, defensive creature ruled by prohibitory external social forces. This person, lacking the capacity for sublimation, is doomed to be led and manipulated by stronger individuals. Freud points out that this capacity for sublimation is present only in a minority, those possessing that rare psychic make-up which elevates them above the common majority.[95] Nietzsche takes a similar line. His distinction between the repressive and the sublimating personality types becomes the axis around which he constructs his two kinds of psychology: that of the extraordinary *Übermensch*, and that of the ordinary man.

At this point it is worth examining the main difference that seems to exist between Freud's conception and that of Nietzsche. Freud, as we have seen, lays emphasis on the unconscious dimension of the sublimatory process — an emphasis which seems far removed from Nietzsche's idea of the autonomous *Übermensch*, since it is almost impossible to concieve of an autonomy which is based on unconscious processes beyond one's rational control. However, this apparent inconsistency may be considerably diminished if we recall that one of the chief aims of psychoanalytic treatment consists in creating the proper

94. SE *21*:79.
95. SE *9*:193.

conditions for the intensification of the sublimated process in the patient. This process relies on the Freudian energetic model, according to which the amount of energy required to repress the instinct is equal to that needed for sublimated activities. In assisting the patient to overcome his repressions by raising them to a conscious level, psychoanalytic treatment helps to free the mental energy that was mobilised solely for repressive acts. The released energy can now be used creatively through sublimative channels (although there is no guarantee that it will be so used). The psychoanalytic enterprise echoes Nietzsche's persistent opposition to excessive repression, in which the liberating processes of sublimation are stifled, deterring the advancement of culture and the creation of the *Übermensch*. For Nietzshce, as for Freud, this was too high a price to pay.

We can now turn to certain Nietzschean texts to examine the way in which they illustrate his own particular views on sublimation. It was not until 1886 that Nietzsche first introduced the term *Sublimierung*,[96] yet his perception of the underlying processes was apparent in his very first philosophical works. Thus the short essay, *Homer's Contest* (1872) already constitutes an analysis of classical Greek culture in terms of sublimation and the displacement of instincts. Here Nietzsche claims that

> Man in his highest and noblest capacities, is wholly nature and embodies its uncanny dual character. Those of his abilities which are terrifying and considered inhuman may even be the fertile soil out of which alone all humanity can grow in impulse, deed and work.[97]

96. MA I — 1; KSA 2: 23.
97. TPN 32; KSA 1: 783.

Following this psychological observation, which regards culture as a sublimation of the beast in man, Nietzsche goes on to consider ancient Greek culture as an historical embodiment of this process. Consideration of a number of historical events leads him to the conclusion that the Greeks, who were thought of as the most humanistic of the ancient cultures, were also characterised by "a trait of cruelty, a tigerish lust to annihilate".[98] At the same time he recognised a Homeric world distinguished by "the extraordinary artistic precision, calm, and purity of line". How to explain this "artistic" mantle which covers "night and terror"?[99] As in *The Birth of Tragedy*, he finds the answer personified in the god of Delphi: Apollo — patron of art and sublimation, who "purified" the Greeks of the "Dionysian barbarian" elements. One of the main occasions for these acts of purification was the widespread Greek institution of "competition" (the classical *agon*), which sublimated the destructive urge into accepted cultural channels. The entire ancient Greek establishment ensured that the struggle never ceased, thus perpetuating these sublimatory acts. Had these opportunities for sublimatory competition been eliminated from the Greek *polis*, nothing would have remained except the "pre-homeric savagery" and the *polis* would have degenerated into Dionysian barbarism. This parallels Nietzsche's attitude in *The Birth of Tragedy* where he emphasises the importance of another Greek cultural institution — the ritualistic presentation of tragedy — and showed how it too constituted a sublimatory process.

In contrast to *Homer's Contest*, where Nietzsche is concerned with sublimation related solely to the aggressive instincts, *The Birth of Tragedy* stresses this mechanism in the context of the sexual, erotic instinct and as an expression of "the sexual omnipotence of nature".[100] Nietzsche later takes up this

98. *Loc. cit.*
99. TPN 34; KSA 1: 784–785.
100. GT 8; KSA 1: 58.

conception of the sexual nature of the drive which nourishes the process of sublimation in *Human, All Too Human*.[101]

Nonetheless, it is to the original line of thought as formulated in *Homer's Contest* that Nietzsche returns. Thus in *Daybreak* (1881) he talks of "the refined cruelty"[102] towards one's (inferior) rivals, expressed in the need to excel. There can be little doubt that the drive towards excellence and the sublimated competition which Nietzsche discovered in the Homeric *agon* of ancient Greece, coupled with the synthesis of the Apollonian and the Dionysian which he found in Greek tragedy, lay at the heart of his formulation of a general principle of sublimation; and it was this principle — when applied to other cultural phenomena such as morality, religion and art — that ultimately led him to the monistic principle of the will to power.[103]

Nietzsche sought a fundamental, monistic psychological principle which would describe and explain the crucial process of "self-overcoming" (*Selbstüberwindung*) and self-control, a pre-requisite for the formation of the *Übermensch*. A first step towards the formulation of this principle was an analysis of those mental mechanisms which are geared towards "self mastery and moderation" of the drives.[104] Nietzsche summarises "six essentially different methods to fight the violence of a drive":

> Avoiding opportunities (for its satisfaction), implanting regularity into the drive, engendering satiety and disgust with it and associating it with a painful idea such as that of disgrace, evil consequences or offended pride, then

---

101. See MA II: 1–95; KSA 2: 415; and JGB 75; 96; 189.
102. M 30; KSA 3: 39.
103. Thus Heidegger, although he disregarded the Nietzschean concept of sublimation, was basically right in maintaining that in GT Nietzsche had already implicitly seen the "artistic phenomenon" as a "most familiar mode of will to power", *Nietzsche*, Vol. I, pp. 70 and 72.
104. M 109; KSA 3: 96. Freud has a parallel description in his 1915 treatise "Instincts and their Vicissitudes", SE *14*:117–140.

dislocation of forces and finally a general weakening and exhaustion.[105]

Thus, one method for overcoming the inner drives is avoidance and denial. This is the course chosen by the monk or the ascetic, and is by its very nature passive and negative. A second method consists in imposing strict Apollonian regularity on the instinctual chaos. This method is characterised by an active ordering principle, although, as with the first method, there is still no element of sublimation. It is only the instinct's external form of expression and initial gratification which is transformed, not its purpose and object. Then there is the method of oversaturation — of giving the instinct free reign until it becomes loathsome. This again bears no resemblance to the sublimation process. A more subtle method attaches a system of negative associations to the instinct through negative operant conditioning as it is called in behavioural psychology. However, this still has nothing to do with repression or sublimation. The fifth method, which Freud calls "displacement" (*"Verschiebung"*) does relate to sublimation insofar as it satisfies the first two conditions of sublimation, namely, modification of the instinct's purpose, and of its object of gratification. However, this method does not necessarily involve any elevation to a higher cultural level, for the displaced instinct could find gratification just as easily *on a plane* as unacceptable and anti-social as the original one. Hence there is no absolute correspondence between displacement and sublimation.[106] The final method listed is that of repression, and the very tone in which Nietzsche presents this possibility makes it clear that he finds it unacceptable.[107]

105. M 109; KSA 3: 98.
106. This description of the displacement of instincts appears in Nietzsche already in 1880 in *Der Wanderer und sein Schatten*, sec.37.
107. "Finally, sixth: he who can endure it and finds it reasonable to weaken and depress his *entire* bodily and physical organization will naturally thereby also attain the goal of weakening an individual violent drive: as he does, for

In contrast to the above methods, condemned as being either sterile or violently suppressive,[108] Nietzsche, later in the same text, offers an aphorism which stresses the productive and valuable nature of those acts which sublimate the instincts:

> One can dispose of one's drives like a gardener and, though few know it, cultivate the shoots of anger, pity, curiosity as profitably as a beautiful fruit tree on a trellis; one can do it with the good or bad taste of a gardener.[109]

Thus the cultivating aspect of the sublimatory act is a corollary of the third element of the process; that is, the elevation of the instinct to a valuable cultural plane. This elevation concludes the process of constructing and shaping the instinct and endows this process with exalted moral meaning:

> One should place before him quite clearly the possibility and the means of being cured (the extinction, transformation and sublimation of this drive).[110]

The three elements of the Hegelian concept of *Aufhebung* and of the Freudian concept of sublimation are succinctly expressed

example, who like the ascetic, starves his sensuality and thereby also starves and ruins his vigour and not seldom his reason as well".

(M 109; KSA 3: 98)

108. Kaufmann, *Nietzsche*, p. 221, in referring to the first five methods says that through them Nietzsche describes the process of "sublimation, as conceived" by him. However, our analysis of the three meanings of the concept of sublimation in Nietzsche and in Freud obliges us to reject this interpretation. Not only does Nietzsche not indicate here in any way the process of sublimation and its artistic creations, but his silence concerning this process in the context of his description of the aggressive-suppressive methods of "combatting vehemence of a drive" clearly implies his understanding of the essentially different nature of sublimation. In the latter, there is neither struggle nor suppression but a productive co-operation with the drive, utilizing it creatively through the mental faculties controlling the acceptable outlets of the instincts.

109. M 560; KSA 3: 326

110. M 202; KSA 3: 176.

here: the elimination of a certain aspect of the instinct, its shaping and elevation, and the preservation of its original, motivating force.

Time and again Nietzsche contrasts the two principal attitudes towards the instincts: creative sublimation versus destructive repression. Believing that both science and religion are dominated to a large extent by the latter, while artistic creation is impelled by the former, he consistently comes down on the side of artistic creation and seeks out sublimative channels for other cultural expressions of basic human instincts.

XI. Socrates the Scientist versus Socrates the Musician

For Nietzsche, however, the path to sublimation through artistic creativity was threatened by the figure of Socrates, who stands as the tutelary genius of all those philosophers seeking repression or "negation of the senses". He personifies both rationalist, repressive tendencies and the superficial optimism of human culture.[111] Yet, why did Nietzsche reject this particular expression of optimism when his entire treatise, in contrast to Schopenhauer's pessimism, is permeated with a strong sense of optimism? To answer this question, we must return briefly to the dualism which Nietzsche envisaged at this stage.

On the one hand there is art, the Apollonisation of the Dionysian, the dominant force in the synthesis. On the other hand there is science, which is exclusively Apollonian, in the guise of a logical drive which claims to be absolute. Nietzsche sides with art and takes up arms against the repressiveness of science. He believes that repression is destructive not only when the restrained drive breaks free of its bonds, but also, and to a greater extent, when this drive is completely destroyed, for in the

111. GT 14.

absence of instinct, culture as a whole will necessarily decline and disappear. The effect of science is to displace instinctual powers, diverting them from life-sustaining Dionysian channels to ultimately valueless (albeit practical) ends. The life-forces are threatened to the point where the very desire to live might ebb away, and thus theoretical Socratic optimism turns "into tragic resignation".[112]

Nietzsche rejects intellectual optimism because it is superficial, and ineffective as a long-term cultural constraint. This view derives from seeing rationalism as a circumscribed phenomenon. Nietzsche here adopts a clearly Kantian motif; it is the nature of rationalism to question and study itself and thereby become embroiled in problems of knowledge which are beyond the capacity of reason itself to solve. The resultant loss of confidence undermines the very enterprise of rationalism and gives rise to destructive sceptical trends which have a paralysing effect on life and action. Logic "finally bites its own tail"[113] and yields to tragic knowledge. The only remedy is for man to return to art.

For Nietzsche, science, or, more precisely, the pretensions and illusions it propagates, harbours another great danger. One of the most powerful of these illusions is the belief on the part of the theoretical man that:

> ... thought, using the thread of causality, can penetrate the deepest abysses of being, and that thought is capable not only of knowing being, but even of *correcting* it.[114]

However, since the chain of causality is infinite, man can never arrive at knowledge of being as such. Thus, after the exhausting

112. GT 15; KSA 1: 102.
113. *Ibid.*; KSA 1: 101.
114. GT 15; KSA 1: 99.

journey to the infinite boundaries of science, the scientist achieves a state in which he "enjoys and finds satisfaction in the discarded covering". The scientist finds the absolute "truth" in his own construction and in the systematic search. He cares "more for the search after truth than for truth itself".[115] Hence the whole endeavour lacks authenticity. It is no more than a "powerful illusion" and being limited in principle it could only ever prove to be a temporarily effective defence. "Tragic illusion" inevitably intrudes upon scientific optimism, making the resultant despair that much greater and its outcome even more destructive. By contrast, art does not pretend to unmask the truth in the sense of giving a rational explanation. Rather it is an authentic activity born out of the genuine problems of life. It contains no self-contradictory or inherently limited rationalist pretensions, and can remain productive by virtue of its creativity and infinite variety. It is in innovative art that Nietzsche seeks the cure for the destructive effects of Socratic rationalism, and it is in his formula, "Socrates who practises music",[116] that Nietzsche aims to circumvent despair and the barbarism that is attendant upon it, a barbarism whose symptoms are already evident. Nietzsche proposed a new synthesis, that of the Dionysian-Apollonian with the Socratic — of the artistic with the rational-scientific. Without repressing any element in this synthesis, he aspires to fuse them together in a creative sublimatory and rehabilitating culture.

Following this demand for a synthesis between art and science, the notion of art takes on a broad significance:

> Will the net of art, even if it is called religion or science, that is spread over existence be woven even more tightly and delicately, or is it destined to be torn to shreds in the

115. *Loc. cit.*
116. GT 15; KSA 1: 102.

restless, barbarous, chaotic whirl that now calls itself 'the present'?[117]

Faced with renewed 'Dionysian barbarism' following the "death of God", a barbarism that threatens European culture, Nietzsche is willing to overlook the essential difference between sublimatory art on the one hand, and religion and science on the other. He is ready to enlist even the latter in the struggle and prefers repressive discipline to a victory of barbarism.

Curiously enough, Nietzsche considered one of the first symptoms of this renewed barbarism, namely Wagnerism, to be the most effective remedy against it, although realisation of his mistake brought a swift and fierce reaction against his former idol. It is worth noting that in the novel framework of Nietzsche's philosophical psychology there is no immanent need for Wagner, and Nietzsche had to resort to the old formulas of Schopenhauerian metaphysics in order to promote the cause of Wagnerism.[118] This was a fact he greatly deplored in the later preface to *The Birth of Tragedy* and in his mature writings.

Nietzsche wishes to come to the aid of "modern man". He begins by ascertaining the reasons for the failure of Socratic culture. The first reason is related to the dialectic tension between the culture's intellectual superstructure and its social reality. In a quasi-Marxist analysis, Nietzsche makes the point that a fundamental tenet of scientific culture is the well-known Socratic saying that knowledge is virtue and that knowledge will lead to virtue. This maxim has led its adherents to adopt a false and superficial optimism which is incapable of withstanding the assaults of historical reality. It fostered the notion that happiness could be achieved through the accumulation of knowledge and

117. *Loc. cit.*
118. It is interesting to note that Schopenhauer himself fiercely opposed any attempt to exploit his philosophy in advancing the Wagner cause. See Karl Löwith, *From Hegel to Nietzsche* (New York, 1967), p. 180.

scientific achievement. However, this culture, "to be able to exist permanently, requires a slave class, but with its optimistic view of life it denies the necessity of such a class".[119] This parallels the Marxist view that this scientific, industrial culture requires for its existence and development an exploited and penurious proletariat. There is a wide discrepancy between this culture's expectation of "the earthly happiness of all" with its "belief in the possibility of such a general intellectual culture", and social reality. The contradiction becomes intolerable when the worker-slave class erupts and sweeps all culture away in a wave of destruction.

> There is nothing more terrible than a class of barbaric slaves who have learned to regard their existence as an injustice, and now prepare to avenge, not only themselves but all generations.[120]

Thus the optimistic rationalism of Socrates destroys not only the Dionysian, tragic culture but also his own — as a result of the inner tensions this very optimism generates. In the first instance, then, the collapse of Socraticism can be analysed in the Marxist terms of a dialectical tension between its ideological superstructure and its socio-economic foundations.

The second reason for the failure of the Socratic scientific culture lies in the ideological contradictions internal to the superstructure itself. Here again the argument hinges on the exaggerated and baseless optimism which characterises scientific culture. It calls into question the claim of science to the absolute and universal validity of its own insights. This is a claim upon which the entire culture is based, and one which ignores

---

119. GT 18; KSA 1:117.
120. *Loc. cit.* On other affinities between Nietzsche and Marx, see Peter Heller, "Nietzsche and Marx in their relation to the Enlightenment", in his *Studies on Nietzsche* (Bonn, 1980), pp. 149–191.

the actual moral and material situation of the individual. Whereas the original Socratic optimism regarded as limitless the epistemic power to grasp reality, later philosophers have imposed limitations on this capacity and have established boundaries which imprison man within a self-constructed prison of knowing. Nietzsche is obviously referring here to Kant's "Copernican Revolution"; Reason's self-criticism setting limits on its own rational knowledge.

This Kantian revolution, which grew out of the philosophical confusion concerning the power of knowledge, ushered in a tragic culture unaffected by "the seductive distractions of science".[121] Thus one could say that a main impulse of Nietzschean philosophy is to extricate man from the decadent pessimism which threatens to undermine him and his culture — a pessimism which, in the history of ideas, has its roots in a powerfully destructive emotional reaction to the Kantian revolution.

Nietzsche's proposed solution is again the therapeutic synthesis of art and science, a solution echoing the conclusion of the original part of The Birth of Tragedy. In light of Kant's circumscription of the area of scientific validity, Nietzsche saw art's opportunity to provide some sort of stability and support. After Kant, the possibility arose of rectifying the distortions in cultural methods of defence, clearing the way for Nietzsche himself to adopt the tragic position of the human being who gazes at tragic and limited existence and knowledge, but no longer needs the contrived optimism of science. Such a man does not negate himself (as Schopenhauer demanded), nor does he seek any "metaphysical comfort". He instead embraces tragic

---

121. GT 18; KSA 1:118. We have here a clear anticipation of Nietzsche's later distinction between the negative enticement (Verführung) of the negative science, and the positive enticement (Versuchung) of "la gaya scienza"; see also Chapter Seven.

art. Nietzsche could perhaps paraphrase Kant's famous words as follows: "I *am obliged to abolish knowledge* in order to pave the way for art". And this is the ideal that Nietzsche presents in order to counterbalance the consequences of the Kantian revolution:

> Let us imagine a coming generation with such intrepidity of vision, with such a heroic penchant for the tremendous; let us imagine the bold stride of these dragon-slayers, the proud audacity with which they turn their backs on all the weaklings' doctrines of optimism in order to 'live resolutely' in wholeness and fullness; would it not be necessary for the tragic man in such a culture, in view of his self-education for seriousness and terror, to desire a new art, the art of metaphysical comfort, to desire tragedy.[122]

The first outlines of the Nietzschean ideal of the *Übermensch* are here already being sketched. Yet, this early solution still contains an element of artistic metaphysical comfort, and the concept of *amor fati* has not yet appeared. The later Nietzsche will transcend this solution, and arrive at the authentic Dionysian man who needs no comfort whatsoever.

122. GT 18; KSA 1:118–119.

CHAPTER TWO

On the Uses and Disadvantages of Psychology for Life

Introduction

Nietzsche's new psychology offers a functional and genetic explanation of art and culture in terms of man's psychological needs. The fiction-constructing Apollonian drive provides man with the artistic and metaphysical comforts he requires in order to survive. From the Dionysian-Greek attitude emerges a psychology that penetrates the illusory "veil of māyā" which adheres to these Apollonian structures.

Nietzsche continues to develop this new psychology in the second essay of *Untimely Meditations.* This time the subject of his analysis is not art but history. In this essay ("On the Uses and Disadvantages of History for Life") Nietzsche focuses on history not as a scholarly discipline with a fixed and rational structure, but as it relates to a particular, human mode of consciousness — the historical consciousness. Thus he treats the problem of history in a manner which is of direct relevance to psychology. Nietzsche's psychological concerns in this essay have a sense of urgency about them which follows from a belief in their relevance to contemporary culture. Just as his interest in the psychology of artistic creativity stemmed primarily from his unsubstantiated hope that the cure for the maladies of his time (the revival of tragic art) would be administered by Wagner, so too his interest in history arose from his diagnosis that the period was one of "the mighty historical movement",[1] especially strong among Germans of the past two generations. Here, then, is a continuation of Nietzsche's attempt to freeze and to suspend the cultural values and the intellectual fashions prevalent in his time. As in *The Birth of Tragedy*, where he tried to carry out a psychologization of "the theoretical man" living in the final stages of Socratic culture, so in the present essay he tries to warn his contemporaries of the psychological dangers lurking in one of the most conspicuous and derivative expressions of "the theoretical culture": historical culture and over-reliance on historicism.

In this persists Nietzsche's insistence that the genuine philosopher must strive to overcome his age. We have seen this attitude in *The Birth of Tragedy*, where he attacked the rationalistic Socratic trend. We will see it again in his struggle against historicism. If Nietzsche saw art as the remedy against science, his answer to the danger of an excess of historical consciousness is the ability to forget, which is a prerequisite for the fully creative life of the powerful man.

Why did the historical consciousness now become the main target of Nietzsche's psychologization? It is quite likely that the critical and sometimes angry reaction of philologists to *The Birth of Tragedy* provided a personal stimulus in addition to his own professed motives; Nietzsche may have felt that it was precisely their proclivity for historical method that had encouraged his critics to reject his first work, as not meeting their 'scientific historical' standards.[2] He may have seen the

1. HL: Foreword (p. 59); KSA 1:246. All quotations from this essay are taken from the English translation by R. J. Hollingdale, in *Untimely Meditations* (Cambridge, 1983), and referred to by chapter and page of this edition.
2. See for example Karlfried Gründer (ed.) *Der Streit um Nietzsche's 'Geburt der Tragödie'* (Hildesheim, 1969); I.H. Groth, "Wilamowitz-Mollendorf on Nietzsche's *The Birth of Tragedy*", *Journal of the History of Ideas* 11 (1950):

philologist's contention that *The Birth of Tragedy* was inadequate as a work of historical scholarship as resulting from the excessively historical *Zeitgeist* of the period. Therefore, Nietzsche's struggle against historicism tries, among other things, to undermine the very intellectual foundation for such criticism. Like *The Birth of Tragedy*, then, this essay is testimony to Nietzsche's desire to overcome the elements of his own personality and profession which inhibited his developing genuine philosophy. If *The Birth of Tragedy* was an attempt to overcome his own 'inner philologist' then this second *untimely* essay is an attempt to overcome the 'historian' within. Nietzsche's Foreword says that "we are all suffering from a consuming fever of history".[3] This is not merely a figure of speech: it is a confession that he suffers himself from this very malady.[4]

I. On the Uses and Disadvantages of Forgetting and Remembering [5]

The first chapter of the essay deals with the mental functions of forgetting and remembering. Memory is the psycho-physiological prerequisite for historical consciousness; it is memory which accumulates the mass of data upon which man attempts to impose order. This organizing activity is vital, for without it the mass would become overwhelming in its weight and arbitrary facticity. Thus the Apollonian principle is enlisted, giving shape to the inchoate material of memory. This process provides the

179–190; M.S. Silk and J.P. Stern, *Nietzsche on Tragedy* (Cambridge, 1981), pp. 90–107.

3. HL (p. 60); KSA 1:246.
4. And see other explicit statements in the Foreword and at the end of the essay (HL 10; KSA 1:324).
5. "Der Nutzen and Nachteil des Erinnerns und Vergessens" — this paraphrase of the entire essay is given by Karl Löwith in *Jacob Burckhardt: Der Mensch inmitten der Geschichte* (Lucern, 1936), p. 35, in a section "Burckhardt und Nietzsche", pp. 11–61.

source of illusion and simulation, of self-deception, denial and repression.

We have already seen that Nietzsche anticipated the psychoanalytic concept of repression. Closely connected with forgetting, repression was presented as a non-authentic, cowardly activity of the weak. Now Nietzsche states this view even more explicitly, declaring that the man who suffers from an excess of memory is forced, in order to maintain his psychological balance, to perform an excess of repressive acts.[6]

By contrast, the "unhistorical man" is overburdened neither by memory nor by the weight of historical consciousness and so is capable of opening himself to a full range of instincts and emotions. Here again one finds contrasted the Apollonian and the authentic Dionysian: the latter possesses no historical memory or consciousness and thus has no need of repression or forgetting.

In *The Birth of Tragedy* Nietzsche still drew support from Schopenhauerian metaphysics, but in this essay on history he anchors his analysis of memory and forgetting in a different metaphysics — that of Heraclitus' doctrine of becoming. The Heraclitean dialectic is vital to Nietzsche, for it allows him to conceive of memory and forgetfulness within the shifting frames of time and space. In a metaphysics of fixed *aeternae veritates* memory's function is to copy reality and hypostatize consciousness. According to Plato, for example, memory is required in order to learn geometry for only through memory do we have access to the fundamental forms of space behind the world of appearance. Such a metaphysics relies on the concept of memory to sustain its commitment to a 'true world' beyond this one, a world outside of the here and now of human experience. In the world of Heraclitean metaphysics, by contrast,

6.   HL 1; KSA 1:249–250.

reality is at every moment in a state of flux, and so provides a suitable home for the authentic Dionysian man, who seeks eternity within the moment. According to Nietzsche, there is no significant metaphysical role for the traditional concept of memory to play, for there is no eternal world in itself beyond the here and now.

Schopenhauer's metaphysics, in which the "blind will" exists as a constant ontological entity beyond phenomena, requires memory as the means of fixing that eternal entity in human consciousness. It is thus not a suitable metaphysics for Nietzsche's present purposes. Instead, Nietzsche's descriptions of the 'unhistorical' state of affairs find more appropriate support in the evolving dynamism of Heraclitus, which is without aim or purpose, structure or fixed patterns. There remains, however, an important distinction between the Nietzschean and Heraclitean perspectives. Heraclitus posits the *logos* as the unifying principle of becoming,[7] while in Nietzsche's scheme this role is played by life itself. On this point, Nietzsche outdoes Heraclitus within his own territory — for the rejected notion of a static *logos* in a world of constant flux and becoming is indeed problematic.

Nietzsche's essay goes on to argue that "the ability to forget" and "the capacity to feel *unhistorically*"[8] are necessary conditions for achieving happiness. The unhappy man is hypothetically exemplified as one condemned to see "becoming" everywhere,[9] and to be eventually lost in its flux. This radical case suggests a psychological principle: forgetting is a

---

7. See especially fragments 197, 198, 199, and 206 in G.S. Kirk and J.E. Raven, *The Presocratic Philosophers* (Cambridge, 1957), pp. 188–191.
8. HL 1 (p. 62); KSA 1:250.
9. *Loc. cit.* This Nietzschean example of *Homo Heraclitus* (possibly inspired by Plato's *Cratylus*) served as the referential basis for a short story by Jorge Luis Borges, "Funes the Memorious", in *Labyrinths* (Penguin Modern Classics, 1970, pp. 87–95). Borges indirectly introduces Nietzsche by saying that the hero of this story is perhaps a "precursor of the superman, a vernacular and rustic Zarathustra" (*ibid.*, p. 87).

prerequisite of all action, and life is impossible without it.[10] This principle, Nietzsche suggests, does not apply solely to weak individuals, but also to whole peoples and cultures. However, proper application of this principle is always conditional on a prior test, which questions "how great the *plastic power* of a man, a people, a culture is".[11] This is an important proviso, for it allows that memory *in itself* is not an absolute evil, just as forgetfulness is not an absolute good. The danger of memory and the positive value of forgetting are direct functions of an individual's or a people's power and of their Apollonian ability to impose meaning and order on the stream of unstructured becoming. An individual's or culture's ability to develop and achieve form is proportionate to its psychological power. Just to the extent that one is capable of confronting and creatively organizing the chaotic flood of past events, may one be in command of memory without resorting to the defensive measures of repression.

Thus Nietzsche presents a new criterion of the *Übermensch*. In *The Birth of Tragedy* the power of a man is measured by how much truth he is able to bear and by how much suffering he is able to endure. In the present essay Nietzsche gives the criterion another form: how much is a man able to remember and assimilate within himself?

The process of forgetting may be an active process deriving from an abundant and positive power, and in this respect it differs from repression. Healthy life spontaneously rejects all those elements that cannot assist it in its growth and self-forming, that hinder its intensification. The need to forget is a

---

10. This idea was already implied in GT 7, where Nietzsche contrasts the "Dionysian man" with Hamlet, for whom "action requires the veils of illusion". Such illusion is also provided by forgetfulness, covering the tragic features of reality.

11. HL 1 (p.62); KSA 1:251. This "plastische Kraft" with its psychological connotations is later (and even in this essay) called "Macht".

basic characteristic of life itself, which requires limits and boundaries for its enhancement. This is the Apollonian principle of organization and order: "A living thing can be healthy, strong and fruitful only when bounded by a horizon".[12] These positive functions of forgetting contrast sharply with repression, which is a reaction of weakness, deriving from an inability to successfully sublimate or transfigure what lies outside, or what is internally threatening.

In *The Birth of Tragedy* Nietzsche had already declared the supreme importance for life of the process of sublimation. But it has also been claimed that sublimation contains the element of obliteration which implies, among other things, a forgetfulness of any events that cannot be assimilated into a new, sublimatory synthesis. In this essay Nietzsche speaks of the organic growth of life, and in this context it is possible to better understand why forgetting should be vital to the act of sublimation and the process of character formation: every process of growth and development contains a component that withers and falls, to be replaced by a new element more suited to its task. In this light, one might be encouraged to regard the Apollonian consciousness as *life preserving* insofar as it is historical and remembering; the non-historical and forgetful Dionysian would by the same token be life negating. Nietzsche is not unaware of apparent tensions which this view suggests and so reminds us of their resolution, declaring that

> the unhistorical and the historical are necessary in equal measure for the health of an individual, of a people and of a culture.[13]

Here we encounter once again the dichotomous psychological

---

12. HL 1 (p.63); KSA 1:251.
13. *Loc. cit.*

structure that had emerged in *The Birth of Tragedy*. It is clear that *both* the Dionysian and the Apollonian are vital to the maintenance of healthy, complete life, just as they were both necessary to the development of artistic creativity and Greek tragedy. The dialectic between the Apollonian and the Dionysian is here retained and elaborated in conjunction with the vitalistic principle determining what should be remembered and what forgotten — "sensing when it is necessary to feel historically and when unhistorically".[14] This dialectic of remembering and forgetting, of Apollonian and Dionysian, will ultimately merge in the new Dionysian character, endowed with positive power. This character is already implicit here in Nietzsche's description of "the most powerful and tremendous nature" standing "in superlative health and vigour".[15]

Developing his psychology further, Nietzsche claims that all human activity may be interpreted as the expression of instincts blocking other possible instinctual expression. The instincts, as he describes them, are engaged in a continual struggle, each fighting to control the others while externalizing itself in the form of a given activity. There is no place for justice or equanimity in these dynamics. To act, it is necessary to forget and to suppress the competing instincts:

> He forgets most thing so, as to do one thing, he is unjust towards what lies behind him, and he recognizes the rights only of that which is now to come into being.[16]

This kind of forgetfulness is the source of instinctual action which was to serve as a therapeutic antidote to both Nietzsche's own and his peers' scholasticism. The activities which emerge from it are spontaneous, intuitive and indifferent to logic, and so

14. *Loc. cit.*
15. *Loc. cit.*
16. HL 1 (p.64); KSA 1:254.

stand opposed to behaviour which has as it genesis rational deliberation based on memory, comparison and analysis. Instinctual action is not only given a preferred status by Nietzsche, but is seen as essential course for human life in the absence of any eternal, ontological entity endowed with metaphysical import. The crucial task of psychology is to describe the conditions for such a life; it makes vital life possible by freezing our beliefs in those metaphysical values which constrict spontaneity. Nietzsche's psychologizations are his means of preserving the Dionysian, spontaneous element in life, and thus of intensifying life itself.

The dialectic of memory and forgetting can be clarified by examination of the dynamic-instinctual model, according to which every activity is merely the expression of the instincts at the expense of the others. Every act of remembering is an active process of some instinct, and is possible only when combined with the forgetting and suppression of other instincts. Memory is impossible in the absence of forgetting — and *vice versa*. Forgetfulness, therefore, is not (as is commonly supposed) a passive state: it is the necessary counterpart of memory. There is no inherent rationality in these mental mechanisms, and Nietzsche articulates them in quantitative and energetic concepts alone. This or that memory appears to consciousness not because of its inherent rational value, but because a particular instinct has temporarily succeeded in overpowering the others, and presses for a particular cognitive expression.

A similar energetic model of mental mechanisms is provided by Freud, who says that "Every instinct is a piece of activity".[17] Moreover, in this "*metapsychological* presentation", which adopts the "economic" point of view, Freud maintains that the processes of repression and recollection, or more specifically

17. SE *14*:122.

the reciprocal relations between the unconscious and the conscious, arise rather from the energetic principles than from the concrete contents of unconscious ideas. When a certain drive mobilizes enough energy (through the *Besetzung* mechanism), it contrives to appear at the conscious level — despite the Ego's efforts to keep it in the unconscious. In other words, irrespective of their actual contents, we recall events and representations of wishes when their driving force succeeds in overcoming the mental energy which kept them suppressed in the unconscious.

An analogous approach is found later in Nietzsche's theory of perspectivism. There is no exclusive validity or truth-value attached to one perspective over another, since none is absolutely true. The dominance of certain perspectives is explained in terms of the interests and force of the drive that moves and sustains any 'interpretation'. Nietzsche's demand for epistemological tolerance is based on this psychologistic approach; strong emotional forces may nourish and promote a particular perspective, but because no truth-value attaches to it absolutely, all perspectives are from a purely cognitive point of view equally valid and legitimate. It is therefore desirable that they should all find avenues of expression, as long as they do not suppress the attitude of epistemological tolerance and power of expression itself.

This dynamic model is also relevant to the validity of history. If human memories are the consequence of the merely contingent domination of one instinct over others, then a conception of history as a purely cognitive and scientific discipline is clearly misguided. The value of history, according to Nietzsche, must therefore be based not on its immanent validity but on the extra-cognitive arena of life itself:

> These historical men believe that the meaning of existence will come more and more to light in the course of its *process*; ... they have no idea that they in fact think and act

unhistorically, or that their occupation with history stands in the service, not of pure knowledge, but of life.[18]

This psychologization of history contains the seed of another of Nietzsche's future ideas, *viz.* the problematic doctrine of "the eternal recurrence of the same".[19] If every act and event, and every memory of an event is only an externalized manifestation of underlying drives; and if, further, these internally competing drives are limited and finite, then it follows that everything that happens is merely an externalized recurrence of the very same instincts and their finite manifestations in history and historical consciousness. Even if all the finitely many impulses within man achieve full expression on occasion, the battle between them never ceases. In the long run, then, the same pattern is repeatedly realized in which a certain impulse expresses itself, disappears under the pressure of another impulse, reappears again, and so on *ad infinitum*. Even if the sequence of appearance is occasionally altered, there is an upper limit to the number of possible configurations (however vast) of a finite set of components. Nietzsche therefore declares that "the past and the present are one, that is to say, with all their diversity, identical in all that is typical".[20]

The distinction in this essay between the "historical" and the "suprahistorical" also suggests the later idea of the *Übermensch*. The "historical man" or the Hegelian type to whom Nietzsche alludes, adopts historical comfort and believes in progress and reason revealed in history. In this respect he is a variation of the

---

18. HL 1 (p.65); KSA 1:255.
19. Exactly what Nietzsche meant by this doctrine has been the subject of much scholarly debate. See e.g. Marvin Sterling, "Recent Discussions of Eternal Recurrence: Some Critical Comments", *Nietzsche-Studien* 6 (1977): 261–291; and Bernd Magnus, "Eternal Recurrence", *ibid.*, 8 (1979): 362–377.
20. HL 1 (p.66); KSA 1:256.

optimistic Socratic character, who believes that science is capable of realizing the supreme good. The "historical man" is weak, lacking Dionysian vitality and requiring external consolations in order to obviate the meaninglessness and chaos of existence. Hegel's belief in the rationality of history is similar to the Socratic conception of science and reason as life-preserving. By contrast, the man who adopts the "suprahistorical vantage point"[21] (like the Dionysian in *The Birth of Tragedy*) rejects the rational and teleological conception of history. In his eyes, there is no significant historical progress. Instead, "the world is complete and reaches its finality at each and every moment".[22] Every single moment for him is completely fulfilled, with no purpose beyond itself. This attitude makes authentic life possible, independent of consolation. The ability to forego various kinds of intellectual comforts becomes for Nietzsche the supreme test of the power of the personality.

II. On the Three Kinds of Historical Consciousness

Nietzsche's essay continues by classifying kinds of historical consciousness according to the extent of memory and forgetfulness each uses and requires. The focus of discussion moves (in a manner typical of Nietzsche's thought) to a description and analysis of different psychological types needing an historical consciousness of one kind or another. Again, Nietzsche's starting point is the distinction between the powerful and the weak character. Each of the three types of historical consciousness may be implemented either in a positive, life-enhancing way or in a negative, destructive one. Like *The Birth of Tragedy*, then, this early essay provides an outline of

21. HL 1 (p.65); KSA 1:254.
22. *Ibid.* (p.66); KSA 1:255.

Nietzsche's fundamental distinction between positive and negative power.

Nietzsche now postulates a close correlation between the personality types and the patterns of historical consciousness:

Each of the three species of history which exist belong to a certain soil and a certain climate and only to that: in any other it grows into a devastating weed. If the man who wants to do something great has need of the past at all, he appropriates it by means of monumental history; he, on the other hand, who likes to persist in the familiar and the revered of old, tends the past as an antiquarian historian; and only he who is oppressed by a present need, and who wants to throw off his burden at any cost, has need of critical history, that is to say, a history that judges and condemns.[23]

Monumental history is necessary to the powerful and active man, who prepares himself for a "great fight" and needs "models, teachers, comforters".[24] This historical approach makes possible a psychological identification with exemplary figures, and reassures those who aspire to greatness, when temporary sickness or hesitancy immobilizes them. Monumental history assists by showing them that "the greatness that once existed was in any event once *possible* and may thus be possible again".[25] The ambitious man is therefore encouraged to reject any gnawing uncertainties and to pursue the path of glory.

The personality that requires monumental consciousness differs from the historical person, sketched by Nietzsche in the first chapter of his essay. The addiction to history provides a pretext to continue life just as it is. *Monumental* history instead

23. HL 2 (p.72); KSA 1:264.
24. *Ibid.* (p.67); KSA 1:258.
25. *Ibid.* (p.69); KSA 1:260.

lends support to the powerful man, an incentive to a great existence that will express his inner power — rather than merely an excuse for being alive. It is clear that the kind of history whose purpose is the glorification of existing power cannot be scholarly, critical and precise. The task of intensification and encouragement requires both a selective assessment of the past, and an obliteration of differences between past and present. The more a man feels that the circumstances of the glorious past resemble present conditions, the stronger is his faith that similar heights are within his own reach:

> How much of the past would have to be overlooked if it were to produce that mighty effect, how violently what is individual in it would have to be forced into a universal mould and all its sharp corners and hard outlines broken up in the interest of conformity![26]

This approach to history as a grand drama is both assimilative and functional; in its script one seeks out "effects in themselves" and ignores the circumstantial differences between the past and the present. In some respects it is the kind of historical consciousness that belonged to Nietzsche himself, who often adopted a monumental standpoint with regard to the past. The history of ancient Greece as well as various exemplary historical figures — Socrates, Jesus, Schopenhauer — are all summoned in order to create a momentous "transfiguration" of our nature and culture.

Given its distorting *modus operandi*, monumental history requires both the mental functions of remembering and forgetting: memory emphasizes the great lines common to the monumental events of the past and the present, and forgetfulness blurs or obliterates the specific differences between past and

---

26. *Ibid.*; KSA 1:261.

present. The selective and organizing nature of this history bears an unmistakable Apollonian stamp; it may be characterized as an historical Apollonian consciouness *for the sake of* the Dionysian. Similarly, in *The Birth of Tragedy* the Apollonian artistic force served the Dionysian "tragic insight".

But the inherent distortions of monumental history generate in it a certain destructive potential. It may harm those men of action who, in their enthusiasm and their pursuit of the heroic, plunge headlong into action, disregarding essential differences between the present and that past. Their danger lies in realizing (too late) that such differences persist stubbornly and may prevent the re-enactment of past greatness. The weaker individual in need of historical illusions is even more seriously threatened; if he tries to assume the monumental consciousness the consequences will be most severe. While powerful men may make of it a positive rationalization, the opposite will obtain for the weak and indolent: the individual who fears great deeds (lest they emphasize his own pettiness) may use monumental history as a false justification for his own *akrasia*, which is to use it as a *negative* rationalization. Such a man will say, "Behold, greatness already exists", and his motto will be "Let the dead bury the living".[27] Nietzsche, then, does not posit monumental history as a good in itself. Its positive or negative value is a direct reflection of the type of person who utilizes it.

The same is true of *"antiquarian"* history, characteristically evidenced in men of a conservative and reverent nature. Its impact is again primarily psychological, providing the individual with a sense of belonging to or being embedded in a cultural and historic tradition. It can thus best serve those who require connectedness with past roots as a vehicle to the development of personal identity. In short, it may strengthen the character

27. HL 2 (p.72); KSA 1:264.

which is too weak to cultivate a robust self-identity from inner resources alone. Nietzsche's description in this essay of this type of historical consciousness makes it clear that history is functioning in a comforting, supporting role similar to the role of art in *The Birth of Tragedy*:

> But this antiquarian sense of the past is of the greatest value when it spreads a simple feeling of pleasure and contentment over the modest, rude, even wretched condition in which a man or a nation lives ... he can live contented and never feel the want of art.[28]

However, antiquarian history contains its own distortions; it too is mobilized in the service of present needs at the expense of accuracy and historical authenticity. This selectivity becomes dangerous, rejecting as it must any elements of the present that exhibit radical novelty or revolutionary change. Only that present which may be elucidated in terms of the past is recognized and acknowledged. The antiquarian position consequently manifests a kind of conservatism which suppresses whatever innovative elements may fail to fit the framework of the past — and this can result in a degeneration of the present. Disallowing new and original perspectives, this conservatism "no longer conserves life but mummifies it".[29]

Nietzsche was of course deeply opposed to any slavishly conventional patterns of thinking; his proposed "revaluation of all values" encourages radically "open" intellectual and existential "horizons". He objects most vehemently to the conservative-antiquarian consciousness when it claims exclusive priority and attempts to dominate alternative attitudes and perspectives. Nietzsche is no reductive "Darwinist", setting the will to survive above all else: the goal of this psychology is not

28. HL 3 (p.73); KSA 1:266.
29. *Ibid.* (p.75); KSA 1:268.

existence for its own sake, but a sublime and powerful existence. This goal is utterly at odds with the merely life-preserving, conservative ambitions of antiquarian consciousness. As his view of monumental consciousness attests, however, Nietzsche does not object to using the past for the sake of the present. It is when the past itself becomes the locus of reference and meaning for life that it becomes anathema to him, for it then works to stifle all that is dynamic in the present and to truncate future possibilities as well.

The antithesis to the excessive dominance of the past is provided in a third kind of historic consciousness: *"critical"* history. This attitude is also designed to serve life and, much like antiquarian history, is particularly instrumental in the life of the weaker individual. But rather than attempting to preserve the past at the expense of the present and future, critical history judges and condemns it. Antiquarian history required an excessive, if selective, degree of memory in order to absorb the past and find comfort in it; critical history also requires memory, but for the purpose of rejecting and casting aside the remembered historical burden. In contrast to the conservative attitude, then, critical history advocates a radical revolution of values which would destroy the sacred icons of tradition and the "pieties" of the past. Having criticised the "mummifying" effects of antiquarian history, however, Nietzsche also voices strong reservations about its extreme antithesis. He recognizes a serious danger inherent in the rejection of all tradition and in the failure to appreciate essential identifications of present with past. The prevailing view of him as simply a radical revolutionary is misconceived; Nietzsche recognized well the positive psychological aspect of conservatism and the importance of retaining a sensitivity of the roots of the past:

For since we are the outcome of earlier generations, we are also the outcome of their aberrations, passions and errors

... it is not possible to wholly free oneself from this chain.[30]

Thus Nietzsche attacks the popular illusion that it is possible to sever oneself completely from tradition, to become a "free spirit" by indiscriminately rejecting one's entire past. For psychological reasons Nietzsche does not believe that such a 'liberation' is even feasible, let alone desirable. He is not at all reluctant, of course, to oppose either the metaphysical traditions of the past or the accepted Christian ethic. But even in this he acknowledges that he draws his "fire, too, from the flame lit by a faith that is thousands of years old".[31] He does not, then, profess to be a nihilist or to seek a complete cleavage with the past and its values. Neither is he a radical revolutionary, freed of the restraints of tradition, and descending into the historical arena from some atemporal, ahistorical pinnacle. Nietzsche's commitment is to a path of transformation which is arduous and painstaking; the rigours of self-education and the anguish of self-conquest constitute a process of slow and difficult evolution. He believes in a steady and persistent educational advance, devoid of grand illusions, which only gradually leads one to new patterns of life and thought.[32]

Nietzsche's own psychology continues to develop in his account of "critical history". Previously, he had maintained that forgetfulness and memory are a function of the struggle between instincts attempting to gain expression in external action. Here he extends this dynamic-instinctual picture to the broader context of human praxis, which has always been characterized by violence (*Gewalt*) and injustice. This is an inevitable move in Nietzsche's thought: if every action is merely an expression of the strength of instinct suppressing other instincts, it follows

30. *Ibid.* (p.76); KSA 1:270.
31. FW 344; KSA 3:577, and see FW 377.
32. HL 3, and see Chapter Three.

that the entire web of human action is characterized not by the measured justice of immanent reason, but by the violence through which an instinct may rise to power. This point finds apt expression in Nietzsche's dynamic-psychological definition of life as "that dark, driving power that insatiably thirsts for itself".[33]

Nietzsche believed that these distinctions between three types of historical consciousness had been passed over by his contemporaries' demand *"that history should be a science"*.[34] Observing that scientific and rationalistic history in Germany was gradually overwhelming this 'triadic' historical consciousness, Nietzsche was prompted to discuss its dangers at length.

Just as aesthetic Socraticism was represented in *The Birth of Tragedy* as an intensification of the Apollonian principle at the expense of the Dionysian, so here scientific Socratic history intensifies the antiquarian and critical types of consciousness while eradicating the monumental element. This tendency upset the delicate balance between history and life, just as in ancient Greece Socraticism distorted the relationship betwen art and life. Despite their respective flaws and potential distortions, each of the three kinds of historical consciousness made its own organic — and necessary — contribution to life. Nietzsche's psychological explications of art and history centre around the primacy of life and aim at its intensification. Scientific history, by contrast, threatens to suppress vitality and spontaneity. The elevation of rational truth over vitality disturbs the sensitive dynamic balance between science and life. Whereas all previous types of historical consciousness collected their data in a selective manner *for the sake of life*, scientific history now indiscriminately pursues and accumulates data, flooding the memory with historical information valued for itself only. The

33. HL 3 (p.76); KSA 1:269.
34. HL 4 (p.77); KSA 1:271.

consequence is, eventually, a disjointed and one-dimensional personality.

An historical consciousness which is oblivious to our psychological needs cannot contribute to a Nietzschean "education" of character. An authentic education requires the assimilation of relevant information *for the sake of life*. Scientific history is mere erudition, concerned with the individual only as a fact-gathering automaton. This deprives the personality of the opportunity to synthesize recollected information into a vital and organic pattern relevant to its needs. A weakened personality results[35] and a schism develops between science and life, form and content. These circumstances leave the way open for the appearance of *barbarism*, which attacks culture itself. To understand these dynamics it is necessary to understand Nietzsche's particular concept of culture. At one point he defines it as:

> a unity of artistic style in all the expressions of the life of a people.[36]

It is the instinctual Dionysian-Apollonian dynamic of unifying and ordering experience into a coherent, organic pattern that makes culture (and the personality) possible. If the instincts are not properly cultivated a pseudo-scholasticism, a kind of intellectual barbarism, will result. In this context, Nietzsche initially discusses the effects of scientific history, but he later also identifies religion, philosophy and science as activities which *may* repress the vital instincts of those who pursue them. Unrestrained, these may perpetrate the decay of civilization. A counterforce is required, and Nietzsche tries to provide one — his psychology. Psychology works to freeze the deleterious mechanisms of pure science, religion and metaphysics and to

35.   *Ibid.* (p.79); KSA 1:274.
36.   *Loc. cit.*

restore the vital powers essential to culture. From this perspective, Nietzsche is clearly anti-nihilistic. The repression of instinct by an excessively rational historicism alienates human character from its own nature; the individual becomes a stage actor who has been cast in inauthentic roles. The philosophical psychologist, however, is able to unmask this performance, exposing the disingenuous ideologies and beliefs which alienate men from their genuine powers. It is important to distinguish this function of psychology from a Rousseauian "return to nature"; it is not a matter of restoring to man a natural goodness which has been repressed by culture.[37] Instead, Nietzsche is suggesting his psychology can cultivate just those features of human character which alone make culture possible.

Modern, scientific history discourages the pursuit of greatness and suppresses the impulse to rise above the mediocrity of one's period. Nietzsche offers an alternative heuristic history which emphasizes the value of the heroic and encourages the powerful man to struggle "against his time". Psychology is thus decisive in determining the course of historical study, demanding that it contribute to the formation of *personality* rather than merely amassing information as an end in itself. But the character of the student of history is equally decisive: he must possess at the outset a personality of sufficient power if his studies are to succeed.[38] At this point, then, Nietzsche's psychology is primarily concerned with prompting a reactivation of personal power; his freezing psychologizations are only a preliminary, if necessary, phase in the process.

In the present essay, Nietzsche rejects a purely objective historicism as quite useless; only a "subjective study" of history — a study which actively engages the personality of the student and is determined by its needs — can provide an authentic

37. See MA I 463, and Chapter Three below.
38. HL 6 (p.94); KSA 1:293–294.

education. In a sense, then, historical study must assume the character of artistic creativity, and admit the influence of instinctual Apollonian *illusion*: history-as-art rather than history-as-science is in Nietzsche's view a solution to the decadence of a lifeless historicism:

> only if history can endure to be transformed into a work of art will it perhaps be able to preserve instincts or even evoke them.[39]

This suggests an historical attitude which is both artistic and responsive to the life instincts. In *The Birth of Tragedy* Nietzsche portrayed the Greek god Apollo in opposition to the "barbarian Dionysus", but these remarks on history suggest that the process is now reversed: artistic history *arouses* the Dionysian instincts and directs them towards vital, heroic activity. If science has dominated life, life must then overcome science by implementing its instinctual aspects. Intolerant of the oppressive constraints of rational science, life will reassert its free and spontaneous nature—as, for example, in creating an authentic morality:

> For speak of any virtue you will ... in every case it becomes a virtue through rising against that blind power of the factual and tyranny of the actual ... It always swims against the tide of history, whether by combating its passions ... or by dedicating itself to truthfulness.[40]

---

39. HL 7 (pp.95-6); KSA 1:296. Thus Kaufmann's observation that here "Nietzsche unmistakably abandons his previous preoccupation with art to turn to values outside the aesthetic realm" (*Nietzsche*, p.142) needs some qualification. As we shall see here, and later, Nietzsche continues to regard artistic values as vitally significant models for the solution of cultural problems. Thus he seeks to apply aesthetic values to other realms of the spirit — here, for example, the historical consciousness.
40. HL 8 (p.106); KSA 1:311.

These remarks surely contain no revolutionary novelty; one need only recall the voluntaristic moral philosophy of Kant, which might well have contributed to Nietzsche's heuristic method. Autonomy is a necessary condition of Kantian morality; man must overcome nature in free, creative, legislative action. For Nietzsche, too, morality requires a free, creative overcoming of the amoral natural given (although without the guidance of "pure practical Reason"). At the same time, morality is possible only against a condition of amoral nature: for Kant moral action only emerges through an act of overcoming nature and responding to the commands of duty. Nietzsche's conception of history is analogous to the Kantian conception of nature in that it exists just in order to be overcome — the morally neutral facticity and quasi-naturalistic laws of history exist in order to be surpassed. The significance of history for the powerful individual lies precisely in his capacity to overcome the natural and given course of events, and to create an alternative pattern of *supra-historical* values. In this respect history is always the servant of supra-history, which constitutes its meaning.

Of the three modes of historical consciousness, monumental history provides the most direct transition to a supra-historical attitude. It is thus natural for Nietzsche to value it more highly[41] than either the antiquarian or critical modes. Monumental history focuses our attention on heroic men who successfully surpassed the limitations of their age, overcoming the natural progressions of history. These are the great, creative legislators who foreshadow Nietzsche's later concept of the *Übermensch*, exemplifying the highest standards of humankind and providing its most exceptional models and paradigms.

41. Even though in the last chapters of the essay he does not explicitly refer to it by this name.

III. Nietzsche Versus Hegel

Nietzsche's preference for monumental history and his emphasis on the *individual* in history are both motivated in part by his rejection of Hegel's historical universalizing "world-processes". The centre-point of Hegelian global history is the Absolute, a rational and objective *telos.* Nietzsche wished to locate the personality of the exceptional individual in its place; his psychology provides an antithesis to Hegel's impersonal *Zeitgeist.* Like Kierkegaard, Nietzsche gives priority to the subjective individual and conceives of his philosophy as specifically post-Hegelian. While Hegel conferred value on the individual only as a vehicle of the historical *telos,* Nietzsche took the primary concern of philosophy to be the existential authenticity of individual working in history:

> The time will come when one will prudently refrain from all constructions of the world-process or even of the history of man; a time when one will regard not the masses but individuals ... No, the *goal* of *humanity* cannot lie in its end but only *in its highest exemplars.*[42]

The Hegelian historical process places the individual and his self-identity in service of the "masses" — the world community in whose metaphysical development he participates. Nietzsche reverses the Hegelian attitude, locating the significance of both history and the masses in their capacity to contribute to the fulfilment of the individual. The exemplary individual is *eo ipso* the supreme goal of the entire process.

Psychology plays a decisive part in Nietzsche's preference for the monumental historical process, for psychology is concerned in the first instance with the person and his self-development. The antithesis of Hegel's universal dialectic — psychologization —

---

42.   HL 9 (p.111); KSA 1:317.

shifts the philosophical focus from the history of the mass community to the historical individual, from absolute reason to the contingent, passionate personality.

In *The Birth of Tragedy* Nietzsche's own method was dialectical, accounting for the work of art in terms of a dynamic oppositional relation in which the Dionysian aroused the Apollonian and united with it to form a synthesis. Now, in spite of his rejection of Hegel's historical dialectic, Nietzsche continues to make use of an analogous dialectical structure: the formation of supra-historical man occurs as a synthesis of the individual and the masses. The mass community and its history comprise one of the two terms required by any dialectical relation, and is indeed essential as the raw material producing the individual, as the obstacle which he must overcome, and as an instrument of practical assistance.

Nietzsche's desire to defend the subjective individual against an objectifying totality, and his personal project of overcoming the intellectual vogue of his own time, both encouraged his criticisms of Hegel. But an even more pressing consideration motivated his thought: the conclusions of the Hegelian narrative implied a form of nihilism, suggesting that human life in the here and now is without value, that the immediate present has no significance:

> for Hegel the climax and terminus of the world-process coincided with his own existence in Berlin ... everything that came after him was properly to be considered merely as a musical coda to the world-historical rondo ... as superfluous.[43]

Nietzsche believed that Hegel had committed the most serious possible philosophical offence, viz., claiming that *this* life is devoid of meaning. If, as Nietzsche sardonically commented, the

43. HL 8 (p.104); KSA 1:308–309.

self-explication of the absolute spirit reached its culmination in Hegel's own existence, post-Hegelian life would lack any point or significance. Indeed, many of Hegel's successors (for example, Eduard von Hartmann) were most eager to discuss the imminent end of the world as the crowning consequence of the Hegelian dialectic. Nietzsche's struggle against this consequence is itself evidence that Hegel's concept of "the end of history" is not to be taken literally. The process of the self-explication of the absolute spirit must continue indefinitely — and if even if it *had* terminated with Hegel, this would hardly have brought about the end of *historical* dialectics.

Nietzsche's rejection of Hegel's rational teleology is at the same time a rejection of the Darwinian theory of evolution.[44] Darwin of course nowhere suggests a specifically *rational* teleology. Nonetheless, the law of selection reductively analyses all innovations and changes within a species in terms of a quantitative increase in survival capacity. In principle, then, even creative innovations in culture could be explained in this way, from which it follows that each stage of evolutionary change is necessarily of greater value than the one preceding. The conclusion is forced, then, that in the history of human evolution no past historical figure, however heroic, can have the same stature as figures of the present day. The more recent is necessarily the more highly valued. When Nietzsche, by contrast, claims that the goal of mankind is the formation of its "highest exemplars", he is not proposing an alternative teleology; his account must abjure the very notion of evolutionary progression in order to allow for the emergence of past exemplary figures:

These individuals do not carry forward any kind of process but live contemporaneously with one another; thanks to history, which permits such a collaboration.[45]

44. See also Chapter Three, sec. VI.
45. HL 9 (p.111); KSA 1:317.

Monumental historical consciousness respects the suggestion that values of the past can be preserved in the present, and the present preserved in the future. It thus provides an alternative to the doctrines of the Hegelian *Zeitgeist* and Darwinian evolution — an alternative which Nietzsche was to later elaborate in his own doctrine of "the eternal recurrence of the same".

Life and instinct are given primacy in Nietzsche's psychology over reason and knowledge. This priority lies at the heart of his critique of Hegelian philosophy, which identifies history and culture with *rationality*. Thus Nietzsche remarks that

> life is the higher, the dominating force, for knowledge which annihilated life would have annihilated itself with it.[46]

Nietzsche in fact not only targets the Hegelian deification of reason, but rejects the entire philosophical tradition of rationalism from Descartes onwards. When he replaces the Cartesian *cogito, ergo sum* by vivo, ergo cogito,[47] he reverses the relation of dependency. One thinks and reasons only because one exists and lives. This expression of the principle of primacy of life is perhaps somewhat crude; it is even reminiscent of the *merely* instinctual Dionysian-barbaric. However, a more sophisticated version aptly characterizes the creative sublimation of culture through the refinement of the instincts: "Only give me life, then I will create a culture for you out of it!"[48]

This formulation of Nietzsche's principle exhibits an affinity with an essential principle of Freudian metapsychology: "where *id* was, there ego shall be".[49] The ego is the cultural agent, creator of civilization — and its protector against the barbarous

---

46. HL 10 (p.121); KSA 1:330–331.
47. *Ibid.* (p.119); KSA 1:329.
48. *Loc. cit.*
49. SE 22:80.

id. At the same time, however, the instincts are not to be simply repressed: this would only impoverish the sublimatory processes and weaken the ego. Nietzsche also vehemently opposes the repressive excesses of erudition, scientism and, above all, historicism. These were, in his view, the instruments of cultural decline. In response, he pursues an effective "delivery from the malady of history"[50] through both the "unhistorical" element of oblivion (forgetfulness) and "supra-historical" instinctual life. These are Nietzsche's antidotes to the illness of his time.

It would be a mistake, however, to interpret these remedies as an attack on rationality as such, or to suggest that he wished to suppress all knowledge and science in favour of a Rousseauian "return to nature". On the contrary, the Apollonian principle of self-knowledge (expressed in the maxim "Know thyself") is an integral part of his psychology. In *The Birth of Tragedy* Nietzsche looked to the Greeks for a model, believing that they had succeeded at grasping the principles by which a culture may creatively "organize the chaos". He returns to them again in this essay, noting that they had masterfully learned to assimilate what was foreign and alien in response to their own authentic needs and requirements. These reflections bring Nietzsche to a guiding principle of his entire psychology:

> Each one of us ... must organize the chaos within him by thinking back to his real needs.[51]

An individual's *Bildung* is comprised of an indefinite number of experiences, ideas and concepts, including a tremendous burden of superfluous information. Through awareness of his authentic needs he may organise and refine this chaos into an harmoniously sublimated whole. Likewise, it is through self-knowledge that a culture can develop "a new and improved

50. HL 10 (p.122); KSA 1:332.
51. HL 10 (p.123); KSA 1:333.

physis".[52] But these transformations are only possible when history is enlisted in the service of the needs of life.

The idea of culture as a refinement on nature (as well as the anti-Hegelian motifs) do not only appear in the second of Nietzsche's *Untimely Meditations.* They are developed further in "Schopenhauer as Educator", a subsequent essay in the same series. Here Nietzsche advocates a similar project of "assisting nature" by promoting philosophers and culture. In overcoming nature, we are actually helping it to achieve its ends. He later rejected this notion (from *The Gay Science* onwards), characterizing nature as a brute given, without direction or purpose. Nonetheless, "Schopenhauer as Educator" contains the concept of *overcoming* which remained central in Nietzsche's thought through all its modifications, and which functions as its unifying thread. Whether Nietzsche is concerned with overcoming nature, or contemporary culture, or ourselves, this theme represents far more than a rejection of the mechanistic Darwinian theory of evolution. This is particularly clear in "Schopenhauer as Educator", where Schopenhauer is less an anti-Darwinian figure than he is an *anti-Hegelian* one.[53] In particular, the essay makes explicit Nietzsche's criticisms of Hegel's conception of philosophy and philosophers.

Hegel thought of philosophical works as an intellectual reflection of their times, apprehended in consciousness. Indeed,

---

52. *Ibid.*; KSA 1:334.
53. Thus Walter Kaufmann's statement, in reference to this essay in particular, and to Nietzsche in general, that the philosopher "was aroused from his dogmatic slumber by Darwin" (*Nietzsche*, p.167) is somewhat exaggerated. It is true that there are several anti-Darwinian elements in Nietzsche's thought, but his greatest intellectual adversary was Hegel rather than Darwin. Without Nietzsche's attempt to furnish a complete antithesis to Hegel, it would be difficult to see him as the precursor of Existentialism. As with Kierkegaard, Nietzsche's Existentialism originated in the attempt to overcome Hegel's spirit of absolutism and his comprehensive philosophical system.

in his famous preface to the *Philosophy of Right* Hegel poetically portrays philosophy as a kind of *Nach-denken* (after-thought): "The owl of Minerva spreads its wings only with the falling of the dusk".[54] Nietzsche challenges this conservative view of philosophy with the figure of Schopenhauer who, he insists, must be admired for having thought and acted *against* his time — for having been untimely indeed. And in numerous other ways Nietzsche uses Schopenhauer as a counterforce to the Hegelian conception. Hegel claimed that a true philosopher must acquire the richest and widest education possible in order correctly to explicate his particular *Zeitgeist*; Nietzsche stresses Schopenhauer's lack of any formal education. Hegel insisted that philosophy should never venture into the arena of *prescriptive* edification — properly limited to the task of mimetic description, philosophy should never give "instruction as to what the world ought to be";[55] Nietzsche identifies Schopenhauer as the model of proper philosophy precisely because of his role as a catalytic agent of transformation and transfiguration of his time. The true philosopher-as-educator is no instrument of historical traditions or intellectual institutions, but rather a revolutionary figure who inspires his generation with exceptional and sublime ideals.

The subject of the philosopher's relations to the state makes the contrast between Nietzsche and Hegel particularly vivid.[56]

---

54. *Hegel's Philosophy of Right*, trans. T.M. Knox (Oxford University Press, 1967), p.13.
55. *Ibid.*, p.12.
56. Nietzsche's critique of the Hegelian position is already fully and explicitly expressed in his lectures *"Über die Zukunft unserer Bildungsanstalten"* (1872). Here Nietzsche declared that it was Hegelian philosophy that provided the rationalization for promoting a philosophy for reasons of the Prussian State (*Vortrag* III). And in the fifth lecture he says that the Hegelian system had recently discovered the formula of self-destruction (*Selbstvernichtung*) of philosophy in its historicism. Ridiculing the key Hegelian statement that "What is rational is actual and what is actual is rational" (*Hegel's Philosophy of Right*, p.10), Nietzsche asks: *"Ist diese Unvernunft wirklich?"* (*Vortrag* V; KSA 1:742)

Hegel imagined the philosopher working in harmony with the state, without tension or competition; since both were supposed to be concrete actualizations of the absolute spirit in the individualistic and collective realms respectively,[57] he thought it proper that they should gradually merge together. Nietzsche's conclusion to his essay on Schopenhauer leaves no doubt about his own opinion of this prospect: he calls for the complete abandonment of cooperative interaction between the two, and specifically demands a separation of the academic institution from the state.

IV. On the Disadvantages of Psychology

We have seen that Nietzsche affirms an ahistorical consciousness, advocating forgetfulness and spontaneous life. At the same time, however, he recommends self-knowledge and his psychological method to eradicate the scientific excesses of his generation. Does this position harbor an inner inconsistency, then, which could undermine his proposed remedy for his culture's maladies?

In *The Birth of Tragedy* Nietzsche had already discussed the freezing power of knowledge; here in his essay on history he claims that illusions are necessary in order to achieve happiness and a life of vitality. Did Nietzsche realize that his psychologistic therapy contained the same elements which had, in his opinion, infected his generation with "the historical malady"? Might not the diagnosis of this malady and its therapy neutralize one another? The psychological attitude actually fosters the monumental historical consciousness, which serves as an antidote to the surfeit of historicism. Nietzsche hoped to use psychology to purge contemporary science, history and

57. Cf. Shlomo Avineri, *Hegel's Theory of the Modern State*, Cambridge University Press, 1972.

philosophy of those nihilistic elements which he believed diminished the vitality of life. Psychology was to help forestall the destructive effects of excessive cognition and to restore the health of man and his culture. But was psychology not itself a kind of cognition, a rational discipline not unlike those he was trying to combat? Might not Nietzsche's method rebel against his intentions and indirectly cultivate the nihilistic trends it was designed to counter? Nietzsche was very much aware of these internal tensions and devoted attention to them in his later works. We will trace some of his arguments as they appear in these texts.

The essay "Schopenhauer as Educator" refers to self-knowledge as the key ingredient of the psychologistic consciousness, but also warns that it is a painful and dangerous path that may injure whoever follows it — and injure him so seriously that "no physician can cure him".[58] Psychologization is intended to free the personality from its dependence on internal repressions and external supports. This process is potentially dangerous, because it dismantles the person's mechanisms of defense, and exposes the vulnerable character. In consequence, the subject may become unable to function properly. This dynamic closely resembles the early stages of psychoanalytic treatment. On entering analysis, the patient exhibits a complex array of self-deceptions, rationalizations and repressive tendencies. As these defence mechanisms are gradually eroded, he may experience a phase of intense anxiety. The analyst, however, is available as a support, guiding him through this traumatic period. Similarly, Nietzsche's essay recommends the assistance of "the exemplary educators" (such as Schopenhauer) as guides through the difficult process of self-liberation. But it remains up to the individual to construct —

58. SaE, Ch. I (p.129).

by himself and for himself — the specific image of such an educator. He must choose an appropriate figure for this role and successfully form a creative relation of identification and internalization. In sum, Nietzsche's first response to the liabilities of psychology appeals to the intimate reciprocal relationship between the psychologistic method and the susceptible personality which it exposes.

The Apollonian principle of self-knowledge is a first principle of Nietzsche's psychology, expressing both its method and its aim: the individual's understanding of his own real needs and authentic nature, assisted by an identification with the exemplary edifying figures of his cultural *milieu*. If the individual succeeds in this project he may himself become an exemplary figure — an "ego-ideal". This dynamic relation is analogous to the relation Nietzsche has described between psychology and the monumental consciousness. The latter can promote a powerful and healthy life for the individual by involving him in an intense relation with heroic figures and extraordinary events of the past. If this relation is based on a penetrating psychological investigation — rather than on naive illusions — the individual will be strengthened, and become better able to contend with the potentially harmful aspects of the psychologistic project.

Nietzsche's own self-education through psychology is well documented in *Human, All Too Human*. This text offers extensive evidence of his own pursuit of an authentic existence and a self-understanding free of defensive illusions. It is only natural that such a personal record should reveal a certain element of doubt and self-consciousness about the potential dangers of the psychological project in which its author was engaged. Indeed, following an aphorism titled "Error regarding life necessary to life", Nietzsche refers to the tension between the path of illusion, on the one hand, and the path of self-knowledge on the other. This text unambiguously expresses his anxiety that psychology, by destroying illusions, might also destroy life itself:

Is it true, is all that remains a mode of thought whose outcome on a personal level is despair, and on a theoretical level a philosophy of destruction?[59]

Could it be that the damage inherent in psychology outstrips its usefulness to life? In this autobiographical note one clearly senses that the question is not merely of theoretical importance to Nietzsche, but is motivated by the intensely *personal* suffering he had experienced in his psychological self-examinations.

How does the author resolve these uncertainties? The response to his doubts and questions is, in the end, characteristically Nietzschean: psychologistic thinking may indeed be dangerous for the weak individual, but for the strong it is the most effective means of achieving greater power and personal authenticity. This answer was foreshadowed in the earlier essay on history, in which Nietzsche emphasized that the value of each mode of historical consciousness was relative to the psychological power of the man who makes use of it. The monumental consciousness, for example, was not appropriate to everyone and could certainly be deleterious to the weak man. Likewise, the positive benefits of the psychological consciousness can only be derived by certain robust individuals; to others it will prove extremely damaging. Nietzsche aptly expressed this double-edged aspect of the psychological method when he remarked of himself, "Whatever does not destroy me, makes me stronger".[60] If psychology does not destroy one, it will restore and invigorate him. Thus the psychological consciousness (like the monumental consciousness) is of *no use at all* for the utterly weak personality. Indeed, such a personality will be naturally disposed to avoid psychological self-scrutiny; as with psycho-analytic treatment, it will find the project too threatening to even be attempted.

59. MA I sec.34; KSA 2:53–54.
60. GD: "Maxims and Arrows".

117

Nietzsche's reservations about his psychological method were also assuaged by its tremendous theoretical import. In addition to its positive existential uses, Nietzsche realized it could contribute crucially to his project of constructing a theory of non-metaphysical life patterns. In particular, he wished to discover essential patterns of a *morality* based on psychological rather than transcendental "maxims".[61] So Nietzsche's ultimate response to the conflict "on the uses and disadvantages of psychology for life" is, then, that the liabilities of psychology are justified by the value it has for the practical task (of forming a powerful personality), and for its theoretical use. The attempt to discern the patterns of an authentic morality was in fact so important to Nietzsche that it stood, for him, as the most compelling reason to persist with his project of personal and cultural "unmasking", even in light of his very serious doubts:

> *Nevertheless* ... the present condition of one certain, single science has made necessary the awakening of moral observation, and mankind cannot be spared the psychological operating table, with its knives and forceps. For now that science rules which asks after the origin and history of moral feelings and which tries as it progresses to pose and solve the complicated sociological problems ...[62]

In Nietzsche's view, an inauthentic morality based on illusions about human nature had developed in the absence of an accurate genealogical-psychological analysis. The overriding ambition of his philosophy was to construct instead an authentic moral pattern, and this ambition provided sufficient courage for him to confront the possible dangers of psychology. Moreover, Nietzsche was so committed to the importance of his psychological method that he came to identify it with his

61. MA I sec.35 (p.39); KSA 2:57.
62. MA I sec.37 (p.41); KSA 2:59–60.

philosophy, and to use it as a central inspiration in his teaching. It is true that his uncertainties about its uses and disadvantages ended only in a kind of Socratic *aphoria* — never reaching a clear conclusion, nonetheless, his strong inclination to take on the Socratic role of "the gadfly on the neck of his generation", diagnosing the ills of contemporary culture, provided a practical solution:

> *How beneficial* ... whether psychological observation brings more advantage or harm upon men. What is certain is that it is necessary, for science cannot do without it ... Whoever feels too wintry in the breeze of this kind of observation has perhaps too little fire in him. Let him look around meanwhile, and he will perceive diseases which require cold poultices ...[63]

Here Nietzsche reiterates the idea that the advantages — or otherwise — of his freezing psychology depend entirely on the relative weakness or strength of the person who attempts it. Psychologization is a necessary therapy — for those who can survive the cure. The practical risk notwithstanding, its very necessity is its justification. It is a risk, Nietzsche insists, we must choose to accept.

63. MA I sec.38; KSA 2:61–62.

CHAPTER THREE

NIETZSCHE AS EDUCATOR

Introduction

Schopenhauer exercised a profound influence on both Nietzsche's early philosophical thought and his personal development. In his essay "Schopenhauer as Educator", the third of the *Untimely Meditations*, Nietzsche acknowledges this debt by applying his psychologizing method to a study of the life and work of this remarkable man. Nietzsche's essay provides special insight into his own early psychology and pedagogy as well, and clearly sets out the basic criteria he exercised in assessing the relative worth and integrity of various exemplary personalities. For these reasons "Schopenhauer as Educator" requires careful inspection.

In the first of his *Untimely Meditations* Nietzsche considered the case of David Strauss.[1] Even in this early work (1873) one can discern the operation of a rigorous "test of character". If this test disclosed conflicts and incongruities between the inner personality and its external manifestations it was unequivocally condemned—and with it, any of its intellectual or cultural progeny. Such was the fate of Strauss: Nietzsche's essay claims to illuminate the fragmentary and inconsistent nature of Strauss's

---

1. "David Strauss, the confessor and the writer", *Untimely Meditations* (trans. R.J. Hollingdale, Cambridge, 1983), pp. 1–55; "David Strauss, der Bekenner und Schriftsteller", KSA 1:159–242.

doctrines, and to reveal a divided personality whose thought manifests various existential contradictions. In consequence, Nietzsche hoped to prevent Strauss's work from exercising any further influence on European culture.

Schopenhauer, subjected to a similar examination in Nietzsche's third essay, fares far better. Nietzsche's method of psychological scrutiny is not significantly different, but the results it yields in this case are very positive indeed. Schopenhauer stands up to scrutiny as a character of exceptional intellectual depth and integrity, and for this reason Nietzsche is finally willing to refer to him as his "educator".

For present purposes, the significance of this essay is that it makes explicit Nietzsche's method of psychologization, which later developed into a comprehensive psychological theory. We have seen that Nietzsche's earliest compositions did not contain any positive, cohesive psychological doctrines; his insights were still sporadic and localized. Although Nietzsche of course continued to make use of an aphoristic method and relied increasingly on specific, isolated moments of insight, these are, in his later writings, woven into a more definite and interconnected theoretical web. It is therefore possible to make perspicuous certain of its general, dominant features. Nietzsche was aware that he needed to consolidate his methodology if it was to ever admit of a focused and coherent application; this resulted in the elaboration of a positive psychology, using the method of 'unmasking' in various cultural domains, and culminating in his concept of the will to power. If we wish to understand how Nietzschean psychologization developed into a genuine psychology of man, we must first explore its method. Nietzsche did not write about his methodology as such; it can be explicated only by considering the uses to which he puts it.

Retrospectively, Nietzsche says that what he was "fundamentally trying to do in these essays [on Schopenhauer and Wagner] was something altogether different from psychology". Nonetheless, he was applying psychologization to these "two famous and as yet altogether undiagnosed types, as one catches hold of an opportunity, in order to say something, in order to have at hand a few more formulas, signs, means of language".[2] He continues these remarks with an historical analogy, saying that "Plato employed Socrates in this fashion, as a sign language for Plato".[3] This is a most instructive comment, illuminating Nietzsche's acute perception of his own intellectual development: Plato's philosophical thinking began with the Socratic dialogues and their dialectical method, and evolved into his own philosophical dialectics and theory of ideas. Similarly, Nietzsche starts with the method of psychologization which gradually evolves into a positive psychology of the will to power. Moreover, this analogy suggests that Nietzsche realised that his psychological investigations did not merely expose the historical figures he took as their subject, but also his own character — Nietzschean unmasking necessarily includes its author's own projections. Every exposure is at the same time a self-revelation, a "personal confession of its author".[4] As he admits himself:

> In "Schopenhauer as Educator" my innermost history, my *becoming*, is inscribed ... at bottom it is admittedly not "Schopenhauer as Educator" that speaks here, but his *opposite*, "Nietzsche as Educator" ... the harsh psychology of the scholar that suddenly emerges in this essay is of some significance.[5]

I. Psychologization in the Service of Authenticity

Nietzsche's essay begins with a statement of the individualistic

2. EH — UB 3; KSA 6:319–320.
3. *Ibid.*; KSA 6:320.
4. JGB 6; KSA 5:19.
5. EH — UB 3; KSA 6:320.

"law that every man is a unique miracle".[6] Nietzsche takes this as an injunction to return to the roots of the genuine individuality and to a spontaneous life, uninhibited by convention. In another psychologistic thesis he claims that human nature is "a thing dark and veiled".[7] Although potentially creative and powerful, man is afraid of expressing himself freely, fully and uniquely, and hides himself behind various dogmas and ideologies. He typically prefers empty and indefinite generalizations to his own remarkable particularity. This is the thesis that motivates and justifies Nietzsche psychologistic method, a method of *unveiling* which attempts to free human individuality from different masks. Psychologization functions as a vehicle of authentic existence by exposing the individual's dependence on external conditioning and internal deception.

Nietzsche applies this method to Schopenhauer in order to illuminate his pedagogical values, but the essay is first and foremost focused on Schopenhauer's psychological nature. It is the personality of a philosopher, Nietzsche claims, which actually educates his readers; the philosopher's character can be made manifest through psychologization. Thus Nietzsche attempts to "see through the book [of Schopenhauer] and to imagine the living man",[8] and offers no references to the theoretical content of his subject's writings. Nietzsche did ultimately reject Schopenhauerian theory,[9] and this may in part

---

6. All quotations from this essay are taken from the English translation by R.J. Hollingdale, "Schopenhauer as Educator", in *Untimely Meditations*, hereafter cited as SaE and referred to by *page* of the English translation. Thus here: SaE 127; KSA 1:337–338. The first version of this chapter was published as "Nietzsche's Early Educational Thought", *Journal of Philosophy of Education* 19 (1985):99–109.
7. SaE 129; KSA 1:340.
8. SaE 136; KSA 1:350.
9. As various observations made immediately after SaE testify, e.g.: MA II, Preface 1; sec. 5; 33 etc.

explain the omission. Nonetheless, it is an omission which highlights his method.

We should not be surprised that Nietzsche admired Schopenhauer while rejecting his philosophy. Nietzsche's attitude to the history of philosophy manifests this feature again and again, most pointedly in his treatment of Socrates. It is also evidenced in his lectures on the pre-Socratic philosophers. In a preface to the publication of these lectures Nietzsche declares, "The only thing of interest in a refuted system is the personal element. It alone is what is forever irrefutable".[10] One might add that "the personal" is also what alone influences those who read philosophy in order to be inspired and educated by it.

A critical challenge to Nietzsche's pursuit of the authentic personality is that of gaining access to the innermost self — the veiled self carefully guarded by a complex of psychological defences. But he does not interpret the Socratic-Apollonian dictum "Know thyself" as a simple prescription for systematic introspection and self-analysis. He has no confidence in the validity and reliability of such introspections; neither does he recommend them as a technique of self-understanding. Instead, Nietzsche prefers a more indirect course, leading into an intensive psychologistic study of exemplary figures and models which assist the development of self-identity through internalization and assimilation:

> Let the youthful soul look back on life with the question: what have you truly loved up to now, what has drawn your soul aloft, what has mastered it and at the same time blessed it? Set up these revered objects before you and

---

10. *Philosophy in the Tragic Age of the Greeks*, trans. Marianne Cowan (Chicago, 1962), p. 25; Die Philosophie im tragischen Zeitalter der Griechen, KSA 1:803.

perhaps their nature and their sequence will give you a law, the fundamental law of your own true self.[11]

II. Nietzsche's "Higher Self" and Freud's "Super-Ego"

A substantive presupposition of the indirect method of self-knowledge is the existence of a mental agency that functions as a focus for the process of identification. This agency is also the locus of internalization of the moral patterns and values of our various educators (parents, teachers, historical heroes and intellectuals). At times Nietzsche refers to this agency as the individual's "true nature":

> Your true nature lies, not concealed deep within you, but immeasurably high above you, or at least above that which you usually take yourself to be.[12]

This notion also figures significantly in the development of Nietzsche's psychological theory in his later writings, and requires some elaboration. In an aphorism titled "Traffic with one's higher self", Nietzsche says:

> Many live in awe of and abasement before their ideal and would like to deny it: they are afraid of their higher self because when it speaks it speaks imperiously.[13]

In *Thus Spoke Zarathustra* Nietzsche stresses the despotic, punitive and ascetic characteristics of the "higher self":

> Always the self [*das Selbst*] listens and seeks: it compares, overpowers, conquers, destroys. It controls, and it is in control of the ego too ... The self says to the ego, "Feel pain

11. SaE 129; KSA 1:340.
12. *Loc. cit.*
13. MA I 624; KSA 2:352.

here!" Then the ego suffers and thinks how it might suffer no more ... The creative self created respect and contempt; it created pleasure and pain ... Even in your folly and contempt, you despisers of the body, you serve your self ... your self itself wants to die and turns away from life.[14]

These self-punishing traits of the "higher self" are the origin of our conscience.[15] For this reason Nietzsche thinks it necessary to somewhat weaken and placate this tyrannical faculty, thereby opening a space for the expression of a spontaneous, free and creative morality—the morality of the *Übermensch*: "I shall not go your way, O despisers of the body!", he declares, "You are no bridge to the overman!"[16]

Nietzsche's idea of the higher self has received far less attention than it deserves. It anticipates Freudian psychoanalytic theory by introducing and defining one of its key terms, viz., the Super-Ego (*Über-Ich*). The higher self parallels the Super-Ego, just as Nietzsche's notion of the Dionysian-barbarian paralleled the Freudian *Id*. To support this analogy we must consider the relations between the *Über-Ich* and Nietzsche's concept in a bit more detail.

In psychoanalysis the Super-Ego functions as the moral agency of the personality, judging it and wielding the power of punishment. Freud sees conscience, self-consciousness and the formation of ideals as formations of the Super-Ego. He introduced the term in 1923 in *The Ego and the Id* as the antithesis of the *Id*. In order to prohibit the unrestrained expressions of the

---

14. TPN, pp. 146–147; Z.I. "On the despisers of the body", KSA 4:40.
15. MA II 2–52.
16. TPN, p. 147.

instinctual *Id*, and to repress its anti-social outbursts, the Super-Ego has separated from the Ego. The *Id*, motivated only by the "pleasure-principle", always presses for immediate gratification. However, an *unregulated* gratification of instinctual drives would inevitably disrupt the Ego; more than this, it would make cooperative social life impossible. The Super-Ego must step in to rescue the individual (and his society) from disastrous collisions with the prevailing norms and conventions of his culture. Yet, if the Super-Ego is to function effectively against the *Id*'s drives it must, like them, operate unconsciously. Thus the Super-Ego is constituted by the *internalization* of parental prohibitions and demands, exercising the powers of observation, criticism and prohibition.[17] It shapes the Ego-ideals and is enriched by cultural agencies such as education, religion and normative morality. In this way the Super-Ego "becomes the vehicle of tradition and of all the time-resisting judgements of value which have propagated themselves in this manner from generation to generation".[18] It impels the Ego to fulfil the ideals of culture or at least not to harm them by the primitive assaults of the *Id*. Freud goes even further and suggests that the Super-Ego is the most subtle of the devices by which society protects itself against the disruptive forces of human aggression. This aggressiveness is turned inward and supplies the stern Super-Ego with the power to keep the Ego, and through the Ego the *Id*, in line: "Civilization, therefore, obtains mastery over the individual's dangerous desire for aggression by weakening and disarming it and by setting up an agency within him to watch over it, like a garrison in a conquered city".[19]

It can be argued, then, that Freud has provided an elaborated theoretical basis to the original Nietzschean insights, describing

17. SE, *23*:116–117.
18. SE, *22*:67.
19. SE, *21*:123–124.

in detail the development of the higher self. If the Super-Ego is indeed formed by various educators through the processes of identification and internalization, then Nietzsche's position is confirmed: to comprehend our own personalities we should first of all examine our educators and their ideals and philosophies. Schopenhauer in fact functioned for Nietzsche as an educator of this sort. Thus the young philosopher pursued self-knowledge by exploring the very ideals and values he had earlier internalized through his identification with him.

III. The "Higher Self" of Nietzsche versus the "Super-Ego" of Freud

There is an essential incongruity between Nietzsche's concept of the higher self and the parallel Freudian idea which signifies one of the basic disagreements between psychoanalytic theory and the Nietzschean existential tradition. According to Freud, the process of internalizing the cultural values imparted by one's parents and educators occurs, for the most part, at an unconscious level. It is thus a deterministic and mechanistic process in which the educators are imposed on the educand by arbitrary circumstances and by the available educational institutions. He is subjected to continuous conditioning by a pedagogic process which he has not freely chosen. This situation accounts for both the strong rigidity of the Super-Ego and its harsh, vengeful reaction to any element which attempts to penetrate the individual's moral-ideal armour.

In contradistinction to Freud, Nietzsche rejects any radical psychological determinism which might deny the possibility of a human authenticity cultivated by the exercise of personal choice and freedom. Instead, his thesis insists that "we are responsible to ourselves for our own existence" and demands that we "refuse to allow our existence to resemble a mindless act of chance".[20]

20. SaE 128; KSA 1:339, and cf. FW 335.

We have the liberty to shape our identity and ideals by freely choosing our educators and exemplary men; indeed, our "educators can be only our liberators".[21] This freedom makes us responsible for our characters just as artists are responsible for their creations, and the path to this creation of an authentic self leads through one's educators. In other words, by subjecting our intuitive admiration for exemplary figures to psychologistic self-analysis we come to realize what we value authentically and who we really are. Only then is the route to self-overcoming and re-creation opened to us. This does not mean, however, that Nietzsche is propagating an educational "ethics of self-realization",[22] or that he regards the role of the educator as that of directing pupils towards their "personal destinies".[23] These ill-chosen terms distort Nietzsche's view, not only of education, but of human existential predicaments in general: they seem to presuppose certain invariant personal 'selves' or 'destinies', static states of being which are ontologically fixed. On the contrary, Nietzsche makes it clear (as we shall see) that *becoming* one's true self is not a matter of living in accordance with a personal essence given *a priori*, but is a perpetual movement of self-overcoming, a free creation of one's own values and perspectives. All these presuppose the persistent overcoming of the rigid higher self which has unconditionally internalized prevalent values and norms.

Nietzsche is well aware of the strong pressures exerted by the conditioning forces inherent in social conventions and educational systems. Hence man's road towards authentic

---

21. SaE 129; KSA 1:341.
22. Kaufmann, *Nietzsche*, p. 158.
23. Haim Gordon, "Nietzsche's Zarathustra as Educator", *Journal of Philosophy of Education* 14 (1980):181–192. For a criticism of this essay's views see David E. Cooper, "On Reading Nietzsche on Education", *Ibid.*, 17 (1983):119–126, and his *Authenticity and Learning: Nietzsche's Educational Philosophy* (London, 1983).

freedom and spontaneous creativity requires two stages. In the first and crucial one, the individual must liberate himself from all the external layers imposed on him by institutional conditioning. Only then, after attaining a kind of *tabula rasa* state, can he proceed to the second stage in which he freely adopts and assimilates moral norms. These norms may well reflect those very traditional values that he had discarded in the first stage; it is not their specific content that matters to the educational process. Personal authenticity is determined rather by the unconstrained *manner* in which they are freely adopted.

The greater part of Nietzsche's philosophy is devoted to the first stage of self-liberation, and so the attention of most readers and commentators is inevitably drawn to his "philosophizing hammers" — the ruthless shattering of contemporary idols and ideologies. Only a minority is likely to be seriously aware that Nietzsche's thinking also presents moral patterns of *positive* power in the second stage. Nietzsche's method of psychologization does indeed deliver "hammer blows", attempting to undermine the effective strength of the prevailing ethos and to shed the enforced higher self. But the method is not employed obsessively or indiscriminately; Nietzsche chooses the objects of his "freezing" manipulations most carefully, and singles out the elements of his own personality which he regards as dispensable. When the process of psychological self-analysis reveals something valuable to himself, he internalizes it again — this time freely and consciously. This was precisely the case in his relation to Schopenhauer. "Schopenhauer as Educator" thus exemplifies the manner in which the process of selection and re-adoption of one's educators and their values takes place.

In spite of this important difference between the deterministic operation of the Freudian Super-Ego and Nietzsche's voluntaristic higher self, the remaining resemblance is still striking. This resemblance is already visible in the common structural rationale in both thinkers, which requires a critical and moral agency as the antithesis to the instinctive drives of the individual. In the context of psychoanalysis the Super-Ego was needed in order to explain the origin of the repressions and defence-mechanisms which enable the Ego to block and divert the instinctual expression of the *Id*. Just as the Freudian Super-Ego is a derivative of the Ego, the Nietzschean higher self is a derivative of the Apollonian element in man, which occasionally enters into a sublimative synthesis with the Dionysian. Thus the real antagonist of the Dionysian-barbarian is the higher self, which has internalized conventional ideals and moral values and urges the Apollonian to fight against and repress the free expressions of the Dionysian-barbarian drives. It is reasonable to assume then that Nietzsche's original dichotomy between the Dionysian and Apollonian elements in *The Birth of Tragedy* already contains the thread of his ideas about a higher and separate moral-social agency, which is the Higher Self. Like Freud, Nietzsche stresses the negative, destructive aspect of this agency. This "conscience" is the source of the guilt-feelings that block spontaneous creativity and transform man into a passive, resentful "slave", characterized by his destructive drives.

IV. Authenticity on Trial: from the "Holy Father" to Schopenhauer

Nietzsche sought positive "moral exemplars and models"[24] as an alternative to this restrictive and repressive morality. He believed that the whole moral system fostered and spread by Christianity had degenerated; this made his project all the more pressing, and its success all the more urgent. He feared that, in the absence of this once powerful moral educator, a nihilistic period would emerge in which all of our values would decline — together with our cultural and social institutions. His search, therefore, should be seen as a search for a new source of values that would replace

24. SaE 132; KSA 1:344.

the declining Christian model. But Nietzsche would still prefer Christianity to the intolerable condition of a valueless society. Here and in other writings he attacks Christianity primarily because it is already in historical decline, and cannot continue to function as "the physician for modern mankind".[25] Today, Nietzsche claims, genuine Christian content has disappeared and only the formal shell is left. Its very presence, however hollow, prevents the resurgence of new moral models. Because it has become a mere form lacking in positive content, Christianity invokes inauthentic "imitated or hypocritical ... morality".[26] Nietzsche tries to revise the prevalent ethos, and to infuse certain norms and modes of behaviour with a new vitality. In modern psychological terms, Nietzsche is seeking substitute authoritarian models capable of reshaping our super-egos, which have become devoid of moral content. This was precisely the function of the 'holy father' of the Vatican, a fundamental father figure, serving as a focus of identity processes and internalization for all Christians. With the influence of such a figure continuing to diminish, a lacuna has appeared that needs to be filled as quickly as possible: without a father — the primary formative source of man's Super-Ego (as Freud also says) — we will be left without morality, tradition or a stable culture. Thus Nietzsche refers to Schopenhauer, and to other exemplary figures, as if they were paternal models, and to the educand as "a son being instructed by his father".[27]

25. SaE 133; KSA 1:345; 346, and see below, Chapter Six, Section VII.
26. Loc. cit. There are affinities here and elsewhere between Nietzsche's diagnosis of Christianity and Kierkegaard's. Cf. e.g. his Attack upon 'Christendom', translated by Walter Lowrie (Princeton, 1944), where Kierkegaard sharply rejects the watering down of Christian faith to a comfortable code of shallow bourgeois ethics.
27. SaE 134; KSA 1:347. This tendency of Nietzsche's is conspicuous in his later aphorism: "If one does not have a good father one should furnish oneself with one", MA I 381; KSA 2:266.

Educators endowed with personal integrity are required to counter a Christianity in which form and content have been disrupted. For Nietzsche, the content must always be life itself. It is not the validity of the philosophical argument that matters, for example, but the validity of the arguing, living person. The more integrally authentic this person is, the more edifying and effective his arguments will be. What counts first is not the specific claims of a philosophy, but the character of the philosophizing: either it does or does not existentially involve the philosopher himself. Therefore Nietzsche stresses the 'how' more than the 'what', and his *ad hominen* approach (towards Schopenhauer and other exemplary individuals discussed in his writings) is no logical fallacy, but a part of a constructive methodology. Nietzsche's prime concern, one may say, is the *psychology* of the person; the philosophy is but a further criterion for the purpose of testing the individual's degree of existential consistency.[28] And indeed, his account of Schopenhauer highlights his view that we should pay more attention to the philosophers than to their philosophies. •

Nietzsche believes that only the authentic personality has any pedagogic-heuristic value. The presence of personal disharmony is destructive to educational processes; if a person is a conspicuous failure with respect to his own self-formation he can be of no genuine help to someone struggling to impose order on his own instincts. Such an "educator" could not successfully function as a positive heuristic model and would instead become a negative and destructive factor. The educand, in such a case, must eradicate the fragmenting influences to which he has been subjected.

Nietzsche's own bitter and disappointing experience with Wagner motivated his penetrating scrutiny of another of his

---

28. The question as to whether this approach implies a genetic fallacy or psychologism will be discussed below in Chapters Four and Six.

most influential educators — Arthur Schopenhauer. Nietzsche delves into Schopenhauer's personality and discovers that his "nature contained a strange and extremely dangerous dualism".[29] On the one hand there was greatness of spirit and genius, but on the other various "all too human" flaws. It is precisely in the latter, however, that Nietzsche discovers Schopenhauer's pedagogical significance, for it is through them that one is able to identify with the philosopher and assimilate his thought: the defects allow us to bridge the gap between ourselves and the exemplary genius. This facilitates the processes of internalization which would otherwise be renounced when confronted by such unattainable and inaccessible greatness. Nietzsche's method of psychologization thus has another function, in addition to that of testing authenticity and harmony of character; it aims to reduce the gap between ourselves and the objects of our inquiry by bringing them down from their Olympian heights and revealing their human dimensions. Such a descent is required, Nietzsche believes, if the project of self-formation is to be aided by exemplary models. The example can only educate us if it stands within reach of our existential human sphere — albeit a little bit above it.

Beyond the educational aims, Nietzsche has a further reason for giving priority to the cultivation of an authentic, integrated personality. Only a consistent and authentic nature, he feels, will be able to perform the special task of all great thinkers: "to be the lawgivers as to the measure, stamp and weight of all things".[30] To the extent that a philosopher's character is discordant and chaotic, these deficiencies will be reflected in his judgements and legislations. Moreover, because culture is the realm of

29. SaE 142; KSA 1:358.
30. SaE 144; KSA 1:360.

"transfigured *physis*",[31] we ought to know the primary nature of the thinker and his culture in order to know to what degree (if at all) his personal transfiguration has succeeded. This is the first criterion of any great philosophy. The method of psychologization functions as the principal means for evaluating the philosopher and his philosophy. By uncovering his innate nature we may be able to realize how far his philosophy has successfully sublimated, formed and changed his essential character.[32] Only a person who has overcome the intractable, given facticity of his own character, is capable of sublimating the raw material of his culture. It is important to recall in this regard that for Nietzsche the overcoming of one's cultural epoch is the highest vocation for the genuine philosopher.

The Dionysian-barbarian (as already indicated in *The Birth of Tragedy*) is the raw material of modern culture to be overcome, sublimated and moulded. The prevailing "savage, primal and wholly merciless" forces "serve the coming barbarism".[33] These barbarian forces had once been tamed and suppressed by the ethical and religious authority of the Christian Church. However, with the decline of Christianity they threaten to break out violently, with much greater destructive effect than ever before. Barbarian instinctuality will have accumulated more and more potential energy during the long years of religious repression; it will, then, inevitably burst forth once the restraints are removed, and the awakening of nationalistic sentiments among the masses

---

31. SaE 146; KSA 1:362.
32. This procedure, of course, is entangled in what might be called in modern terms "a hermeneutic circle" [cf. e.g. Paul Ricouer, "The Model of the Text", *Social Research* 38 (1971):529–562]. In order to establish the philosopher's primary nature, we must turn, in the majority of cases, to his philosophical writings, through which we shall also be able to judge the changes in his character. The only way partially to escape this circle is to make use of biographical (or in rare cases autobiographical) studies; however, these again usually draw most of their material from the writings.
33. SaE 149; KSA 1:366–367.

will only stimulate and encourage the eruption. With the decline of the moral authority of the Church, human society is in great danger of an impending chaos in which all forces and drives will be at war. Nietzsche attempts to forestall this deterioration by searching out a new and inspiring model of authority, capable of effectively confronting the Dionysian-barbarian forces. He examines three such models in an attempt to see which of them might be fit to move people towards "a transfiguration of their own lives".[34] His inspection of these models constitutes a succinct review of the earlier psychological distinction between the Dionysian and the Apollonian, and between the various kinds of historical consciousness. The full characterization of these three character patterns thus represents the culmination of Nietzsche's early psychology.

V. On the Three Models of Transfiguration

Nietzsche's first model — the "man of Rousseau" — exemplifies the Dionysian-barbarian type, which "has promoted violent revolutions".[35] This is the person who tears at the sublimated cultural fabrics while attacking traditional conventions and institutions. Rousseauian man, lacking Apollonian moderation, exhibits the spontaneously erupting activity that strives to return to nature and to pre-cultural life. Nietzsche is convinced of the inevitable failure of this pattern and for its antithesis he turns to "the man of Goethe".

Goethe symbolizes the purely Apollonian reason. This is a theoretical man who thrives solely on (and for) *theoria.* He rejects every kind of violence and direct activity and devotes himself to contemplation. The passive element of the Goethian model is

---

34. SaE 150; KSA 1:369.
35. SaE 151; *Ibid.*

dangerous to its disciples, since it will eventually lead into decadence, and the loss of will for any meaningful action and positive change. He will subsist on residues from the past, contributing nothing to events around him. From this perspective, he is a person who has adopted the 'antiquarian' conservative consciousnesss. At this point, Nietzsche therefore rejects the Goethian example, as endangering life, though his view of Goethe radically improved in his later work.[36]

Neither the Dionysian-barbarian Rousseau nor the Apollonian Goethe are satisfactory models; instead Nietzsche opts for a synthesis of these types — as in *The Birth of Tragedy* he had preferred the synthesis of the Dionysian-barbarian and the Apollonian. Here this synthesis is represented by the "Schopenhauerian man", who exemplifies the "heroic" life and the reconciliation of the Dionysian and the Apollonian. Put differently, he proposes a "monumental" type of consciousness, which is *praxis* in service of *theoria*. Schopenhauerian man acts out of a theoretical principle without escaping to the so-called scientific ideal of knowledge for its own sake. While pursuing personal truthfulness (*Wahrhaftigkeit*)[37] he is living a life full of struggle and conquest of himself and his culture. This is the authentic person whom Nietzsche affirms as a monumental model for those to be educated, the person who asks himself the most "unusual" questions: "Why do I live? What lesson have I to learn from life? How have I become what I am?".[38] Nietzsche himself assimilated this exemplary figure as a model for his own life and thought — as evidenced by *Ecce Homo*, his last

---

36. See, e.g., MA II 2–99; M 190; 197; FW 103.
37. SaE 152; KSA 1:371. This concept of *'Wahrhaftigkeit'* (truthfulness) is actually the equivalent of the later key existentialist concept of 'authenticity', which as such does not appear in Nietzsche's writings, and see also Chapter Four, below, (esp. footnotes 6 and 7), and cf. my forthcoming book: *Authenticity and Inauthenticity* (London, Unwin Hyman).
38. SaE 154; KSA 1:374.

autobiographical work subtitled "*How One Becomes What one Is*".

The educating models do not merely constitute supreme super-historical ideals demanding theoretical analysis; they also influence and shape the every-day lives of their educands by providing a normative model of existence which, when assimilated, become a formative, moral life pattern.

The most prominent adversary to the process of self-formation and sublimation is the perpetual — and senseless — pursuit of happiness. Nietzsche thus declares (agreeing with Kant) that to the extent that we pursue happiness we differ from animals only in the degree of our consciousness of seeking it. And since Nietzsche's professed moral and educational ideal is to "emerge out of animality",[39] we must strive to transfigure our natures. This ambition implies that we must overcome our quest for happiness, a quest which originates in our instinctual nature. Nietzsche believes, again with an almost Kantian attitude, that happiness as a *natural* phenomenon has no redeeming value, and that we must overcome our natures in order to become aware of what is genuinely worthy. However, our preoccupations with such ideals as 'the state', money-making, sociability and scientific progress now function as convenient ways of evading this awareness. Only the exemplary figures who have subdued their animalistic facticity are capable of awakening us from our naturalistic, unconscious slumbers. Only "the *philosophers, artists and saints*"[40] can help us to extricate ourselves from our given situations and work towards a sublimated culture.

This argument has a further aim which demands consideration: combating the "true but deadly"[41] Darwinian theory.

39. SaE 158; KSA 1:378.
40. SaE 159; KSA 1:380.
41. HL 9 (p. 112); KSA 1:319.

VI. The Formation of the "Higher Self" in a Darwinian World

Nietzsche attempts to supersede the blind mechanism of natural selection by regarding philosophers, artists and saints as the highest models of culture. If exceptional individuals whose lives are directed towards *progress of character* can be deliberately cultivated by their surrounding environment, they may function as an effective alternative to the deterministic Darwinian processes. For this reason Nietzsche makes use of quasi-Darwinian terms when he observes that with the appearance of philosophers, artists and saints "nature, which never makes a leap, has made its one leap in creating them".[42] It is no accident that his anti-Darwinian framework makes reference to the three "models of transfiguration" discussed above. Their dynamic interaction represents a vanquishing of natural giveness and necessity, metamorphosing innate nature into another and a "transfigured *physis*" (namely, into a sublimated personality). This motif has already been encountered in Nietzsche's descriptions of artistic sublimation in *The Birth of Tragedy*. It is again encountered in the discussion of philosopher and saints, who perpetually overcome the given raw materials of their own characters and times.

Moreover, within this almost Kantian attitude to the nonnatural essence of morality, Nietzsche presents the philosopher, artist and saint as representatives of the mental agency of the higher self. The instinctual *Id* and the rational Ego are both unsatisfactory because they originate and reside in the *natural* domain. Human drives and instincts are clearly expressive of given nature, as is the human ego insofar as it is merely the

---

42. Sae 159; KSA 1:380 ,and see BA: Fourth Lecture; MA II 2–198. This is an almost direct quotation from Darwin's epoch-making book. where he refers to that "old canon in natural history, *'Natura non facit saltum'"*; Charles Darwin, *The Origin of the Species by Means of Natural Selection* (London, 1872), p. 209.

thinking and acting arm of the *Id*. Only the formation of the third mental agency — the higher self — distinguishes man from beast, constituting and realizing a domain of moral, supra-natural ideals. Philosophers, artists and saints are distinguished by their dynamic and formative higher selves, the antithesis to Darwinian mechanistic laws, and they are therefore the agents of culture *par excellence*. They assist mankind in "its redemption"[43] from nature by overcoming its persistent facticity and providing uniquely human ideals. The first outlines of Nietzsche's later idea of the *Übermensch* are adumbrated here: "that final and supreme becoming-human" — the great educator of mankind who heroically redeems it from its imprisonment in Darwinian nature.

Nietzsche's anti-Darwinian outlook is developed further, again in terms of some of Darwin's own concepts. He argues that in observing the "animal or plant world" one may learn that it "is only concerned with the individual higher specimen, the more unusual, the more powerful". The Darwinian influence is quite clear, but Nietzsche attempts to invert it and to graft the notion of natural selection onto human culture. The inverted account proposes a "selection" of highly exceptional individuals as the embodiment of the ideals which are being deliberately cultivated. From this issues Nietzsche's categorical imperative:

Mankind must work continually at the production of individual great men — that and nothing else is its task.[44]

This imperative also complements Nietzsche's ideal of the "transfiguration of nature". A genuinely human culture must be liberated from a deterministic framework of heteronomous purposes. The road to such liberation leads through an

43. SaE 161; KSA 1:382. We shall deal with this religious concept of redemption (*Erlösung*) in Chapter Six, sec. VII.
44. SaE 161; KSA 1:383–384.

140

overcoming of natural givenness and the blind mechanisms which govern it. Thus Nietzsche reiterates the idea that "the goal of [mankind's] evolution lies, not in the mass of its exemplars and their well-being ... but rather in those apparently scattered and chance existences"[45] of great exemplary, individuals. Humanity is capable of becoming conscious of the final goal, but it must not leave its realization to mere chance. Instead, it should deliberately "seek out and create the favorable conditions under which those great redemptive men can come into existence".[46] We recognize here an idea central to the early Nietzsche, i.e., that humanity should consciously assist nature in reaching its goals, thereby overcoming nature itself.

It is also clear that this idea is not solely directed against Darwinism as such. In Nietzsche's eyes it also suggests a solution to a most crucial contemporary problem — the danger of nihilism and the disappearance of all values in concert with the "death of God". We must create new *immanent* goals to replace the perished transcendental order if we are to salvage humanity from a valueless, empty and mechanistic existence. This concern is the primary motivation for Nietzsche's emphasis on the cultivation of exemplary individuals, and for his later ideal of the *Übermensch*.

At this point we can already detect the emergence of an intuition absolutely basic to Nietzsche's thought: the intuition of complete immanence[47] according to which there is only one world and one nature. Transcendental entities or supra-natural powers do not exist. There is no "pure reason", no other world, no domain different than or superior to our own. Thus everything that belongs to man and his culture, that can contribute to

---

45. SaE 162; KSA 1:384, and see Chapter Two, sec. III.
46. *Loc. cit.*
47. Explicitly formulated in sections 108–125 of *The Gay Science*, and see also Chapter Four — Introduction.

Nietzsche's moral ideal of the qualitative progress of mankind, must originate from and be located within an exclusively human context. As we shall see, this is exactly another function of Nietzsche's positive psychology which explicates immanent human goals and provides their *raison d'être*.

In order to turn mankind in this new direction, however, Nietzsche is first obliged to psychologically freeze other ideals and values which are deflecting human effort from its utmost goal. He is obliged to expose prevalent pseudo-ideals and false values which dissuade us from adopting them. His method of psychologization thus becomes vital for the restoration of a superior culture. The ideals that Nietzsche wishes to cultivate and the pseudo-ideals that he attempts to freeze are especially pertinent to the education and formation of the individual. His alternative is a pedagogical model for the higher self of every man; he wishes not just to transform nature into a humanistic super-culture, but also to transfigure the inchoate Ego and *Id* into a fruitful and genuine higher self. These ambitions issue in his injunction to humanity to "look beyond itself and to seek with all its might for a higher self as yet still concealed from it".[48] Nietzsche's philosophical thought thus runs on two parallel tracks: the sociological-historical, which deals with human culture in its totality, and the psychological which is concerned with the education and cultivation of the individual within a cultural context. The goal of the latter is precisely the cultivation of a genuine higher self.

48. SaE 163; KSA 1:385.

Part Two:

PSYCHOLOGY OF POWER

CHAPTER FOUR

FROM PSYCHOLOGIZATION TO A PSYCHOLOGY OF POWER

Introduction

Thus far Nietzsche has restricted the employment of psychologization to his analyses of art, science and the historical consciousness. In *Human, All Too Human* the method is extended to the areas of religion, morality and philosophy. The writing of this text coincided with a period of personal crisis in Nietzsche's life, caused by his disenchantment with the romantic ideologies of Schopenhauer and Wagner whom he had previously revered. These aphorisms, then, reflect Nietzsche's own existential emancipation, in which psychologization is exercised to fashion an authentic life, free of any illusion. Psychologization is here functioning as the author's self-therapy, no less vital to his life than to his philosophical thought. It was essential to the success of his own "revaluation of all values", his "overcomings", to the recovery of his mental stability, and to the discovery of a genuine self no longer overshadowed by the idols of his cultural tradition.[1]

---

1. Nietzsche is well aware of the benefits conferred by psychologization on his life and thought, and he maintains (in MA II — Preface) that there is nothing better than self-analysis as a therapeutic means against conflicts, excessive romanticism, and all kinds of dependencies and illusions.

The young Nietzsche had conferred on Wagner the symbolic status of an adopted father. The revelation of Wagner's spiritual bankruptcy thus initiated an acute crisis in Nietzsche which forced him to undertake a psychologistic self-examination or "self-treatment".[2] It was this process which led to the development of his positive psychology. In this respect Wagner influenced Nietzschean philosophy no less — and perhaps even more — than Goethe, Socrates, Jesus and Schopenhauer. Just as the death of Freud's father served as a catalyst to the development of a full-fledged theory of psychoanalysis through the process of self-analysis (in *The Interpretation of Dreams*), Nietzsche's self-analysis clarified the form and technique of his psychological doctrine. In both instances, then, private circumstances contributed to theory construction through a process of "generalization". Nietzsche acknowledges that this is the course of every "free spirit". "What has happened to me", he says, "must happen to everyone in whom a *task* wants to become incarnate and 'come into the world'".[3] The collapse of his earlier idols made it only natural for Nietzsche to ask himself the crucial question of his mature philosophizing: "Can *all* value not be turned round? And is good perhaps evil?"[4]

The route to "redemption", to intellectual autonomy, "self-decision" and "self-control" is not easy. To attain these aims, Nietzsche had to first freeze the internalizations which had restrained him; he needed to "overcome himself" in order to restructure himself and become a "free spirit". Experience had

---

2. *Selbst-behandlung*, MA II — Preface, and *ibid.*, V3.
3. MA I — V7; KSA 2: 21. Since his personal conflict and the accompanying psychosomatic symptoms functioned as catalysts for the unfolding of his self-psychologization and his psychological teaching, Nietzsche tended to stress the advantage of illness in achieving insight (see, e.g., *ibid.*, V4). This, as he remarks, is the origin of the inter-relations between illness, psychology, the theory of perspectives and the "revaluation of all values".
4. MA I — V3; KSA 2: 17.

taught Nietzsche, however, that this could not be achieved by eagerly embracing some alternative dogma and metaphysics. He was determined to "live experimentally" before commiting himself anew to any specific norms and values. This is a decision to live *aphoristically*, in the Socratic sense of *aphoria*: to be ruled by an attitude of intellectual and emotional suspension. Only such an experimental life will allow a truly perspectival attitude, and only such an attitude can satisfy Nietzsche's existential imperative: "You shall become master over yourself, master also over your virtues".[5] The method of psychologization is most conducive to this attitude, for it helps both to freeze the non-authentic elements of one's personality, and to test and scrutinize the other components which can contribute to the formation of the authentic character.

It should be noted here that the notion of authenticity does not entail any anachronistic fallacy when applied to Nietzsche's thought: the central part of his morality of power deals extensively with the "authentic" as the term was used by later Existential thinkers.[6] Authenticity is not, in this context, comparable to truth as an external correspondence between propositions and states of affairs; neither does it refer to an internal coherence between sentences. It is instead a notion identifying a state of harmony between the innermost self and its external manifestations, whatever form and content they may possess. If genuine selfhood is repressed, a state of alienation develops between the person and his actions; the "core" of the personality becomes disassociated from social and ideological commitments which — instead of expressing it — work to suppress and deny it. And although Nietzsche does not explicitly use this term, it is possible to locate the origin of his later

---

5. MA I — V6; KSA 2: 20.
6. This notion of *authentisch* is virtually the synonym of the Nietzschean (see Chapter Three) and Heideggerian term *eigentlich*.

distinction between truth and authenticity in various passages distinguishing *"Wahrheit"* (truth) and *"Wahrhaftigkeit"* (truth-fulness).[7]

★ ★
★

When Nietzsche's early, naive admiration and idolization of Wagner[8] were supplanted by distaste and condemnation, he experienced a period of acute ambivalence. This experience perhaps provided the personal motivation for his claim that philosophy's most basic and perennial question is:

'How can something originate in its opposite, for example, rationality in irrationality, the sentient in the dead, logic in unlogic... living for others in egoism, truth in error?'[9]

This is a typically dialectical question, and contrasts vividly with the traditional philosophical preoccupation with essences which, for example, would regard everything sublime and good as originating solely from the "thing in itself". The dialectical approach enabled Nietzsche to situate his important concept of sublimation in an appropriate philosophical context. Recognizing it as peculiarly appropriate to his ends, he adopted and used it in a long series of psychological analyses, which he termed "a *chemistry* of the moral, religious and aesthetic conceptions and

7. See e.g.: "a proof of truth is not the same thing as a proof of truthfulness and that the latter is in no way an argument for the former!" (M: 73; KSA 3: 72). See also FW: 357; KSA 3: 600, and JGB: 1 where Nietzsche uses the concept of *"Wahrhaftigkeit"* in a negative sense because of its relation to *"der Wille zur Wahrheit"* (KSA 5: 15).
8. See, e.g., Roger Hollinrake, *Nietzsche, Wagner, and the Philosophy of Pessimism* (London, 1982), and Ernest Newmann, *The Life of Richard Wagner* (New York, 1946), vol. 4, pp. 1866–1883.
9. MA I — 1; KSA 2: 23.

sensations".[10] The resultant analysis of human emotions represents his psychologization, later exemplified in psycho-analysis as well. This method, as we have already seen, requires the concept of *"Sublimierung"*, (originally belonging to chemistry), which functions as the theoretical starting point for analyses aiming to distil and refine the complex elements of our mental life. Psychologization is precisely such an analytical method, focussing on descriptions of immanent features of the world rather than reverting to metaphysical principles or to an ontological bifurcation of Being into the immanent and transcendent. Nietzsche's "historical philosophizing" deals with the genesis and functional development of world-views and cultural realms; he employs it as an antithesis to any metaphysical view of man as *"aeterna veritas"* or metaphysical construction of "eternal facts"[11] and absolute norms. As discussed above, however, Nietzsche does not fully embrace Hegel's historical attitude, and clearly indicated his misgivings concerning certain aspects of the Hegelian program.[12] Nevertheless, the nucleus of Hegelian historicism is in part preserved, and it is apparent that Nietzsche understands the relevance of an historical perspective to his psychologistic-genetic attitude. Genealogy calls for history, and in order to supply it Nietzsche is ready to adopt (with qualifications) Hegel's version of historicism, although he continues to reject other elements of Hegelian philosophy — in particular its idealization of rationality. At the time of writing *Human, All Too Human*, it was easier for Nietzsche to turn to Hegel as a theoretical resource than in previous works. He had completely disowned the Schopenhauerian metaphysics which had operated as an anti-

10. *Ibid.*; KSA 2: 24.
11. MA I — 2: KSA 2: 25.
12. *Loc. cit.*; and see Chapter Two, sec. III.

Hegelian weapon, and had come to realize that it was Hegel, rather that Schopenhauer, who might assist the formulation of his own insights.

In any event, Nietzsche now sought to analyze the general character of metaphysical belief, with special attention to the metaphysics of Schopenhauer. This project was partly prompted by the need to give account of his own former fascination, while freezing or suspending the "metaphysical need"[13] that had so powerfully motivated it.

I. The Dream: A Royal Road to the Unconscious in Nietzsche and Freud

Nietzsche wished to undermine the influence of metaphysics by revealing the specific needs and mental predicaments which move men to contrive it. His main instrument of denunciation is the phenomenon of dreaming:

The man of the ages of barbarous primordial culture believed that in the dream he was getting to know a *second real world*: here is the origin of all metaphysics. Without the dream one would have had no occasion to divide the world into two. The dissection of it into soul and body is also connected with the oldest idea of the dream, likewise the postulation of a life of the soul, thus the origin of all belief in spirits and probably also of the belief in gods.[14]

If we look, for example, at Descartes' *Meditationes de Prima Philosophia* (1641) we will find considerable evidence supporting the notion that dreams play a vital role in the formation of

13. MA II 2–16; KSA 2: 550.
14. MA I — 5; KSA 2: 27.

metaphysics.[15] Nietzsche's assertion that dreams provide an impetus for the distinction between body and soul is also essential to the Cartesian view. Descartes, too, one may recall, started the reconstruction of his dualism with an argument identifying reality with dreams. He believed this gave sufficient reason for scepticism about the existence of a material world, but failed to refute the reality of the soul; indeed, the dream hypothesis even confirms its continuous existence. This is but one example from the history of philosophy supporting Nietzsche's suggestion that the dream phenomenon serves as a primary route leading thought into the arena of metaphysics.

Nietzsche sought, as far as possible, to replace the transcendental, metaphysical viewpoint with a strictly immanent account. He thus began to analyze the dream phenomenon in order to invalidate it as an overture to metaphysics. His method of psychologization in this way functions as a concrete alternative to the various attempts to explain the world in metaphysical notions:

> As soon as the origin of religion, art and morality is so described that it can be perfectly understood without the postulation of *metaphysical interference* at the commencement or in the course of their progress, the greater part of our interest in the purely theoretical problem of the 'thing in itself' and 'apearance' ceases to exist.[16]

Anticipating Freud's *Interpretation of Dreams* (1900) by almost twenty years, Nietzsche proceeds to apply psychologization to an extensive analysis of dream phenomena. Both he and Freud

15. Especially in the First and Second Meditations, and, on dualism, in the Sixth. See Jacques Maritain, *Le Songe de Descartes* (Paris, 1932), where he maintains that the rationalism of modern philosophy originated in three dreams dreamt by Descartes on 10th November, 1619. See also Plato, *Theaetetus*, 158A; *Timaeus*, 46a and d.
16. MA I — 10; KSA 2: 30.

maintain that the distortions of memory are the essence of the dream. These transformations of remembering are subject, according to Freud, to "the laws of dream-formation",[17] which he calls the "Dream-Work" *(Traumarbeit)*. The latter is a complex mental operation which transforms the genuine and latent dream contents, thereby producing the manifest dream as remembered on waking. This Dream-Work is responsible for what Nietzsche calls the "confusion and capriciousness"[18] of the manifest dream, and it differs in essence from conscious and rational thinking. He mentions several mechanisms which implement the "transvaluation of psychical values" between the manifest, conscious level of our mental functioning and the latent, unconscious level of our deepest desires.[19] When he maintains, for example, that a dream "continually confuses one thing with another on the basis of the most fleeting similarities",[20] he is actually describing the basic mechanism of the Dream-Work that Freud called "condensation" (*Verdichtung*)[21] and "displacement" (*Verschiebung*).[22] With the inclusion of symbolism (in both Nietzsche and Freud), these are the mechanisms by which the unconscious in masked and disguised, and which comprise the most primitive modes of human thinking. In this context it is

17. S.E., *17*: 51, and *ibid.*, 4: 11.
18. MA I — 12; KSA 2: 31.
19. Compare Freud's statement: "The dream-work is not simply more careless, more irrational, more forgetful and more incomplete than waking thought; it is completely different from it qualitatively ... It does not think, calculate or judge in any way at all; it restricts itself to giving things a new form ... That product, the dream, has above all to evade the censorship, and with that end in view the dream-work makes use of a *displacement of psychical intensities* to the point of a transvaluation of all psychical values" (*The Interpretation of Dreams*, S.E., *5*: 507). This last phrase is by no means an accidental one, and Freud later admitted borrowing it from Nietzsche (S.E., 4: 330; *5*: 655).
20. MA I — 12; KSA 2: 31.
21. S.E., *6*: 58ff; *4*: 293–295; *8*: 164; *15*: 191.
22. S.E., *15*: 174.

appropriate, then, that Nietzsche mentions "mythologies" and say that in dreams we all resemble "this savage".[23] Freud likewise frequently compares archaic modes of thought with the "primary processes" of dreaming, and even quoted Nietzsche in this context:

> Behind this childhood of the individual we are promised a picture of a phylogenetic childhood — a picture of the development of the human race, of which the individual's development is in fact an abbreviated recapitulation influenced by the chance circumstances of life. We can guess how much to the point is Nietzsche's assertion that in dreams 'some primeval relic of humanity is at work which we can now scarcely reach any longer by a direct path'.[24]

For his own part, Nietzsche confirms the primacy of man's paleological thinking over his logical procedures, and suggests that the rational history of mankind is only a late derivative of its nonrational, primitive history. His "revaluation" is thus effected, maintaining that human reason originated from unreason, and that the human mind is rooted in primary, irrational mental processes. Another way of putting the point in the Nietzschean framework may be this: the genesis of the Apollonian is in the Dionysian-barbarian, and is directly derived from it on the phylogenetic level of the whole culture as well as on the ontogenetic level of the individual. In *The Birth of Tragedy* Nietzsche wished to maintain a delicate balance between the Apollonian and the Dionysian; we now find this balance

23. MA I — 12; KSA 2: 32.
24. S.E., *5*: 548–549. Freud is apparently referring to the last sentence of Nietzsche's aphorism *"Dream and culture"*: "Thus: in sleep and dreams we repeat once again the curriculum of earlier mankind" (MA I — 12; KSA 2: 32).

153

deliberately upset to the advantage of the latter. In his first books Nietzsche's reply to the question "What is the origin of the Apollonian?" was partial and inadequate. He now offers a more positive response: It is in the Dionysian, the *arche* of all human and cultural expression.[25]

As some of his other aphorisms show, Nietzsche does not conceive of the analysis of dreams solely as a means of freezing the "metaphysical drive". As for Freud, dreams are of interest for their own sake, and provide a source of significant psychological insights. For instance, the aphorism "The logic of dreams" explores a rich array of psychological motives; moreover, it makes use of psychologization to generalize the ontogenetic analyses in terms of the wider phylogenetic and cultural context. It also contains several specific ideas that are echoed in Freud:

> In sleep our nervous system is continually agitated by a multiplicity of inner events... the dream is *the seeking and positing of the causes* of this excitement of the sensibilities, that is to say the supposed causes... Everyone knows from experience how quickly a dreamer entwines with his dream a sound that strongly impinges upon him from without, the ringing of bells or the firing of cannon, for example... He accounts for the sound in terms of the dream, so that he *believes* he experiences the cause of the sound first, then the sound itself...
>
> Man still draws in dreams to the present day, for many millennia mankind also drew *when awake*: the first *causa* that entered the mind as an explanation of anything that required explaining satisfied it and was accounted truth...

25. Later Nietzsche tries to solve the problem of the origin of the Apollonian by regarding it — together with the Dionysian—as belonging to the monistic principle of the will to power, which includes both the Dionysian element of the driving force and the Apollonian capacity to form and organize this force into a creative power.

The poet and the artist, too, *foists upon* his moods and states of mind causes which are certainly not the true ones; to this extent he recalls an earlier humanity and can aid us to an understanding of it.[26]

Here Nietzsche is maintaining that one of the auxiliary factors in creating dreams is the somatic condition of the sleeper, namely, the set of physical stimuli that have aroused his nervous system. This contention traps Nietzsche into a circular argument, since he attempts — in the same aphorism — to explain the genesis of the concept of causality by the use of this same concept. Freud's *Traumdeutung* also devoted some space to "The Somatic Sources of Dreams"[27] and suggests that the external physical stimuli act as additional sources of dream stimulation. According to Freud, one of the purposes of dreaming is to prolong sleep.[28] This could in part explain why the dream deals with potentially disruptive external stimuli by incorporating them into the manifest dream context, thus deferring the awakening. In the aphorism quoted above, Nietzsche maintains that the dream quickly incorporates any strong stimulus — "such as the ringing of bells or the firing of cannon". In a strikingly coincidental account, Freud refers to the example of a dream in which a potential interruption — the pealing of bells — was successfully interwoven into his dream content, preserving the state of sleep.[29] Freud's analyses concur with and confirm Nietzsche's view that the dreamer attempts to create a rational, causal framework for external stimuli by incorporating them into the narrative of dream.

The agreement between Nietzsche and Freud is sustained not only in piecemeal references to specific dreams, but also in

26. MA I — 13; KSA 2: 32–35.
27. S.E., 4: 220–240.
28. *Ibid.*, p. 233ff.
29. S.E., 4: 232.

connection with more general psychological principles. A central Freudian thesis, for example, subsumes all our mental functioning under two main headings: the *"Lustprinzip"*[30] which governs the irrational and primary processes in dreams, neurotic symptoms and mythical primitive thinking; and the complementary *"Realitätsprinzip"*,[31] which dominates the secondary, normative and logical thought processes, and most of the everyday activities that take the conditions imposed by the outside world into account. Nietzsche does not use these terms, but he suggests the same underlying idea when he declares that "the dream is a relaxation for the brain, which has had enough of the strenuous demands in the way of thinking such as are imposed by our higher culture during the day".[32]

As yet, these particular parallels have not taken us to the core concept binding Nietzsche's and Freud's analyses of the role of dreams in psychological theory — the concept of the unconscious. It was during Nietzsche's analysis of the dream phenomenon that he first developed and located this concept at the center of his own psychology, a move which clearly anticipated the Freudian psychoanalytic model. Nietzsche's attempt to uncover rational patterns in the dream — the most irrational mode of ordinary thinking — produced his conviction that our mental life is not entirely visible or accessible, and that most of it occurs at unconscious levels. The revelation of the

30. S.E., *5*: 574, 616; *14*: 120–121; *18*: 63; *19*: 160.
31. S.E., *11*: 218–226; *14*: 134–135.
32. MA I — 13; KSA 2: 34. Nietzsche's remark at the end of this aphorism about "the poet" and "the artist" as exemplifications of primitive thinking recalls many Freudian references to artistic creation as illustrating the paleological, primary processes governed by the *Lustprinzip*, see Chapter One, sec. X.

unconscious provided a direct challenge to the Cartesian tradition which identified soul with consciousness, and assumed the latter to be utterly transparent — "clear and distinct". Nietzsche's emphasis on the unconscious therefore contained important ramification for the western philosophical tradition.

For Freud, dreams were the "royal road"[33] to the unconscious. Similarly, Nietzsche believed that the analysis of the dream phenomenon did not only uncover the archaic, paleological patterns — the dimensions of pleasure and reality — but also could enable one to reach into the irrational, unconscious realm of the mental life. Indeed, after his preliminary dream analyses in Part One of *Human, All Too Human* the notions of *"das Unbewusste"* and *"unbewusst"* appear in his writings with increasing frequency.[34]

"That which we sometimes do not know or feel precisely while awake" Nietzsche tells us, "the dream informs us of without any ambiguity".[35] Dreams, seemingly meaningless and chaotic, contain significant information about ourselves of which we would otherwise be completely unaware. This accounts for the amazement and surprise we sometimes feel when on waking we recall our dreams:

33. *"The interpretation of dreams is the royal road to a knowledge of the unconscious activities of the mind"* (S.E., 5: 608)
34. This central concept of Nietzsche's psychology is unfortunately almost completely ignored in Richard Oehler's various indices and in his *Nietzsche-Register* (Stuttgart, 1943). Karl Schlechta's *Nietzsche-Index*: FNW — V (München, 1965), though helpful, is also incomplete in this respect. At first Nietzsche used a synonymous concept — *"unwillkürlich"* (e.g.: MA I — 54; KSA 2: 74; MA I — 81; KSA 2: 86); however, at the same time, and then more frequently, he preferred *"unbewusst"* (the "unconscious hypocrites", MA I — 51; KSA 2: 72), saying that "We unconsciously seek for the principles and dogmas that are appropriate to our temperament", describing this fact as the "unconscious comedy" (MA I - 608; KSA 2: 345). In the second volume of *Human, All Too Human*, Nietzsche frequently uses this notion of *"unbewusst"* (MA II 1–119, 126, 144, 147, 320, 339, 383; MA II 2–9, 23, 33, 41, 45, 62, 212, 228, 282, 295, 339), and the term occurs also in his later writings.
35. MA II 1–76; KSA 2: 408.

Our dreams are... chains of symbolic scenes and images in place of the language of poetic narration; they paraphrase our experiences or expectations or circumstances with such poetic boldness and definiteness that in the morning we are always astonished at ourselves when we recall our dreams".[36]

Nietzsche conceives of the dream as a symbolic text, conveying data about the most hidden aspects of mental life in a figurative and disguised language. If we are to understand ourselves, then, we must learn how to decipher this text and to read its genuine meaning.[37] Since Nietzsche regards the psyche as unconscious for the greater part, he does not believe that introspection alone can penetrate it. Moreover, he also recognizes that the need for disguise issues from the dream's attempt to express immoral and forbidden desires. Thus the dream must be cautious; it must carefully deceive the censorious moral agency. In a posthumously published fragment (written several years before *Human, All Too Human*) Nietzsche commented insightfully on the immoral content of many of our dreams, and noted the existence of a moral agency that represses and prohibits our unconscious manifestations:

Man permits himself to be lied to at night, his life long, when he dreams, and his moral sense never tries to prevent this.[38]

36. MA II 2–194; KSA 2: 639.
37. It should be noted that this aphorism (*loc. cit.*) refers to the third mechanism of the "dream-work" symbolism. Freud devotes much space to this concept, arguing that dream uses symbols in order to present forbidden, unconscious elements to the consciousness. Symbolism is thus an effective means of expressing repressed mental content, since it offers the most convenient material for disguising the unconscious. It is the most primitive pattern of cognition. See also Ernest Jones, "The Theory of Symbolism", in *Papers on Psycho-Analysis*, 5th ed. (London, 1950), pp. 93–104.
38. "On Truth and Lie in an Extra-Moral Sense" (TPN pp. 43–44; KSA 1: 876–877).

For both Nietzsche and Freud the dream reveals the unconscious text underlying our conscious mental life, and discloses the principal content of this text: man is essentially a coil of stormy drives, lusting for satisfaction in reality.

> If all the drives were as much in earnest as in *hunger*, which is not content with *dream food*; but most of the drives, especially the so-called moral ones, *do precisely this* — if my supposition is allowed that the meaning and value of our *dreams* is precisely to *compensate* to some extent for the chance absence of 'nourishment' during the day... Waking life does not have this *freedom* of interpretation possessed by the life of dreams, it is less inventive and unbridled — but do I have to add... that there is no *essential* difference between waking and dreaming?... that all our so-called consciousness is a more or less fantastic commentary on an unknown, perhaps unknowable, but felt text?[39]

The notion that the unconscious meaning and *raison d'être* of dreams is the partial fulfilment of forbidden desire had customarily been considered an exclusive discovery of psychoanalysis. Even this brief outline of Nietzsche's theory of dreams, however, demonstrates that this is not the case. His theory already contains the insight that man is a constellation of drives seeking satisfaction and that the common mental activity of dreaming unburdens the individual by expressing these drives. Dream-work constitutes a compromise between the repressive cultural mental agencies which restrict the arena of permissible thought, and the dissatisfied drives pressing for satisfaction. Overt expression in conscious thought is disallowed; dreams therefore provide the language of the desires which can find no

39. M 119; KSA 3: 112–113.

voice in waking life. This is evidently a rather remarkable anticipation of psychoanalysis. In *The Interpretation of Dreams* Freud himself gives highest priority to the discovery that dreams function as wish-fulfilments for desires which are otherwise prohibited and repressed by moral agencies.[40] Moreover, the commonality of dreaming in all people — both 'healthy' and neurotic — and the common features of their dream mechanisms led Freud to conclude that no essential difference obtains between the normal and the neurotic personality: we are all neurotic in varying degrees. This too is suggested by Nietzsche in the passage cited above: if dreams are expressions of drives, as are all other cognitive mental phenomena, there is no essential distinction between dreaming and waking cultural life.[41]

Are culture and morality, then, also manifestations of drives? The meta-psychological foundation developed by both Nietzsche and Freud on the basis of investigation of dreams indeed construes them as such. Both eventually took their guiding question to be: what drive is seeking to express itself in phenomenon X or Y, in this value or that morality? Precisely what drive is seeking satisfaction through a particular pattern? Freud's answer is that the *Libido* impels most of our mental and spiritual actions. Nietzsche's most frequent response refers to the *will to power:* this drive and its derivatives were to become (as will soon be seen) the positive principle of his psychology.

Freud was later to endorse several findings noted in Nietzsche's analysis of dreams — although the former claimed priority of discovery. It is even reasonable to suggest that Nietzsche approached the threshold of the Oedipal complex, the

---

40. S.E., 5: 550–572.
41. See: "*Quidquid luce fuit, tenebris agit,* but the other way around, too. What we experience in dreams ... belongs in the end just as much to the over-all economy of our soul as anything experienced 'actually'" (JGB 193; KSA 5: 114).

core of Freud's theory of neurosis. Certainly the following aphorism lends considerable support to this possibility:

> You are willing to assume responsibility, for everything! Except, that is, for your dreams! What miserable weakness, what lack of consistent courage! Nothing is *more* your own than your dreams! Nothing *more* your own work! And it is precisely here that you rebuff, and are ashamed of yourselves, and even Oedipus, the wise Oedipus, derived consolation from the thought that we cannot help what we dream! From this I conclude that the great majority of mankind must be conscious of having abominable dreams.[42]

Unlike the early Freud, however, Nietzsche was not primarily concerned with psychopathology. He did not require the postulation of an Oedipal complex — or any other complex — for the development of his psychological doctrine. His central concern was rather the decline of western culture and its upcoming nihilism; he wished to create a healthy morality and immanent standards that might reverse the contemporary trend toward decadence. To understand and provide a therapy for this culture it was necessary for Nietzsche to expose the drives that had constituted it, and to inquire into how he might shape these

---

42. M 128; KSA 3: 117–118. The Oedipus complex was postulated by Freud through similar analyses of dreams, especially his own (S.E., *5*: 398–399). He also refers to Jocasta's famous saying: "Many a man ere now in dreams hath lain with her who bare him" (S.E., *4*: 264; Lewis Campbell's translation of *Oedipus Rex*, line 982ff). It is reasonable to assume that Nietzsche, so versed in classical Greek literature, knew this sentence, and probably understood its psychological meaning and that of the whole play. Moreover, Freud himself maintains in a letter to his friend Fliess, in his first reference to the Oedipus complex, that "the Greek legend seizes on a compulsion which everyone recognizes because he feels its existence within himself" (S.E., *1*: 265). On Nietzsche's sympathy towards Oedipus see Eric Blondel, "Oedipus bei Nietzsche", *Perspectiven der Philosophie* 1 (1975): 179–191.

instincts and redirect them toward healthier and more creative channels. The goal of his psychologization is to explicate the relations between our fundamental mental composition and its cultural manifestations.

II. The Purpose of Nietzsche's Psychologization: to "Freeze" the Metaphysical Drive

Nietzsche's investigation of psychodynamics eventually crystallized into a metapsychological doctrine, and became one of the main instruments in the full development of his philosophy. In more than one instance, as has been seen, Nietzsche moves from particular applications of the psychologistic method to positive psychological hypotheses about the nature of the human psyche. He required such hypotheses to justify his method, and to summarize and generalize the partial, discrete results arising from its application. There is a resulting difficulty in distinguishing the method from the doctrine; they exhibit a circular and interdependent structure. This difficulty becomes increasingly formidable, for Nietzsche did not trouble to articulate his method explicitly, or even to identify and define its multifarious components. One must, therefore, distill the general and essential features of his psychological teaching from his specific psychologistic analyses, focussing especially on those aphorisms which directly state a psychological thesis or principle. Such theses either function as a necessary prolegomena to a future psychologization, or present a sort of generalization from findings already derived from its application.

The following aphorism exemplifies a psychologistic thesis expressing a fundamental point of theory which has emerged from applications of the method:

> Thus there come to be constructed habitual rapid connections between feelings and thought which ... are in

the end no longer experienced as complexes, but as *unities*. It is in this sense that one speaks of the moral feeling of the religious feelings, as though these were simple unities: in truth, however, they are rivers with a hundred tributaries and sources.[43]

Nietzsche had already considered the connection between "feelings" and "thoughts" in the context of his dream investigations, regarding dream as the language of desire. Here he projects this notion on to other human cultural manifestations, such as morality and religion, inferring an atomistic thesis of the psyche. This atomization of the soul is a necessary basis for the analytic-psychologistic method described earlier as a chemistry of the moral and religious sentiments.[44] However, this assertion regarding the relation between feelings and thoughts does not yet adequately explain how and by what mechanism such a connection is at all possible. One of the aims of Nietzsche's psychologization was finding some reasonable solution to this problem.

A partial answer was provided by Nietzsche's quasi-Kantian statement that this phenomenal world has acquired its meaning and "color" by the operation of the intellect on the basis of various human needs and emotions.[45] Thus, behind the categories of the intellect and its synthetic *a priori* judgments Nietzsche posits the psychological-emotive functions of the "Human-All-Too-Human" in a way similar to his distinction between the Apollonian and the Dionysian categories.[46]

It is not open to Nietzsche, however, to perform a "transcendental deduction of the categories"; unlike Kant, he is unable to

---

43. MA I — 14; KSA 2: 35.
44. *Ibid.* — 1.
45. MA I — 16.
46. See Chapter One, fn. 48, and MA I — 19.

offer us a "Schematism" or an *a priori* argument about the existing bond between mental needs and the intellectual products satisfying them. Instead, he is obliged to turn to the *a posteriori* realm, and to attempt to expose psychic needs and their relations to ideas by means of purely empirical speculations. His psychologistic method is thus applied to intellectual patterns in order to reveal this interrelation.

There are evidently certain post-Kantian epistemological problems posed for the theoretical application of Nietzsche's method. More importantly, it is limited in practical effectiveness:

Rigorous science is capable of detaching us from this ideational world only to a limited extent ... inasmuch as it is incapable of making any essential inroad into the power of habits of feeling acquired in primeval times: but it can, quite gradually and step by step, illuminate the history of the genesis of this world as idea — and, for brief periods at any rate, lift us up out of the entire proceeding.[47]

Psychologization is unable to liberate us completely from our attachments (for example, attachments to metaphysical viewpoints) since this devotion is sustained by powerful psychic needs almost impossible to overcome by the theoretical understanding alone.[48] Nietzsche is thus compelled to concentrate on "cooling down" and *freezing* these needs. He must curtail their imperious domination by attaining an "indifference *against* faith"[49] and the state of *ataraxia* (freedom

---

47. MA I — 16; KSA 2: 37–38.
48. Witness Spinoza's attempt to transform the understanding into a powerful and positive *"affectus"* since only then might it be able to overcome the negative emotions:
    "An emotion can only be controlled or destroyed by another emotion contrary thereto, and with more power for controlling emotion." (Benedict de Spinoza, *The Ethics*, Part IV, Prop. VII, trans. by R.H.M. Elwes, New York, 1955)
49. MA II 2–16; KSA 2: 550.

from disturbance of mind or passion). To ultimately subdue the metaphysical drive (his own as well as ours) Nietzsche himself adopted — and prescribed for his entire culture — the instrument of freezing psychologization. In the process, he had to forgo the direct refutation of intellectual beliefs. Because these beliefs serve to satisfy certain powerful psychic needs, an attempted refutation would have provoked an emotional resistance motivated by those same needs, resulting in a reinforcement of the very dogmas one wished to refute. For this reason Nietzsche preferred the method of freezing psychologization to rational disputation:

> Do not deride and befoul that which you want to do away with for good but respectfully *lay it on ice*, and, in as much as ideas are very tenacious of life, do so again and again. Here it is necessary to act in accordance with the maxim: 'One refutation is no refutation'.[50]

In addition to the psychologistic freezing of the metaphysical impulse, an alternative must be provided which is capable of functioning as a reliable substitute. But in the first instance, the relevant needs and psychic interests served by metaphysics must be defined:

> To feel more irresponsible and at the same time to find things more interesting — that is the twofold benefit for which he believes he has metaphysics to thank. Later on, to be sure, he acquires no trust of the whole metaphysical mode of explanation; then perhaps he sees that the effects he has experienced attained equally well and more

---

50. MA II 2-211; KSA 2: 644; and see Nietzsche's description of his "free-thinking" (*Freigeisterei*) as of "a highly perilous wandering on glaciers and polar seas" (MA II 1-21; KSA 2: 387); and his declaration that MA — as a book "for free spirits" — expresses the "inquisitive coldness of the psychologist" (MA II Preface 1; KSA 2:371).

scientifically by another route: that physical and historical explanations produce that feeling of irresponsibility at least as well, and that his interest in life and its problems is perhaps enflamed even more by them.[51]

In referring to "physical and historical explanations" Nietzsche suggests that offering the psychological explanation might replace the mental function of the metaphysical explanation and successfully satisfy the "metaphysical drive". This transformation from metaphysics to psychology would ensure that the human needs and interests met by the former would not suffer deprivation, and this would facilitate the freezing of the metaphysical values and mode of thinking.

In this respect Nietzsche is far removed from any modern philosophical tradition advocating the annihilation of metaphysics by the power of either *logos* or silence — the traditions inspired by Carnap and Wittgenstein, for example, offering sophisticated proofs that metaphysical questions have arisen out of linguistic fallacies or the "bewitching" and misleading uses of everyday idiom. Nietzsche would argue that these anti-metaphysical projects do not adequately respond to the metaphysical drive that has a profound and powerful psychical basis: they fail to abolish the *need* for metaphysics, and so the metaphysical *Eros* will emerge once more, like the phoenix, from the ashes.

III. The "Freezing" Psychologization is Free of the Genetic Fallacy

At this point one might argue that Nietzsche's psychologistic treatment of metaphysics (and other intellectual manifestations)

---

51. MA I — 17; KSA 2: 38, and cf. MA II 1–12, where Nietzsche also indicates other human needs that are satisfied by metaphysics.

clearly involves a *genetic* fallacy: it tends to judge the value and validity of any given philosophical position by reference to non-cognitive functions and motives. In short, it might be claimed that his ambitious program of overcoming metaphysics by means of genetic psychologization is irrelevant to any serious attempt at logical refutation. The antagonist might also remind one that the genesis of a belief "that P" — our *motives* for believing P — have nothing to do with the *rational* validity of P. This being the case, the project of uncovering the psychic motives that drew man to some complex of metaphysical commitments can never inform questions of the falsity or truth of those commitments themselves.

Nietzsche might defend himself by contending that the objective of psychologization is not *intended* to produce a rational refutation. The first purpose of the genetic uncovering of psychic factor underlying metaphysical beliefs is to freeze the motivating force or driving power — not to provide proof of their logical invalidity. He is aware, in any case, of the danger of the genetic fallacy and so abstains from suggesting that his psychologizations are *equivalent* to refutation.[52] On the contrary, he explicitly rejects the claim that metaphysical beliefs are strictly false:

52. Moreover, he is not blind to the possible abuse of psychologization by people who might try to evade a direct intellectual confrontation with a viewpoint they find unacceptable (see MA II 1–39; KSA 2: 398). The very fact that Nietzsche himself persistently uses this method indicates, at least, his belief that he does not abuse it. His warning against the danger of genetic fallacy, and his confidence that he has avoided it is even more pronounced in the following passage:

   If there is anything in which I am ahead of all psychologists, it is that my eye is sharper for that most difficult and captious kind of *backward inference* in which the most mistakes are made: the backward inference from the work to the maker, from the deed to the doer, from the ideal to him who *needs* it, and from every way of thinking and valuing to the *want* behind it that prompts it. (NW: "We Antipodes"; TPN: 670, and see FW 370.)

In regard to philosophical metaphysics, I see more and more who are making for the negative goal (that all positive metaphysics is an error), but still few who are taking a few steps back; for one may well want to look out over the topmost rung of the ladder, but one ought not to want to stand on it.[53]

One ought, then, to observe metaphysics from the outside, from a psychologistic perspective; but this is not an attempt to use its own arguments to reject and refute it. The overcoming of metaphysics, therefore, is not to be effected by disproving its internal validity nor by criticizing it from an alternative rational standpoint. Nietzsche understands that anyone who wishes to refute metaphysics in this manner will only become more deeply entrapped. Rational refutation of a philosophical or metaphysical position requires that one at least recognize its claims to truth and validity: but if we take into account the sceptical ramifications of Nietzsche's theory of perspectives, it is clear that he cannot (nor would wish to) refute any given theory or set of beliefs. However problematic the concept of truth may be in Nietzsche's philosophy, it is evident that he rejects the notion of truth as objective and immutable — and direct refutations require a *prima facie* commitment to precisely this notion. He prefers instead to offer a pattern of life which has no *need* for metaphysical consolations, and to impose this pattern he is first obliged to freeze the metaphysical drive by psychologistic means. The viability of his particular method may of course be questioned: why should we accept the genetic argument and its underlying assumptions if there are not truths, but only perspectives? This problem will be considered later. For present

---

53.   MA I — 20; KSA 2: 42; and see Chapter Seven below for the comparison of this notion of the ladder with Wittgenstein's *Tractatus*.

purposes, it will suffice to say that the acceptance of Nietzsche's arguments does not depend on their *truth-value*, for with respect to rational validity they are no more nor less preferable than the views he attempts to "put on ice". They are acceptable only if, like Nietzsche, we adopt a certain existential perspective — a lived attitude — that will enable us to exemplify in our life a particular pattern; and this pattern, Nietzsche argues, is latent in every individual. If we allow ourselves to be enticed into accepting the proposed life perspective, it is not because we recognize it as objectively true, but because of its success in reactivating the elements of our inherent authentic power (*Macht*) which were previously repressed by other, antagonistic psychological features.

The following passage clearly articulates Nietzsche's understanding of his project of freezing as categorically distinct from a project of rational refutation:

Perhaps the *scientific* demonstration of the existence of any kind of metaphysical world is already so *difficult* that mankind will never again be free of a mistrust of it. And if one has a mistrust of metaphysics the results are by and large the same as if it had been directly refuted and one no longer had the *right* to believe in it.[54]

Nietzsche's main concern in his applications of the psychologistic method is to evoke a *mood* of deep suspicion and distrust regarding metaphysics:

The question of the origin of our evaluations and tables of the good is not at all equivalent to their *critique*, as is so

54. MA I — 21; KSA 2: 42. Therefore I am in a complete agreement with David E. Cooper's observation that "Nietzsche, incidentally, is not guilty of any 'genetic fallacy' (at least in any crude form)", *Authenticity and Learning*, 1983 p. 24.

often believed: however certain it is that the insight into some *pudenda urigo* brings with it the feeling of a lessening of value in what originated in such a way, and prepares the way for a critical mood and attitude towards it.[55]

The appropriate affective mood would, in his view, be tantamount in practice to a direct refutation: its lived consequences would be the same. Such a transformation of one's mental attitude to metaphysics would undermine the metaphysical drive, and in this way Nietzsche's purpose would be achieved without commiting any fallacies — genetic, logical or otherwise. The evocation of a psychic (rather than strictly philosophical) doubt in the viability of metaphysics would freeze man's motivation for believing it and would check his efforts to repeatedly resurrect its various manifestations. An authentic and healthy culture would then emerge, a culture no longer relying on dubious metaphysical comforts and able to function creatively without the traditional philosophical crutches.

This authentic "new culture"[56] can be constructed only if Nietzschean psychologization is employed in an almost Popperian fashion: just as Popper aims at undermining the credibility (and the associated incentive power and influence) of scientific theories rather than directly refuting them, Nietzsche insists that for both the individual and science the "... truest allies must be doubt and distrust":

Nonetheless, the sum of unimpeachable truths, which have survived all the assaults of scepticism and disintegration

---

55. WM 254. By speaking about "a critical mood and attitude" Nietzsche refers rather to state and "pathos" of mind about which more will be said in Chapter Six.
56. MA I — 24; KSA 2: 45.

can in time become so great ... that on the basis of them one may resolve to embark on 'everlasting' works.[57]

Once again, it is clear that Nietzsche does not aspire to logically refute metaphysical (or other) theories, but rather to undermine their impact on our lives with his "destructive analysis". Only the theories and ideologies that survive this analysis, with their influence unimpaired and our belief in them unshaken, could contribute usefully to a new, purified and authentic worldview. The psychologistic method thus functions as a kind of foundry, refining our beliefs and selecting attitudes that withstand tests of credibility, emerging intact and even more powerful than before.

Nietzsche's method found a powerful contemporary ally, namely the world historical process that was bringing about "the death of God" — a metaphysical being who had functioned as the main source of inspiration to the construction of metaphysical philosophy. The shadows of the deceased God (one being metaphysics itself) were extremely slow to disappear, however, as they still served powerful and pervasive psychic needs. Although God as such had died, the need for him unfortunately remains quite alive. In order for humanity to take its fate and future into its own hands, it had to dispel these lingering shadows. The constitution of a new metaphysics could not accomplish this, as it would only create yet a further shadow; psychology, on the other hand, may function to support humanity's aspirations to achieve complete spiritual autonomy. Here one can locate another explanation of Nietzsche's indirect method of attacking the prevailing metaphysics. To engage in a direct confrontation would have required the development of

---

57. MA I — 22; KSA 2:43, and cf. Karl R. Popper, *The Logic of Scientific Discovery* (New York, 1959), and *Conjectures and Refutations: The Growth of Scientific Knowledge* (London, 1963). See also another "Popperian" statement: "It is certainly not the least charm of a theory that it is refutable; it is precisely thereby that it attracts subtler minds" (JGB 18; KSA 5: 31).

some new metaphysical posture, and any success it might have enjoyed would have left him with his destructive instrument still in hand, another metaphysical system, another redundant shadow of the dead God.

Nietzsche is therefore again prompted to act obliquely; rather than struggle directly against metaphysics he realizes he must undermine the mental sources which feed the metaphysical need: "A philosophy can be employed either to *satisfy* such needs or to *set them aside*".[58] The second route is clearly preferable.

Since the metaphysical urge originates in irrational needs, it cannot be eliminated by the rational means of logical refutation or the exposure of internal inconsistencies. Irrational forces are quite immune to the arguments of reason. Otherwise they would not be so unreasonable!

One error after another is coolly placed on ice; the ideal is not refuted — it *freezes* to death — here, for example, 'the genius' freezes to death; at the next corner, 'the saint'; under a huge icicle, 'the hero'; in the end, 'faith', so-called 'conviction'; 'pity' also cools down considerably — and almost everywhere 'the thing in itself' freezes to death.[59]

This freezing of emotions is the ultimate objective and praxis

58. MA I — 27; KSA 2: 48. Nietzsche's attempt at undermining metaphysical needs is again evidence of his objection to Pragmatism. In MA I — 30 Nietzsche, aware of the genetic fallacy and trying to avoid it, says that even if some opinion might be capable of bestowing happiness and other advantages, it does not necessarily follow that it is "by itself good and true" (KSA 2: 50). Thus even if some system of metaphysics satisfies man's "metaphysical need" and brings about some benefits, this does not mean that it is true. On the other hand, despite Nietzsche's own belief that metaphysics is harmful and inhibits the reactivation of man's authentic powers, he does not insist that this conviction provides him with enough ground for declaring metaphysics false or invalid.

59. EH III — MA 1; KSA 6: 323.

of Nietzsche's method of psychologization; there is no basis for the accusation of genetic fallacy, which applies only in an argumentation explicitly attempting to refute the rational validity of any given statements by genetic, psychologistic or socio-logical means.

IV. Psychologization as Salvation from Salvation

Nietzsche's psychologization is more than a means of overcoming metaphysics or revaluating all values. It also fulfils a specifically existential function by addressing the psychic needs of man, easing the burden of his life,[60] giving him peace of mind and "cooling" him.[61] These existential effects flow directly from the capacity of psychologization to freeze the metaphysical need, a need which has never been adequately satisfied by metaphysics itself: every "metaphysical comfort" is subsequently shattered by the collapse of the metaphysical system which provided it. A state of disquiet and discontent naturally ensues, perpetuated by the individual's scepticism about the adequacy of any metaphysical system. This has been the historical predicament of philosophy, but if Nietzsche's method can successfully freeze the need for metaphysical consolation and support he will have helped to relieve us of a profoundly distressing condition. Rather than pursuing comfort through metaphysics, we may be able to achieve a condition of repose — of perpetual peace of mind. In this respect, then, Nietzsche offers a kind of existential salvation precisely by redeeming man from his need for salvation.[62] The "salvation from salvation" was

---

60. MA I — 35; KSA 2: 57.
61. MA I — 56; KSA 2: 75.
62. Spinoza, for instance, sought a metaphysics that would enable him to "enjoy continuous, supreme, and unending happiness", and would grant peace of mind and "a great comfort" ("On the Improvement of the Understanding", trans. R.H.M. Elwes, op. cit., vol. 2, pp. 3–5). Nietzsche

to become a central motif of Nietzsche's mature philosophy. This motif is especially pronounced in *The Gay Science*, in Nietzsche's description of the death of God and the need to vanquish his shadows, and in *On the Genealogy of Morals*:

> But some day ... he must yet come to us, the *redeeming man* ... he may bring home the *redemption* of this reality: its redemption from the curse that the hitherto reigning ideal has laid upon it.[63]

Nietzsche expounds the many personal benefits and "blessings" conferred on us when the psychologistic "axe" finally eradicates the metaphysical need.[64] Man's present condition is conceived as a state of illness, and that need — as a primary symptom — requires the treatment of "icepacks".[65] Only this method can enable us to be "steady, inoffensive, moderate".[66] Psychologization is a personal therapy prescribed for anyone suffering a perturbing intellectual or ideological fever; it is a prescription for the restoration of a healthy tranquility through personal emancipation.[67]

V. From the Psychologistic Method to the Psychology of Power

Although Nietzsche refers to his method by various names, he rarely ever calls it a "science".[68] Of special interest, however, is

---

wishes to attain almost the same goal, but by diametrically opposite means: by eliminating the need for metaphysics.

63. GM 2–24; KSA 5: 336.
64. MA I — 37; KSA 2: 61.
65. MA I — 38; KSA 2: 62.
66. *Loc. cit.*
67. Actually Nietzsche's method of psychologization is also a kind of group therapy, treating the cultural neurosis of his period (MA I — 244; KSA 2: 204).
68. But, e.g., "Chemistry" (MA I — 1; KSA 2: 24, and see the Introduction above); 'historical philosophizing" (MA I — 2; KSA 2: 25); "physiology and

his characterization of it as "the art of psychological dissection and computation".[69] It is particularly significant in this context that Nietzsche picks out La Rochefoucauld as an example of a psychological artist, referring to him as "the great master of the psychological maxim".[70] He greatly admired La Rochefoucauld, but while often describing him as an artist, never identifies him as a *scientist*. La Rochefoucauld, for all his polished and penetrating aphorisms, developed no positive psychological doctrine set of systematic principles to support his insights. In his *Réflexions, ou Sentences et Maximes morales*[71] he stresses the importance of self-scrutiny and integrity, and offers an enlightening analysis of various disguised or unconscious manifestations of self-interest. In this respect La Rochefoucauld resembles a physician who provides a brilliant diagnosis of one's disease but fails to suggest any effective remedy. The absence of a positive therapy (in the form of a systematic psychological doctrine) prevents Nietzsche from allowing him the status of scientist; it also in part justifies his criticism of the predominantly pessimistic and suspicious outlook reflected in La Rochefoucauld's aphorisms.[72]

Nietzsche himself, by contrast, offers his method of psychologization as "one of the means of bestowing charm on existence and relieving and mollifying it".[73] Moreover, his reference to this method as *"Kunst"* — which is both craftsmanship and art — confers on it a position much like that of art in *The*

the history of the evolution of organisms and ideas" (MA I — 10; KSA 2: 30, and see MA I — 17); "backward inference" (FW 370; KSA 3: 621); "psychological observation" (MA I -36; KSA 2: 58; *ibid.* — 38; *ibid.* — 61), etc.
69.   MA I — 35; KSA 2: 57.
70.   *Loc. cit.*
71.   Ed. Jean Lafond (Paris, 1979).
72.   MA I — 36; KSA 2: 59.
73.   MA I — 36; KSA 2: 58.

Birth of Tragedy. The art of tragedy and the art of psychologization both function in a consoling and therapeutic role in man's mental life. Nonetheless, when Nietzsche employs his method in analysis of the genesis and annals of the moral sentiment he attempts to provide a positive solution to the problems exposed by his earlier investigations. At this point psychologization is more properly conceived of as a psychological science.[74] The subsequent exercise of psychologization in the sphere of morality issues in a complete set of positive principles: the psychology of the weak man and his *"Sklaven-Moral"*, the psychology of the powerful man and his *"Herren-Moral"*, and underlying them the monistic principle of the will to power. All of these elements constitute a positive psychology or science of power — of which more will be said later.

This transformation from psychologization to psychology is mainly implicit and *a posteriori*; it occurs only when Nietzsche recognizes that his method required a positive and fairly comprehensive psychological doctrine if he was to successfully substantiate and intensify its therapeutic aims. Specific principles and criteria must be made explicit if the method is to be practically viable. In articulating his method (as we have already seen) Nietzsche had already appealed to certain psychological principles, i.e. the unconscious, sublimation and repression. He now perceives that this assortment of positive concepts may combine into an organic whole which, if not consistent *de jure*, may nonetheless endow his "science" of psychology with a *de facto* applicability.

Nietzsche's psychological findings are not accidental,

---

74. MA I — 37; KSA 2: 59–60, and see ff. When Nietzsche here and elsewhere in this book speaks of *"Wissenschaft"* he is not referring to empirical science (as Danto implies by saying that at this time Nietzsche "considered himself to be practising a science", *Nietzsche as Philosopher*, p. 69 and ff.) but mainly to his own psychology. See also MA I — 38.

arbitrary or particularistic: his theses are consolidated and unified by a pivotal principle of mental life — the concept of *Macht*. It is the discovery, explication and consistent application of this principle which represents the culmination of Nietzsche's positive psychology. Regarding man as an instinctual, creative creature (a *homo faber*), Nietzsche was led to describe him in terms of the will to power. His preliminary energetic-dynamic model of the human psyche and its sublimatory creative processes, especially in the moral arena, now takes on a more perspicuous structure through the monistic principle of an instinctual, creative power capable of supervising, restraining, assimilating and molding forms. Nietzsche's early psychologizations revealed the Apollonian-Dionysian complex of drives and emotions as the nucleus of both the individual and his culture, imposing creative, organic forms on the rhapsody of stimuli produced from both within and without. It is this same nucleus, now baptized as the will to power, which becomes the exclusive demurgic principle in Nietzsche's mature philosophy. From this point forward, Nietzsche's thought will be concentrated on this particular instinctual substratum underlying all primary cultural manifestations: science, philosophy, religion and morality. The will to power, in other words, is a striving Dionysian will molding itself through Apollonian forms. Nietzsche's *On the Uses and Disadvantages of History for Life* presents morality as an expression of the creative conquest of the natural elements in man and his environment. Since only power can overcome power, the very existence of morality and culture must mean that man is himself no less than a will to power — in this case a will to morality and an autonomously creative culture. In this way Nietzsche derives both a summation and generalization of the process of morality as self-overcoming, as well as the organization of man's chaotic instincts, out of his seminal idea of culture as a "transfiguration of nature". The psychological notion of the "Higher Self" must also be included in this unified cluster, for it is responsible for the struggle (mainly by means of repression) with the instincts, and for the internalization of moral values. In Nietzsche's later philosophizing this "Higher Self" is also articulated in terms of the comprehensive concept of the will to power. In the following chapter these moves will be explicated in detail.

As the reader may have observed, a psychological perspective has been adopted in the interpretive reconstruction of Nietzsche's early teaching. In consequence, we are able to view the mature philosophy as a consistent development of preliminary investigations. The coherent progression from the psychologization of the first stage to the psychology of the second imparts a natural, organic unity to the entire Nietzschean construction.[75]

75. Thus there seems to be no great need for a criticism based on a consideration of the several distinct and contradictory attitudes that appear to exist in Nietzsche's philosophy. A good case in point is Karl Jaspers' interpretation of Nietzsche. His two books and several essays on Nietzsche, however informative and illuminating, do not distinguish between the earlier and later views, but rather tend to a synchronic presentation stressing the seeming contradictions and ambiguities.

CHAPTER FIVE

FROM FORCE TO POWER

Introduction

The key to the meaning of the will to power is Nietzsche's notion of self-overcoming. *"Selbstüberwindung"* is a concept which originated in Nietzsche's recognition of the role of sublimation. Sublimation, as the mental mechanism which orders and subdues the instinctual drives, is responsible for the attainment of "Self-mastery".[1] Until this point Nietzsche's thought has been guided by a retrospective examination of his own personal self-conquests; now, however, he has identified a specific pattern of existence in which these conquests are construed as instances of a general principle, being interpreted as manifestations of the will to power.

This move is well illustrated in *Thus Spoke Zarathustra* which contains his first detailed discussion of the will to power. In the chapter titled "On Self-Overcoming" Nietzsche discusses the will to power in terms of an unceasing will to overcome oneself:

And life itself confided this secret to me...: I must be a struggle and a becoming and an end and an opposition to ends... Whatever I create and however much I love it —

---

1. M 109; KSA 3; 96, and cf. Chapter One, Section X.

soon I must oppose it and my love; thus my will wills it.[2]

As a *perpetual* willing, the will to power negates the already formulated (Apollonian) forms and replaces them with other creations. Dialectical self-overcoming is the clue, then, to Nietzsche's mature philosophizing. It can be construed in part as an indirect "confession" of his own triumph over the negative elements of his character and culture. As he says himself:

My writings speak *only* of overcomings: 'I' am in them, together with everything that was inimical to me.[3]

Certain parts of Nietzsche's personal and intellectual biography are radically transformed by his sublimatory philosophizing; some are preserved intact, others are eliminated, while others are elevated beyond the merely biographical — his own Self-overcoming itself being finally explicated as a manifestation of the universal principle dubbed *the will to power*.

Nietzsche's notion of self-overcoming also contains a reconstrual of the meaning of maturity and spiritual growth. In

2. ZA II sec. 12; TPN: 227; KSA 4: 148. Thus the essential relations between Nietzsche's concept of the will to power and his notions of *Selbstüberwindung* and "opposition" bring me to agree with Wolfgang Müller-Lauter's persuasive interpretation regarding *"Gegensätzlichkeit"* as a fundamental feature of the will to power. See his *Nietzsche: Seine Philosophie der Gegensätze und die Gegensätze seiner Philosophie* (Berlin, 1971), pp. 10–33.

3. MA II-Preface 1; KSA 2: 369. We may assume here that these "inimical" elements of *Zeitgeist* include the strong religious sentiments that Nietzsche inherited from his Lutheran father and pious surroundings, his metaphysical-transcendental inclinations (Schopenhauer), his romantic predilections (Wagner), and the nihilist-pessimistic world outlook prevalent at that time in European culture, inspired by the "death of God", and Darwinian doctrine. We should add to these cultural trends Nietzsche's own racial and nationalistic-chauvinistic prejudices, so widely shared at the time of his youth. Nietzsche's basically by positive views on Jews and his anti anti-semitism are discussed in my "Nietzsche on Jews and Judaism", *Archiv für Geschichte der Philosophie* 67 (1985): 139–161.

the later stages of character development one must have overcome whatever elements are alien to the inner, organic personality — the elements that precluded authentic creativity and freedom. If, then, one were to ask Nietzsche, "What is the purpose of this Self-overcoming?", he would answer succinctly: to achieve maturity and power. In this respect the will to power is of a piece with the will to selfhood — the will to become such a free and creative person capable of devising his own values and realizing them in his actions without timid hesitations or uncertainties. The optimal will to power is realized in the *"Übermensch"*. On the other hand, if this will is diminished in quality one's tendency to escape from self-development and to identify with the "herd" — or various available political or religious ideologies — will intensify. An individual with a truly sound psychic make-up is endowed with a will to power of higher quality and greater vitality. His will expresses the "master morality", in contrast to the "slave morality" typical of those possessing lesser power or *Macht*, although the latter may be endowed with greater physical force or *Kraft*. The distinction between *Kraft* and *Macht* is crucial to any understanding of Nietzsche's mature and positive doctrine of power: it represents his philosophical emphasis on the transition from physical force to mental power.

I. Force Versus Power in Nietzsche

The term *Kraft* is introduced in a passage which deals explicity with the will to power as the will to autonomous and creative selfhood. This aphoristic passage describes the dramatic turning-point in Nietzsche's life and thought when he was disabused of his Wagnerian illusions and began the process of intellectual and personal emancipation. He refers to this as a period of *"a great liberation"* and describes it as the "first outbreak of strength (*Kraft*) and will to self-determination... will

181

to *free* will".[4] Here Nietzsche clearly equates "strength" and "force" with "self-determination" and freedom. And since the notion of autonomoy includes these two concepts, it follows that force is equivalent to autonomy.

This concept of *Kraft*, however, is not identical to that of *Macht* as later formulated by Nietzsche in the idea of the will to power. One might argue, then, that any equivalence between *Macht* and autonomy is unconvincing, at least on the authority of the above passage. *Kraft* and *Macht* are etymologically quite distinct, but at this stage Nietzsche makes no effort to differentiate between them and treats them as equivalent. Only later did he come to see the need to make a fundamental distinction between the two terms, finding *Kraft* inadequate to convey his philosophical intentions. It was subsequently replaced by the pivotal concept of *Macht*, and in order to understand this latter concept it is useful to trace the connotations of both terms and to analyse the reasons why the one supplanted the other.

Nietzsche's notion of *Kraft* constitutes a primitive energy, a latent and indefinite state which only functions when activated within a concrete situation.[5] The transition from *Kraft* to *Macht* is thus a transition from the potentiality of force to its actualization. Blind *"Kraftquellen"* are transmuted and become *"mächtig"* (powerful) through a concrete expression in a specific cultural and historical context.[6] The transition from a primal, inchoate driving-force into a rationally formulated power is essentially Nietzsche's original characterization of the sublimatory process: the Apollonian shapes and directs the "Dionysian-barbarian"

---

4. MA I — V3; KSA 2: 16–17.
5. See, e.g., MA II 1–226; KSA 2: 481–482. This connotation of "Kraft" actually agrees with current everyday German usage, as in the expression: "schlummernde Kräfte im Menschen wecken". And see "Kraft" in *Duden: Das grosse Wörterbuch der deutschen Sprache* (Mannheim, 1978).
6. MA II 1–226, *loc. cit.*.

and thereby achieves cultural value and esteem. This distinction between "force" and "power" indicates clearly that *power is a sublimated force.* The connection between *Macht* and sublimation is underlined in the following:

> They took this all-too-human to be inescapable and instead of reviling it, preferred to accord it a kind of right of the second rank through regulating it within the usages of society and religion: indeed, everything in man possessing *power* they called divine and inscribed it on the walls of their Heaven.[7]

The *"Naturtrieb"*[8] is simply the primordial, "barbaric" force and only its sublimated cultural manifestations are endowed with effective and actual power.

Nietzsche later calls this sublimation "Victory over strength (*Kraft*)", which is the title of an aphorism pertinent to our discussion. A section of this runs as follows:

> We are still on our knees before *strength* — after the ancient custom of slaves — and yet when the degree of *worthiness to be revered* is fixed, only the *degree of rationality in strength* is decisive: we must assess to what extent precisely strength has been overcome by something higher, in the service of which it now stands as means and instrument![9]

While the "slave" worships brute strength, only a force sublimated by rational Apollonian elements, and thereby elevated to a culturally valuable level, should merit our admiration. This is qualitative power, the most intense

---

7. MA II 1–220; KSA 2: 473, and cf. *ibid.*, sec. 219.
8. *Loc. cit.*
9. M 548; KSA 3: 318.

expression of which is the "genius",[10] in whom this force is inwardly directed towards the creation of selfhood.[11] This harks back to the idea in *The Birth of Tragedy* that man is of value only as an "aesthetic phenomenon", although here one finds the added dynamic element of the transmutation of *Kraft* into *Macht*. Special mental resources are required to achieve this "victory over strength", this process of self-sublimation. But with this "triumph" we become a supreme work of art: an actualised *Macht*. The authentic selfhood of the *Übermensch*, like that of "the exceptional Greeks",[12] is achieved by his ability to bring about within himself a "transfiguration of nature", a purification *("Reinigung")* of the primitive, raw element of force into refined, creative power. Those who give vent to their brute force or naked agression do not belong in the category of the *Übermensch*.

Nietzsche valued the psychic more highly than the physical. This is evident even in those passages dealing with "the blond beast"[13] that have sometimes been used to give a distorted reading of Nietzsche's attitude towards physical strength, suggesting he worshipped pure violence:

> In the beginning, the noble caste was always the barbarian caste: their predominance did not lie mainly in physical strength [*Kraft*] but in the psychic — they were more *whole* human beings (which also means, at every level, 'more whole beasts').[14]

Another fragment shows how Nietzsche associates "force" with unsublimated Dionysian instinctuality:

10. *Loc. cit* in *Schopenhauer as Educator* "the saint", "the philosopher" and "the artist" best exemplified this self-control and self-overcoming.
11. Thus accomplishing this "spectacle of that strength which employs genius *not for works* but for *itself as a work*", M 548; KSA 3: 319.
12. MA II 1–221; KSA 2: 474.
13. For instance: GM I — 11; II — 17; GD VII sec. 2.
14. JGB 257; KSA 5: 206 (My slightly revised translation).

To demand of strength that it should *not* express itself as
strength, that it should *not* be a desire to overcome, a
desire to throw down, a desire to become master, a thirst
for enemies and resistances and triumphs, is just as absurd
as to demand of weakness that it should express itself as
strength. A quantum of force [*Kraft*] is equivalent to a
quantum of drive, will, effect — more, it is nothing other
than precisely this very driving, willing, effecting.[15]

Triumph over blind nature and basic instincts, including the
drive towards agressive supremacy, is a sign of the powerful
personality and of authentic selfhood. Nietzsche's discovery (in
Daybreak and later works) that current morality was simply an
artful disguise of the drive towards domination and subjection
caused him to reject it, for it was not a genuine manifestation of
power.

Macht, with its connotations of determination and freedom, is
better suited to the notion of power as a sublimated and creative
force, than is *Kraft*, with its implications of undefined potentiality.
This point is amplified in *"Nachgelassene Fragmente"*, part of
which was posthumously compiled and published as *The Will to
Power*.[16] In a series of aphorisms rejecting a "mechanistic"

15. GM I — 13; KSA 5: 279.
16. My occasional references to this problematic collection do not imply that I
accept Bäumler's description of this selective compilation of experimental
notes from Nietzsche's notebooks of the years 1883 to 1888, not authorized
for publication, as his final, "systematic" and most fundamental work (Alfred
Bäumler, "Nachwort" zur *Kröner Taschenausgabe* Bd. 78, 1930). On the
other hand, I cannot fully agree with the diametrically opposite view of Karl
Schlechta, who, trying to cleanse Nietzsche of the Nazi elements ascribed
to him by Bäumler, maintains that "in 'Der Wille zur Macht; nichts Neues
steht" (Karl Schlechta, "Philologischer Nachbericht", *Friedrich Nietzsche
Werke*, 1977, Bd. V, s. 55), and thus suggests that the book is hardly worth
reading. See also his *Der Fall Nietzsche: Aufsätze und Voträge*, München,
1958, pp. 99–115; and compare Tracy B. Strong's view that "At best, the
book serves an indexing function", *Friedrich Nietzsche*, p. 220. In my own
exposition I do not use this collection as representing Nietzsche's mature,

interpretation of the world in favour of a "dynamic" one, Nietzsche expresses his dissatisfaction with the concept of "force", which lacks the requisite connotations of intentional, deliberate, creative direction:

> The victorious concept "force" (*Kraft*), by means of which our physicists have created God and the world, still needs to be completed: an inner will must be ascribed to it, which I designate as "will to power" (*Willen zur Macht*), i.e. as an insatiable desire to manifest power; or as the employment and exercise of power, as a creative drive, etc.[17]

Nietzsche rejects the notion of "force"; it is a quantitative concept derived from descriptive mechanistic physics, which fails to account for qualitative processes:

> 'Mechanistic interpretation': desires nothing but quantities; but force is to be found in quality. Mechanistic theory can therefore only *describe* processes, not explain them.[18]

The conative aspect of the process of overcoming, which includes the sublimatory overcoming of oneself, is inseparable from the idea of the "will to power". On the other hand, this aspect is absent from an indefinite and naturalistic idea of force, though the latter does include the notion of change brought about by its external activation. It is an aspect also associated with the concept of will, a feature which in part motivates the attempt to assimilate both terms: "The only force (*Kraft*) that exists is of the same kind as that of the will: a commanding of other subjects, which thereupon change".[19] However, what we

authorized and explicit philosophy, but rather to get a closer look at his philosophical laboratory, where various ideas were tested, refined and rejected.
17. WM 619.
18. WM 660.
19. WM 490.

have here is "a commanding", which is a conative-conscious act, far removed from the idea of a natural and mindless force. Nietzsche therefore had to abandon this attempt at assimilation. More importantly, blind force lacks that element of power essential to Nietzsche — Its Apollonian rational creativity. Furthermore, power includes the notion of "pleasure in creating"[20] which is not the primary motive, but an epiphenomenon accompanying the consciousness of creatively implementing power.[21]

A concept of force derived from the natural sciences and suited mainly to cosmology and the description of natural processes is inappropriate to psychological theory. The notion of the will to power, however, unifies under one heading a large number of psychologizations and psychological observations. It is a term which grows out of many specifically psychological phenomena, such as sublimatory creation, self-overcoming, will, drives, intentional activity conscious of its own goals, moral *praxis*, ascetic religious patterns etc. This unifying notion of the will to power was to become the core of Nietzsche's comprehensive psychology.

It is in his 1888 'declaration of intentions' — partly realised in his writings of that and the previous year — that Nietzsche testifies to the centrality of the will to power in the "Unitary conception of psychology". There he discusses the monistic theory "that the will to power is the primitive form of affect, that all other affects are only developments of it", and that "all driving force (*Kraft*) is will to power, that there is no other physical, dynamic or psychic force except this".[22]

The reason Nietzsche ultimately rejects the concept of physical force (apart from its inappropriateness in dealing with

20. WM 661.
21. WM 702.
22. WM 688.

psychological phenomena) is that is lacks intrinsic dynamic intensification. The concept of force cannot be used to explain the basic psycho-biological phenomena of growth and maturation by means of overcoming:

> The will to power... defines limits, determines degree, variations of power. Mere variations of power could not feel themselves to be such: there must be present something that wants to grow and interprets the value of whatever else wants to grow.[23]

Self-overcoming and sublimation require an indefinite investment of energy for the cancellation, preservation and elevation of a given activity. The concept of force, however, is associated with the preservation of a certain amount of energy within a closed system.[24] This renders it inappropriate to a dynamic approach, one which generalises the biological notion of continuous growth into a comprehensive psychological theory. To put it differently: the concept of force obeys the dictum *Ex nihilo nihil fit*, in that the effect contains nothing which did not already exist in the cause. Sublimation, self-overcoming and the effort of the psyche to intensify itself cannot be bound by such mechanistic principles. Causal explanations do not apply in the mental domain of the human will, and one is quite justified in speaking of the phenomenon of the dialectical intensification of life, due to the operation of the will which elevates it to a qualitatively higher level and "degree" of power:

> In our science, where the concept of cause and effect is reduced to the relationship of equivalence, with the object of proving that the *same* quantum of force (*Kraft*) is present on both sides, *the driving force is lacking*: we observe only

23. WM 643.
24. See, for example, WM 1062 and 1064.

results, and we consider them *equivalent* in content and force".[25]

This rejection of the conservationist aspect of the concept of force is connected to certain of Nietzsche's reservations about Spinoza's concept of *Conatus*. As Nietzsche understands it, this concept paralyses any dynamic change or development:

> Spinoza's law of 'self-preservation' ought really to put a stop to change: but this law is false, the *opposite* is true. It can be shown most clearly that every living thing does everything it can, *not* to preserve itself, but to become *more*.[26]

Mere preservation of being leads to stagnation. The will to power is will for growth and selfhood, the will to overcome anything that curbs the being's intensification or affirmation. This is incompatible with the law of the conservation of energy of classical physics:

> The will to *accumulate force* (*Kraft*) is special to the phenomena of life, to nourishment, procreation, inheritance — to society, state, custom, authority... Not merely conservation of energy, but maximal economy in use, so the only reality is *the will of every centre of force to grow stronger* — not self-preservation, but the will to appropriate, dominate, increase, grow stronger.[27]

The aspects of "force" imbued with the element of "power" are already present in the manifestations of the will to power. Thus, although Nietzsche replaced the concept of force with the notion of power, the latter actually includes the former as the raw

---

25. WM 688 (italics as in the German text).
26. *Loc. cit.* (italics as in the German text).
27. WM 689 (italics as in the German text).

material, a set of instincts and potential energy (reminiscent of Aristotle's treatment of matter as the capacity to receive "forms"). The substratum upon which the processes of sublimation operate is the force, and the element that forms and moulds this force is the will. Force is the necessary — but not the sufficient — condition for the display of power. The (Dionysian) force together with the (Apollonian) forms provide the necessary and sufficient conditions. This synthesis of Nietzsche's earlier dualistic principles into the monistic principle of the will to power shapes his mature, positive psychology.

According to various notes (not authorized for publication) it seems that Nietzsche was not content with a psychology which had now become "the morphology and *the doctrine of the development of the will to power,*[28] but wished to return to the Schopenhauerian formula and generalize the psychological phenomenon of the will to power into a comprehensive metaphysical cosmology. This contrasts with his published writings in which he objects to Schopenhauer's cosmology of "the will in itself" as "a primeval mythology".[29] This aphorism (and others) indicates that Nietzsche could not subscribe (at least not openly) to a cosmological and metaphysical doctrine of the will to power, firstly because he limits willing to "intellectual beings" only, and secondly because he regards the concept of "substance" as an advantageous fiction.[30] Hence, in contrast to Schopenhauer, Nietzsche does not identify "being" with "willing". In his view the latter is solely "a mechanism",[31] a functional psychological system, within which the will is not an

---

28. JGB 23; KSA 5: 38.
29. FW 127; KSA 3: 483.
30. See, for example, FW 111. Such statements, among other things, brought Danto to maintain that Nietzsche replaced "the ontological category of *entity*"by "an ontological category of *power*" (*Nietzsche as Philosopher,* p. 172, *et passim*).
31. FW 127; KSA 3: 483.

entity but a function — merely another action. In Nietzsche's authorised writings, then, the will to power is based upon distinctly psychological and anthropological principles.

Nietzsche's attempt to locate man and culture within a metaphysics of the will to power is expressed mainly in the posthumous collection, *"The Will to Power"*.[32] Presumably Nietzsche was not satisfied with these notes and ideas. Being aware of the contentiousness of such generalized speculations, he did not include them in any of his finished books,[33] Nonetheless he does occasionally nod in that direction, and even makes the demand, for example, "that psychology shall be recognized again as the queen of the sciences".[34]

The preeminence of the role played by psychology in Nietzsche's thought is exemplified in his (untimely) attempt to psychologise nature by projecting the human will to power onto the entire cosmos. Nietzsche universalizes the strong man as "a monster of energy (*Kraft*), who demands a monster of a task",[35] describing "this world" as "a monster of energy (*Kraft*),[36] a chaos in which every element consumes the other in a perpetual struggle for dominance and control. Just as the human "monster of energy" sublimates its own tremendous force, creating the "Übermensch", so the entire *'"Dionysian world"* creates itself "out of the play of contradictions back to the joy of concord (*Einklang*)", thereby becoming *"the will to power — and nothing besides it!"*.[37] Dionysian energy and Apollonian sublimation exist

---

32. Especially in sections 618–715, "which has no parallels" — as Kaufmann rightly says in his translation — "in Nietzsche's books", WM, p. 332, fn. 53.
33. With the possible exception of JGB 36, where he conducts a speculative "experiment" (*"den Versuch"*, KSA 5: 54) regarding the entire world as the "will to power and nothing else" (KSA 5: 55).
34. JGB 23; KSA 5: 39.
35. WM 995.
36. WM 1067.
37. *Loc. cit.*

not only in the psychology of man and culture, but in the cosmos itself. Man as the will to power is only a limited human fragment of the universal process.

This unofficial cosmology implies Nietzsche's view that the will to power also manifests itself in the wish to impose interpretative perspectives on the whole of nature so as to control it through a set of cognitive projections:

> The will to power *interprets*... In fact, interpretation is itself a means of becoming master of something.[38]

Man as will to power, capable of moulding himself and his surroundings, is not only conscious of that fact, but immediately attempts to project and generalise this insight (or self-interpretation) on to the whole cosmos. This universal projection should then be understood as another heuristic-didactic clarification of the fundamentally psychological consequences of the will to power. Because such an understanding lends no philosophical legitimacy to Nietzsche's *"Versuch"* he excluded such cosmological speculation from his published work.

II. From *Libido* to *Eros* in Freud

Certain parallels can be drawn between Nietzsche's shift away from a concept of force as an arbitrary and primitive energy towards the notion of power as a sublimated, creative force, and Freud's motives for moving from the early notion of *libido* as brute, sexual energy to the concept of *Eros*, which is central to his late metapsychology.

However, we must first turn to Nietzsche's treatment of force in the sense of sexual energy:

> The artist is perhaps necessarily a sensual man... This

---

38. WM 643.

notwithstanding, he is on the average, under the pressure of his task, of his will to mastery (*Meisterschaft*), actually moderate, often even chaste. His dominant instinct *wills* this of him: it does not permit him to expend himself in any casual way. The force (*Kraft*) that one expends in artistic conception is the same as that expended in the sexual act: there is only one kind of force.[39]

This force is not identical with purely biological, sexual energy — Freud's *libido*— which lacks any qualitative aesthetic element. Rather it is the will to power, including also the erotic component. The latter is manifested in part by the capacity of the "instinct" to undergo sublimation, recreating new structures on a qualitatively higher level. Nietzsche emphasises the erotic, creative aspects of the will to power by referring to the process of incessant growth in which the will strives for new and original arrangements of its components. In this respect, all the processes of psycho-biological maturing and development are sublimated acts of dispensing with the already given and making use of the inherently vital remainder, elevated to a qualitatively higher level:

> An incarnate will to power, it will strive to grow, spread, seize, become predominant — not from any morality or immorality but because it is living and because life simply *is* will to power.[40]

Freud's later metapsychology also vividly portrays the Nietzschean conception of the erotic element of the will to power undergoing a process of sublimation and inciting a qualitative "expansion, incorporatiom, growth".[41] In order to stress his

---

39. WM 815 (my slightly revised translation).
40. JGB 259; KSA 5: 208.
41. WM 704.

concern with something other than a merely biological drive, Freud's final version of his dualism between the life and death instincts introduces the old philosophical and mythological antithesis between *'Eros'* and *'Thanatos'*. He shifts from the concept of the biological *libido*, which emphasises the quantitative, energetic and inchoate aspects of instinct,[42] to the Platonic notion of *Eros*, which illuminates its qualitative, formative features — themselves manifested in the construction of new and more inclusive vital unities. This shift constitutes a broadening and refinement of the meaning of sexuality in his work. Freud came to realise that the biological, quantitative concept of *libido* does not contain the subjectively qualitative and creative elements that appear, for example, in sublimation (which nevertheless needs *libido*-energy in order to take place).[43] He therefore had to extend the notion of *libido* in order to encompass these important aspects, just as Nietzsche had to extend the concept of force to include both the driving energetics of force and the particular characteristics of qualitatively sublimated instinct.

Freud undertook the shift from *libido* to *Eros* in order to coordinate his theory of instincts with the concept of sublimation, as well as to emphasise culturally sublimated manifestations of sexuality rather than its direct expressions. Furthermore he makes this transition with the intention of developing a comprehensive metapsychology which will give us

42.   Inasmuch as the sexual drive represents a force exerting pressure, libido is defined by Freud as the energy of this drive. This quantitative aspect dominates his 'libido-theory':

"*Libido* is an expression taken from the theory of the emotions. We call by that name the energy, regarded as a quantitative magnitude (though not at present actually measurable), of those instincts which have to do with all that may be comprised under the word 'love'." (Freud, SE *18*: 90, and cf. SE *7*: 217).

43.   See, for example, "The Libido Theory", SE *18*: 256.

an economical and parsimonious genesis of an entire culture.[44] In *"Jenseits des Lustprinzips"* (1920), when introducing this new dichotomy between *Eros* and the death instinct, Freud states the main aim of his "metapsychology" as being "the most complete description"[45] of the mental processes. To this end, the major elements are grouped under three headings: the "topographical" aspect (the division of the psychic apparatus into a number of sub-systems such as the Unconscious, the Preconscious and the Conscious, and the three agencies, Id, Ego and Super-Ego); the "dynamic" aspect (which regards mental phenomena as the result of the conflict and combination between instinctual forces); and the "economic" model (which describes the psychic phenomena in terms of the distribution and circulation of instinctual energy which is capable of increase or decrease).

Freud himself recognized that his metapsychology relied on "speculative assumptions", attempting to put forward a total system which alone could account fully for "the facts of daily observation".[46] This attempt is similar in aim to certain trends of systematic speculation in philosophy, and originates in Freud's initial "longing for philosophical knowledge".[47] His attempt to

44. Thus I agree with Herbert Marcuse's contention in *Eros and Civilization* (London, 1969), that Freud's "Eros signifies a quantitative and qualitative aggrandizement of sexuality" (p. 166), by which "the biological drive becomes a cultural drive" (p. 170). However, it is hard to accept another part of his argument, that "the aggrandized concept (*Eros*) seems to demand a correspondingly modified concept of sublimation" (*ibid.*, p. 166), since, from the first, Freud's theory contained a pronounced disproportion between the (qualitative) concept of sublimation and the (quantitative) concept of *libido*, and by his shift from libido to *Eros*, Freud attempted, *inter alia*, to bridge this gap.
45. SE *18*: 7.
46. *Loc. cit.*, and see SE *14*: 181.
47. Freud's letter of 2.4.1896 to his friend Wilhelm Fliess: "As a young man I knew no longing other than for philosophical knowledge, and now I am about to fulfil it as I move from medicine to psychology." *The Complete Letters of Sigmund Freud to Wilhelm Fliess: 1887–1904*, translated and

outline a metapsychological system (an implicit substitute for metaphysics) in which the principle of *Eros* plays a crucial role, serves to locate psychoanalysis midway between the natural sciences and philosophy.[48] It could be argued, then, that Freud, through his speculative metapsychology, tries to raise psychoanalysis to the level of philosophy, whereas Nietzsche wished to replace philosophy with psychology by means of his metapsychological principle of the will to power.

In spite of Freud's deeply ambivalent attitude towards philosophy, he often deliberately approaches it. This ambivalence is quite pronounced even in the essay introducing his *Eros* principle from the metapsychological perspective:

> It is of no concern to us in this connection to enquire how far, with this hypothesis of the pleasure principle [*Lustprinzip*], we have approached or adopted any particular, historically established, philosophical system ... On the other hand we would readily express our gratitude to any philosophical or psychological theory which was able to inform us ...[49]

In this context, Freud mentions "the discovery" of "an investigator of such penetration as G.T. Fechner".[50] Yet he has someone other than Fechner in mind when he refers to a "particular ... philosophical system". Similarly, he is not just thinking of Plato when he introduces the concept of *Eros* which

edited by Jeffrey Moussaieff Masson (Harvard University Press, Cambridge, Mass., 1985), p. 180.
48. See SE *19*: 217, where Freud asserts that psychoanalysis stands in a "middle position between medicine and philosophy".
49. SE *18*: 7.
50. *Ibid.*, 8. Freud refers here to a late book by Fechner, *Einige Ideen zur Schöpfungs- und Entwicklungsgeschichte der Organismen* (Leipzig, 1879), although in fact Fechner published his doctrine in a much earlier philosophical article "Über das Lustprinzip des Handelns", *Zeitschrift für Philosophische Kritik* (Halle, 1848), 1–30; 163–194.

"would coincide with the *Eros* of the poets and philosophers".[51]
Even before he mentions the *Symposium,* Freud refers obliquely
to Nietzsche when he speaks of

> the belief that there is an instinct towards perfection at
> work in human beings, which has brought them to their
> present high level of intellectual achievement and ethical
> sublimation and which may be expected to watch over
> their development into super-men. I have no faith, however,
> in the existence of any such internal instinct and I cannot
> see how this benevolent illusion is to be preserved.[52]

Several editions of *The Will to Power,* appeared[53] and attracted
much attention during the years in which Freud was developing
his metapsychology, but we have no direct evidence that Freud
ever read it. In any event, Nietzsche did not call his will to power
"an instinct towards perfection",[54] although he did identify it
with intensified life-instincts, just as Freud identified *Eros* with
"Lebenstrieb". Despite the close relationship between the will
to power and the development of the *Übermensch* and the
resemblance between Nietzsche's monistic principle and Freud's
Eros, it is difficult to prove that Freud's metapsychology was
directly influenced by Nietzsche. Some indirect influence seems
very likely; what concerns us here, however, is not the historical
relationship between Freud and Nietzsche and their respective

---

51. SE *18*: 50, and see SE *23*: 245, where Freud mentions the Ancient Greek
philosopher Empedocles in connection with his discussion of the concepts
of *"Eros* and *destructiveness".*
52. SE *18*: 42.
53. E.g.: The "Grossoktavausgabe" in Vols. XI; XVI (1911); the "Musarionausgabe", Vols. XVIII; XIX (1920–1929); Kröners Taschen edition, Vol. 78
(1930).
54. It is interesting to notice that one contemporary commentator has also
perceived the notion of the will to power in this way: "*First,* the will to power
... is essentially a striving to transcend and perfect oneself" (Kaufmann,
Nietzsche, p. 248).

thought but the existence in both of an immanent logic to the introduction of their key concepts.

Freud rejects the quasi-Nietzschean "belief that there is an instinct towards perfection", and proposes as an alternative "the efforts of *Eros* to combine organic substances into even larger unities".[55] He denies the "instinct towards perfection" (which supposedly leads to the Nietzschean "super-man") regarding it as a "benevolent illusion", because he (wrongly) assumes that Nietzsche optimistically believed in progress and rational *telos*, leading to the perfection of man and culture.[56] Instead, Freud endorses the Darwinian scheme of arbitrary, immanent development:

> The present development of human beings requires, as it seems to me, no different explanations from that of animals.[57]

Unwittingly, Freud's thought here closely approximates Nietzsche's own, which also generalizes the psychological principle of the will to power to apply to the animal world. All considered, Nietzsche is indeed closer to blind Darwinian evolution than to rational Hegelian progress, and his affinity with Freud is particularly strong at precisely that point at which the latter thought himself most radically distanced. Here we encounter Freud's antithesis between the destructive and regressive death instinct and the creative, expanding life instinct. Although he did not believe in perpetual, rational development and conscious self-perfection, one cannot infer that Freud did not believe in change (which after all occurs even at the level of the individual who undergoes psychoanalysis). Yet the principle

55. SE *18*: 42–43.
56. So Freud had certainly not read Nietzsche's aphorism from *The Will to Power* entitled: "Against determinism and teleology" (sec. 552).
57. SE *18*: 42.

of change in Freud is closed and exhaustive rather than open and optimistic, because it includes a thanatic psychological and cosmological principle which checks the growth of *Eros* and causes it to regress. A similar type of closed change is to be found in Nietzsche's "eternal recurrence of the same", which restricts the infinitely open change of the will to power.[58] Indeed, since the will to power and *Eros* are restrained by a similar "enemy", they come to resemble each other even more intimately.[59]

III. The Revealing of Power in Weakness

Until *Human, All Too Human*, Nietzsche had investigated individual phenomena without committing himself to any

58. Certain Nietzsche interpreters have disregarded the close relations between the two most important ideas in his later work, the will to power and eternal recurrence, even sometimes maintaining that the two notions are completely separate (e.g. Tracy B. Strong, *Friedrich Nietzsche*, p. 261). However, Nietzsche himself declares, for instance in EH III ZI; KSA 6: 335, that eternal recurrence forms the "fundamental conception" of *Zarathustra*, which is the book where the idea of the will to power is introduced for the first time, and in the process of describing it he returns on several occasions to eternal recurrence. Furthermore, in the *"Nachgelassene"* drafts for the intended book *Der Wille zur Macht* (years 1882–1885) a plan for a section on "the eternal recurrence" usually appears before a chapter entitled "The will to power". The compilation WM concludes with a chapter on "The Eternal Recurrence", following Book Three, which deals with the various manifestations of the will to power (as knowledge, in nature, in society, and as art). It seems that these locations of the idea are not incidental, and imply that eternal recurrence brings these open manifestations of the monistic principle to a close.
59. Another possible resemblance between Freud and Nietzsche may be found in that Freud formulated his highly speculative idea of *Thanatos* on the empirical basis of the phenomenon of *"Wiederholungszwang"* (Repetition Compulsion), as a result of which a person tends compulsively to repeat old experiences — especially the distressing ones. It is quite likely that Nietzsche's experiences of this kind acted as a personal basis for his *"ewige Wiederkehr"*, being the antithesis of the will to power, as *Thanatos* opposes *Eros*.

specific principle: his psychologizations up to this point had only been particularistic applications of a speculative method rather than the development of a doctrine and had not yet yielded the concept of power. It is only when Nietzsche turns to an analysis of the feeling of pity and the tendency of the weak to arouse sympathy that he discusses (for the first time) the psychological meaning of power:

Observe children who weep and wail *in order that* they shall be pitied, and therefore wait for the moment when their condition will be noticed; live among invalids and the mentally afflicted and ask yourself whether their eloquent moaning and complaining, their displaying of misfortune, does not fundamentally have the objective of *hurting* those who are with them: the pity which these then express is a consolation for the weak and suffering, inasmuch as it shows them that, all their weakness notwithstanding, they possess at any rate *one power (Macht): the power to hurt.*[60]

It is noteworthy that Nietzsche does not use the concept of *Kraft* in this context, preferring the more psychological notion of *Macht.* It is also quite significant that the 'discovery' of the will to power appears precisely in an analysis of the motives of the weak and miserable; it is a revelation of power in weakness which expressly refers to the *"Versuch einer Umwertung aller Werte"*[61] effected by Nietzsche's psychologizations. A powerful person may at times spontaneously manifest the power at his disposal, but the *desire* for power is more clearly evidenced in the behaviour of those in whom power is wanting and who require some kind of external affirmation. But where do such individuals find the power to exploit their weakness through

---

60. MA I — 50; KSA 2: 70–71. Other indexes to Nietzsche's complete writings omit this context in which the concept of *Macht* appears so significantly.
61. A subtitle of the collection *Der Wille zur Macht* published in 1901.

such manipulative dynamics? It cannot be the case that the weak person starts without any power at his disposal: the very need for power indicates the existence of some primary source of power. So conceived, "power" in the Nietzschean psychology cannot be quantitatively variable from one person to another; the difference between the weak and the powerful (or the "slave" and "master") is not a quantitative one of degree. Power is a feature of every individual's constitution, and the variations are rather to be accounted for in terms of *qualitatively* distinct ways in which it is expressed. The main characteristic of power in Nietzsche is that it is not susceptible to any quantitative assessments in terms of force. The nature of the difference between the "man of power"[62] and the "powerless"[63] is a difference in the qualities or forms through which a constant resource is manifest.

Some interpreters have nonetheless suggested that relative, quantitatively variable assessment is appropriate to Nietzschean power, claiming that "the 'powerful' and the 'powerless' agree in desiring *more* power".[64] This characterization is clearly inappropriate. Nietzsche's powerful man makes no attempt to acquire *more* power, but wishes only to be conscious of and to enjoy the free expression of the power he already possesses through its spontaneous re-activation.

Why is all *activity*... associated with pleasure? Because before it an obstacle, a burden existed? Or rather because all doing is an overcomig, a becoming master, and *increases* the feeling of power (*Machtgefühl*)? Ultimately, it is not only the feeling of power, but the pleasure in

---

62. MA I-44; KSA 2: 66.
63. MA I-45; KSA 2: 67.
64. Kaufmann, *Nietzsche*, p. 185. This statement is surprising, since Kaufmann himself distinguishes between "force" and "power".

creating and in *the thing created*; for all activity enters our consciousness as consciousness of a 'work'.[65]

If the notion of "powerful master" and "powerful slave" had been quantitative and relative, Nietzsche would have been unable to explain how the historical domination of the powerful, master morality by the weaker, slave morality could have occurred.[66] Moreover, if the value of power depended on an estimation of quantitative degree, Nietzsche would clearly have committed a naturalistic fallacy, analysing the specifically ethical value of a property (what ought to be) in terms of its natural characteristics (what naturally is).

At this point one might pose directly the obvious question: Why, after all, does Nietzsche disapprove of the weak who do their best (according to their inherent nature) to acquire power from others by means of their weakness, while approving of the powerful individuals who cannot help but manifest their power — even at the expense of others? This question must certainly be answered, but first we must consider Nietzsche's morality of power in more detail.

Nietzsche's discovery of the power inherent in weakness, and particularly of the benefits attaching to neurotic illness by the *"Geistig-Gedrückten"* anticipated Freud's own conclusion about the neurotic's means of obtaining satisfaction. Freud discussed the *"Krankheitsgewinn"* and the *"Flucht in die Krankheit"*, referring to the complex of direct or indirect satisfactions that a patient derives from his illness. Like Nietzsche before him, Freud introduces these notions in the context of the phenomenon of pity:

> Experience shows without doubt that when once a poor man has produced a neurosis it is only with difficulty that

---

65. WM 661.
66. GM III-13, and see Chapter Seven.

he lets it be taken from him. It renders him too good a service in the struggle for existence; the secondary gain from illness which it brings him is much too important. He now claims by right of his neurosis the pity which the world has refused to his material distress, and he can now absolve himself from the obligation of combating his poverty by working.[67]

Freud also discusses neurosis in terms of compensation which the sick person demands from his surroundings. Again like Nietzsche, he stresses the aggressive features of neurosis and the willful desire of the neurotic to dominate others through the vehicle of his illness.[68] Neurosis is thus revealed as an attempt to gain commiseration and compensation from a hostile environment. This resembles Nietzsche's descriptions of the "aesthetic" or "metaphysical consolation". Because the pursuit of consolation through illness is a neurotic symptom, it is not difficult to understand why Nietzsche tended to identify metaphysics with neurosis and disease, and why he perceived it as an illness requiring a therapy and a cure. Contemporary religious, moral and metaphysical solutions thus become symptoms of an impoverished will to power, which in its weakness strives to extort pity and seeks such consolations as may appear gratifying.

Nonetheless, the ascetic-religious attitude as a complex expression of power has not been unequivocally rejected at this stage of Nietzsche's work. Indeed, when he speaks (in *Human, All Too Human* of the *"Selbstüberwindung"* of the Jesuits, one can clearly detect a note of admiration for their religious

---

67. SE *12*: 133, and see SE *7*: 42 and 43 (n) where Freud defines more specifically his ideas about the primary and secondary gains from illness and discusses the "flight into illness". He returns to this theme in SE *9*: 231, where he calls the process "a *consolation*".
68. SE *16*: 382–385.

expression of self-overcoming.[69] As a direct manifestation of power, Nietzsche commends their example remarking that "No power could maintain itself if its advocates were nothing but hypocrites".[70] This suggests one reason for Nietzsche's criticisms of the sense of pity evoked by the weak: the weak individual may be hypocritically using his alleged powerlessness precisely as a vehicle for gaining power over others, for dominating his environment, and for escaping into neurosis. As a temporary means of gratification these manipulations may serve some point, but they must eventually be exposed as unreliable and ineffectual methods of self-affirmation. If it becomes apparent to others that the neurotic is exercizing a forceful and tenacious control over them by exploiting his illness, they will typically turn against him and refuse to console or pity him. Whenever an individual's means of acquiring and sustaining power depend on the responses of his environment — rather than on his own internal resources — they cannot promise any long term satisfaction. If he were to redirect his power, however, and successfully exercise authority over himself rather than attempting to exercise power over his environment, he would be in a far less vulnerable situation. Freud expresses a very similar idea:

> The help provided by a neurosis has as a rule no better success with the patient. This may be because dealing with a conflict by forming symptoms is after all an automatic process which cannot prove adequate to meeting the demands of life, and in which the subject has abandoned the use of his best and highest powers.[71]

Both Nietzsche and Freud recommend a direct and independent

---

69. MA I-55; KSA 2:75.
70. *Ibid.*: 74.
71. SE *16*: 385, and cf. SE *12*: 133.

struggle with external (social and economic) or internal (psychological) distress as the most reliable solution; in the long term it is the only way to ensure and affirm the *inherent* power of the individual personality. A character which develops exclusively through the formation of dependent relations with others can never become genuinely mature: it will not have developed its *own* power to its maximum potential. The affirmation of the self cannot be completed without the overcoming of its weak and regressive elements. Nietzsche emphasizes this point when remarking that the strength (*Kraft*) of the Catholic Church lies in the strength of its particular representatives who "continually establish further pillars of their power"[72] by using their inherent power in a life project of self-overcomings. Only these 'servants' of the Church exemplify the truly powerful personality — and only such a personality can be sufficiently inspiring to exercise the requisite influence in the education of others.[73] Here, as elsewhere in Nietzsche's writings, psychic power emerges as primary.

IV. The Weakness of Power in Confrontation with Force

Nietzsche has rejected the psychological tendency to manipulate the external environment in an attempt to exploit and conquer it, and has instead proposed an internal process which rechannels personal power towards the challenge of self-overcoming and self-transformation. As in his essay on Schopenhauer, then, he

---

72. MA I-55; KSA 2: 74.
73. This statement is again clear evidence for Nietzsche's distinction between external "force" and intrinsic personal "power", that is, between concrete political and social achievements and the dynamic psychological powers behind them. It is obvious then that a ruler who holds sway over the fates of millions of human beings testifies to the existence of a strong and external political force, but this does not necessarily signify that he himself is a "master" or an *Übermensch* endowed with a genuine will to power.

favours the figure of the *saint* who radically manifests this process. This positive attitude towards asceticism gradually underwent a change, however. He came to see asceticism as a defective method insofar as it fails to sublimate the instinctual drives; it is not a method which is capable of the move of creative-erotic assimilation in which these drives are transformed and elevated. The ascetic saint (or Jesus) does effect a kind of self-overcoming, and possesses an exceptional personal power. This power is used, however, to the end of a one-sided repression and extirpation of other drives. The result is a perpetual cycle of self-abnegation which can never culminate in an act of affirmation. Nietzsche's earlier distinction between repression and sublimation thus re-emerges in the moral and religious context, both of which may allow a man to treat "himself not as *individuum* but as *dividuum*".[74] The division of the personality and the repression of many of its essential elements is characteristic of the prevailing ethical norms, preventing man from achieving personal harmony and checking the full expression of his inherent power. For these reasons Nietzsche is compelled to reject any specifically *repressive* morality.

The discussion of the ascetic morality requires a third concept of force in addition to *Kraft* and *Macht*: the concept of *Gewalt* (violence) is now introduced:

> For certain men feel so great a need to exercise their strength [*ihre Gewalt*] and lust for power that, in default of other objects or because their efforts in other directions have always miscarried, they at last hit upon the idea of tyrannizing over certain parts of their own nature...
> In every ascetic morality man worships a part of himself as God and for that he needs to diabolize the other part.[75]

74. MA 57; KSA 2: 76.
75. MA I-137; KSA 2: 131.

The concept of power as *Macht* is thus located between two extreme poles: quantitative, static Kraft at one end, devoid of rational and creative sublimation, and the excessively dynamic and brutal *Gewalt* on the other, suppressing and annihilating all the other vectors of force. *Macht*, however, contains the meaning of cancellation as well as creative assimilation. Put differently, creative power is a compromise between an unrestrained and destructive play of the instincts, and their hostile repression. By describing ascetic attitudes in terms of violence, Nietzsche emphasizes that they actually constitute a violence performed on power itself. The ascetic does finally achieve a kind of tranquility by willing one drive to dominate the others until they are all eradicated; but this tranquility is achieved at the expense of all dynamism and personal anarchy, annihilating the sublimatory creative energy. The genuinely powerful individual, by contrast, is continually readjusting the forces of his own personality, calling on different drives to motivate positive action, and using the natural instinctual chaos as the material for a creative, productive life. The essential difference between the *Übermensch* and the ascetic saint, then, may be formulated in terms of the distinction between *Macht* and *Gewalt*, sublimation and repression. It should be noted, however, that repression also is an operation requiring a kind of force in the overcoming of drives, and so is accompanied by a subjective experience similar to that characteristic of sublimation:

> The saint practises that defiance of oneself that is a close relation of lust for power and bestows the feeling of power even upon the hermit.[76]

The similarity in one's subjective experiences of repression and of sublimation can in large part account for Nietzsche's early

76. MA I-142: KSA 2: 138.

enchantment with the ascetic, and explain why he mistakenly identified it as an exemplar of personal power. It can also help to clarify why the image of the saint typically produces responses of extreme respect and reverence from others: they admire the difficult self-conquest, failing to distinguish the kind of self-conquest achieved through negative force (*Gewalt*) from that resulting from a positive, creative sublimation (*Macht*). Only the latter can culminate in genuine, personal power, and it comprises a distinct spiritual realm as well, rendering the personality more delicate and sublime. In practical contexts, however, this personality may be less able to survive in an environment which exercises violent force (*Gewalt*) against him, although he may possess an intrinsic and genuine power, unlike those others who wish to dominate him.

A portrait of the powerful personality emerges which depicts it as more vulnerable in direct confrontation with brute force, precisely because of its spiritual and rational element. This feature serves to clarify an apparent paradox in Nietzsche's doctrine of the will to power — the paradox suggested in a question posed by the preceding section: If Christianity (whose exemplar is the ascetic saint) represents a suppressed and declining will to power and a decadent system of instinctual drives, how did it defeat and overwhelm the elements that express an authentic will to power? If Nietzsche had been a pragmatist,[77] historical domination — the *successful* manifestation of power — might have been his central criterion of power. But Nietzsche is clearly not pragmatic in this way; an authentic power is not always obliged to show itself in terms of success in a world where force typically dominates spirit. Spiritual power, which was Nietzsche's concern, is of course often vulnerable to the pressures of brute physical force: no paradox actually exists

77. See, for example, MA I-227.

here. This is often the case on both the individual plane (the *Übermensch* versus the saint) and the historical-cultural plane (the ancient Greeks versus the barbarians; the superior pagans versus Christianity). When the religious personality redirects its intense force outwards, away from repressive self-tyranny and towards the domination of others, success is assured *a priori*. It sets out to suppress and destroy[78] precisely those others who are engaged in creative activity and are using their inner resources for self-formation, rather than self-denial. These others retain their superior power, notwithstanding the fact that they exercise less force:

> Even today, many educated people think that the victory of Christianity over Greek philosophy is a proof of the superior truth of the former — although in this case it was only the coarser and more violent (*Gewaltsamere*) that conquered the more spiritual and delicate.[79]

Although the qualitative power of the individual or the society is no guarantee of its material success and victory, it nonetheless ensures a spiritual and cultural superiority. For this reason Nietzsche is careful to distinguish between the history of power (spiritual and intellectual progress) and the history of force (physical and material domination). It is precisely those who have been in the weaker position relative to the history of force who have been responsible for cultural advances relative to power: "It is the more unfettered, uncertain and morally weaker individuals upon whom *spiritual progress* depends".[80] This is not a renunciation of Darwinian theory of course, for the latter refers primarily to the material domination assured by the survival of the strongest (those possessing *Kraft*). Nietzsche

78. MA I-114.
79. MA I-68; KSA 2: 80-81.
80. MA I-224; KSA 2: 188.

offers rather a complementary perspective, treating "spiritual progress" as a function of agents who are wanting in force:

> To this extent the celebrated struggle for existence does not seem to me to be the only theory by which the progress or strengthening of a man or race can be explained.[81]

The creative and spiritual dimensions of genuine power make it more vulnerable in the "battlefields" of life which are governed by the rules of crude force, and in which victory is conferred on those who possess material strength. But for Nietzsche "life is no argument":[82] it is not paradoxical to consider *Macht* superior to *Kraft* and *Gewalt*. In his own way he aspires to the Socratic value of encouraging only the good life, rather than preserving life as such.

This psychological attitude to power, qualitatively defined, provides an answer to another question, more far-reaching than the question of the victories of Christianity: How did "slave morality", representing decadence and decline, succeed in taking over the "master morality" of the powerful?

V. Autonomous versus Heteronomous Power

To find a reasonable solution to this problem Nietzsche had of course to regard the concept of power in qualitative terms, and to assume that energetic and mechanistic quantities were irrelevant to its solution. The strength of the powerful is not due to a greater degree of force, just as the weakness of the powerless is not simply represented in lower magnitudes of energy. Power and weakness do not signify different *quanta* but a different direction of the operation of power and distinct modes of derivation and intensification. It is useful here to recall the

81. *Loc. cit.*
82. FW 121; KSA 3: 477.

famous Kantian distinction between autonomy and heteronomy. Nietzsche himself uses this distinction implicitly in his analysis of those individuals who use their power hypocritically to manipulate their external environment, for example, by evoking pity in others. The domination of another for purposes of exploitation is a manifestation of weakness, implying that the dominating person is unsure of his inner power and is compelled to renounce its direct and spontaneous activation. He rejects psychic autonomy and authentic self-expression, opting instead for a dependence on others which he sustains through indirect techniques of exploitation and domination. Nietzsche observes this same pattern in the wider historical-cultural context of religion and morality. A weak — and possibly persecuted — social group or sect may attempt to subjugate the powerful by indirect means, just as the weak person extorts pity from the powerful as a means of absorbing some of his strength and undermining his autonomy. If religious and moral values emphasizing pity and justice are internalized by the powerful personality they will inculcate feelings of guilt and humiliation. In this way the weaker obliquely draw the powerful down to their own level, and so avoid the challenge of elevating themselves through self-development. What authority the weak may thus obtain is not, then, internally located. The powerful personality, by contrast, autonomously and creatively legislates its own values and laws, and becomes a model for others only through his successes in self-formation. If he innocently prescribes laws to others as well, it is not because he needs to dominate them as a method of enhancing his own authority; such prescription is only the natural expression of the power he already possesses. Thus Nietzsche says that "to be a lawgiver is a more sublimated form of tyranny";[83] that is, the law-giving of the powerful is an

---

83. MA I-261; KSA 2: 215.

expression of an autonomous, refined will to power — and not a direct act of violence (*Gewaltakt*) or an indirect, heteronomous tyranny.

The manipulative methods by which the weak press for domination always avoid any direct confrontation with the powerful. They do not engage in conflict as such, but move obliquely, attempting to penetrate the power structure from within: religious and moral norms based on the inculcation of guilt feelings provide them, then, with an ideal vehicle with which to undermine that structure's foundations. The "slaves" employ "the instincts of cowardice, cunning and canaille",[84] their aspiration being to gain domination over those in power.[85] But how is it that the genuinely powerful, autonomous agent internalizes these corrupting values and yields to the *ressentiment* of the weak? Why does his power not guarantee a self-legislating creativity which would be resistant to such internalizations?

Nietzsche recognized the seriousness of this question and tried hard to respond to it; his answer, however, is neither definite nor unequivocal. In *Human, All Too Human* he suggests that the highly developed spiritual and intellectual component of power may in some sense weaken even the most superior personality. Because he is genuinely free and independent, he is unlikely to adhere to any rigid and inflexible complex of norms: the values he possesses are open to examination and susceptible to being "overcome". He will, then, be more vulnerable to the surreptitious indoctrinations which the weak use against him. His freedom from any given tradition induces a kind of frailty, for it allows him to oscillate perpetually between whatever possibilities he may encounter. In historical praxis, this dynamic may produce an

84. WM 864.
85. MA I-111; KSA 2: 114.

impressionable personality, susceptible to manipulation and exploitation:

> Compared with him who has tradition on his side and requires no reasons for his actions, the free spirit is always weak, especially in actions; for he is aware of too many motives and points of view and therefore possesses an uncertain and unpractised hand. What means are there of nonetheless rendering him *relatively strong*? How does the strong spirit (*esprit fort*) come into being?[86]

The problem may be recast as that of turning spiritual power into a concrete historical force: How can the Hamlet figure, the *Übermensch*, be transformed into a decisive and active character? Is it possible to preserve the spirit of a Hamlet in the form of a Faust? Nietzsche's solution focusses on the social fabric woven of religious and moral dogma which produce a psychological pattern characterized by guilt, vengeance, and bad conscience.[87] These are the weakest threads of culture, responsible for the corruption of power and intellectual progress. In emphasizing these elements, Nietzsche is implicitly admitting that there can be no absolute psychological autonomy: even the most powerful are not impervious to influence by the environment with which they interact. The revaluation of prevalent cultural norms is essential to the evolution of the *Übermensch* psychology because even the arena of the "authentic legislator" may be penetrated by environmental values

---

86. MA I-230; KSA 2: 193.
87. Nietzsche's struggle with the phenomena of guilt feelings and bad conscience goes back to the beginning of his philosophizing. Already in GT (Chapter One) he criticized the mechanism of repression activated by guilt, and in subsequent essays he attempted (by psychologization) to soften the "higher-self" responsible for conscience formation (including the bad conscience). In MA again he is involved in a fierce crusade against these manifestations: see MA II 1–42, 2–38, 52; MA I-107; MA I-39.

and forces. The absolutely autonomous will to power is, therefore, no more than a regulative idea — one which provides the model for approximation, but which can in principle never be perfectly and fully realized.

Indeed, Nietzsche always refers to the will to power as something that is never absolutely satisfied. It is a perpetual movement of the whole organism in relation to everything that it encounters, a movement to assimilate it, overcome it and mature with it. By nature this activity is incessant, for its range of operation is infinite and in principle inexhaustible. The only constraint on the range is the feature of the "eternal recurrence of the same": but even this contraint only creates a *circular* pattern of continuous activity, without beginning or end. Although Nietzsche wished to approximate the ideal will to power as closely as possible by translating power into a concrete historical force, he did not aim at exhausting or fully realizing its potential. There can be no final conclusion to the Nietzschean dialectic of power.

VI. Power versus Violence

The second volume of *Human, All Too Human* places even greater emphasis on the spiritual and qualitative characteristics of power, establishing more clearly the distinction between power and simple force. As we have seen, Nietzsche describes man as an Apollonian-Dionysian power, organizing the world around him in his own image and in accordance with his own uniquely human categories. He is assisted in this project by an intellectual capacity to construct theoretical perspectives,[88]

88. Almost from the beginning of his treatment of power phenomena, Nietzsche identifies perspectivism with power: "You shall see with your own eyes the problem of *order of rank*, and how power, and right, and spaciousness of perspective grow into the heights together" (MA I Preface 6; KSA 2: 20–21).

which enable man to assimilate nature by anthropomorphizing it. In this way intellectual activity, it is suggested, serves the psychological need for power. These needs are met even if they do not achieve victory in the practical arena of the history of force:

Power without victories — The strongest knowledge (that of the total unfreedom of the human will) nonetheless is the poorest in successes, for it always has the strongest opponent, human vanity.[89]

This is not, of course, an endorsement of radical determinism. Nietzsche is only pointing out that the concept of unfreedom is a cognitive vehicle of spiritual power to the extent that it combats human narcissism: only the individual who has overcome his own narcissism has truly realized his own power. Nietzsche clearly rejects the notion that the full development of selfhood can be identified with self-love.

One observes a growing tendency in Nietzsche's thought to spiritualize the notion of power. This tendency has its origins in the Apollonian-rational component, and its development now

Consequently, any comprehensive discussion of Nietzsche's theory of perspectives or, which is the same, his implicit theory of knowledge, has to start with the will to power, which is the only paradigm, and the foundation of knowledge; see Ruediger H. Grimm, in *Nietzsche's Theory of Knowledge* (Berlin, 1977), and Martin Heidegger, *Nietzsche*, Vol. III, "Will to Power as Knowledge and as Metaphysics" (New York, 1979).

89. MA II 1–50; KSA 2: 401. This passage is a basis for understanding Nietzsche's subsequent admiration for Spinoza, whom he discovered one year later:

I am really amazed, really delighted! I have a precursor, and what a precursor! I hardly knew Spinoza ... Not only is his whole tendency like my own — to make knowledge the most *powerful passion* — this most abnormal and lonely thinker is closest to me in these points precisely: he denies free will, ...

Letter to Franz Overbeck (July 30, 1881) in: *Selected Letters of Friedrich Nietzsche*, ed. and trans. Christopher Middleton (Chicago, 1969), p. 177.

seems to be a part of his attempt to distinguish power from the other, tangentially related concepts of *Kraft* and *Gewalt*. This movement serves to secure a central location for the concept of *Macht* in the context of his whole philosophy.

Nietzsche's first compositions (and the attendant method of psychologization) already portrayed Man as a complex of instinctual drives, each of which strives continually to dominate the others. Such a portrayal naturally suggested acts of violence as inherent in all life activities — including those manifesting power. The internal logic of this early psychology required Nietzsche to distinguish acts of brute violence (*Gewalt*) from the elements of *Gewalt* necessarily included in the various sublimated process of *Macht*. The spiritualization of power helps to satisfy this requirement, by providing the criterion of self-overcoming:

> Writing ought always to advertise a victory — an overcoming of *oneself* which has to be communicated for the benefit of others; and there are dyspeptic authors who write only when they cannot digest something.... Through their anger they try unconsciously...to exercise violence (*Gewalt*) upon the reader — that is, they too desire victory but over others.[90]

Here, as elsewhere,[91] Nietzsche explicitly identifies the use and exploitation of others with violence (*Gewalt*), contrasting this

90. MA II 1–152; KSA 2: 441 (my translation). Nietzsche's own works are not intended to wreak violence on the reader, since they are evidence (as he says) of his own self-overcomings for the sake of the positive enticement of that reader. Hence we may assume that the brutal distortion of his writings by Nazi commentators, and their exploitation as an ideological basis for propaganda and external conditioning, would have been regarded by Nietzsche as an act of violence upon himself, and upon the readers of these 'adapted' writings.
91. For example, JGB 259, etc.

external manifestation of gross force with power. The latter exhibits no violence as such, for its strength is directed towards an internal expression of self-overcoming. Internalized power must also be free of masochistic violence, since it must not completely annihilate individual characteristics but rather creatively sublimate them.

Nietzsche's emphasis on the development of selfhood and the intrinsic use of the energy provided by the will to power are illuminated in the following passage:

> "Will a Self"— Active, successful natures act, not according to the dictum 'Know thyself', but as if there hovered before the will a commandment: thou shalt become a self.[92]

Nietzsche's rejection of the Apollonian maxim is entirely consistent with his mistrust of direct introspection as a method of penetrating and revealing the innermost personality.[93] Self-knowledge is necessarily mediated by one's past experiences and future intentions; at any given moment one is characterized by a flux of consciousness and volition, projecting and propelling away from the 'specious present'.[94] Man is a historical product through which the past continuously flows in a hundred channels.[95] Therefore, the dictum "wolle ein Selbst" is directed

---

92. MA II 1-366; KSA 2: 524.
93. We have encountered this mistrust several times (see Chapter Three); it is repeated here and in MA II 1-223.
94. For example: "In reality ... all our doing and knowing is not a succession of facts and empty spaces, but a continuous flux" (MA II 2-11; KSA 2: 546). This almost Heraclitean picture, which still shapes Nietzsche's attitude in MA, gives a deeper meaning to the psychological will to fix and consolidate itself, and thus attain its selfhood and self-determination within this anarchic and chaotic environment. The question arises (although it is outside our present context): what is the ontological status of this will? Is it not merely another "metaphor" and abstract generalization (MA II 1-5), or is it a philosophical myth — for it cannot be an entity or a substance within the Heraclitean flux.
95. MA II 1-223; KSA 2: 477.

not only towards the future; it also refers backwards, demanding an affirmation of ourselves as we have already been formed. Nietzsche's attitude of *amor fati* makes this reaffirmation of the past quite explicit. It is an attitude devoid of any negative fatalism for it expresses the essential element of will. His notion of the "eternal recurrence of the same" likewise points to a will to power which attain selfhood *ex post facto*. This willing of the self is of course not confined to the past; it is impelled forwards as well, assimilating and internalizing future elements that are external to the will. Without this second, futural movement the entire process would eventually become frozen,[96] and fail to realize a continuous, maturing dynamic.

While the process of self-overcoming is (by definition) free of violence, other processes of assimilation and internalization do manifest it to a degree, particularly those which employ force against an object external to the self.[97] Recognizing this, Nietzsche imposes three important constraints on the violent ramifications of the will to power.

First, Nietzsche maintains that a genuine process of assimilation does not entail sheer negative destructiveness; the will is constrained insofar as the external object must not be entirely obliterated, but rather preserved in part by being creatively sublimated. For this reason Nietzsche set creativity against rejection and negation: "All rejection and negation...point to a lack of fruitfulness".[98] One may say, then, that the violent implications of the creative assimilation of external entities only

---

96. Nietzsche, therefore, rejects all the patterns of *akrasia* and *ataraxia* since in them the will pathologically wishes to reach the freezing point of ennui: "At the freezing-point of the will" (MA II 1–349; KSA 2: 520).
97. Therefore fully positive power, which does not need an external reinforcement, is free of this dimension of violence, whereas negative power, dependent upon external objects, expresses a certain degree of violence.
98. MA II 1–332; KSA 2: 515.

challenge their relative autonomy — but do not obliterate them. A second constraint limiting the violence of assimilative acts follows from Nietzsche's insistence that these acts are not concerned with physical violence directed against concrete objects: what is used and assimilated is not the object as such, but one's own mental impression or experience of it. Consequently, power is not identified in the individual's ability to master others by force in acts of confrontation.[99]

The most important constraint, however, issues from the purpose or goal of the affirmation of power. The point is not to change or reform the external object with the intent of destroying it, but ultimately to transfigure the agent of assimilation himself. Acts of violence may be typically instrumental in forcibly changing or transforming others; but the instrumental use *of* others within a context of self-transformation and self-overcoming must be manifest in *sublimated* expressions of the will to power. These sublimated expressions are exactly what those "strong individuals" lack who treat

> ...not only nature but societies and weaker individuals too as objects of plunder: he exploits them as much as he can and then goes on.... His demonstrations of power are at the same time demonstrations of revenge against the painful and fear-ridden state of his existence: then again, he wants through his actions to count as being more powerful than he is.[100]

The actions of man who is preoccupied with revenge cannot be properly motivated by the attitude of *amor fati*; he therefore lacks the truly positive power which Nietzsche's psychology

---

99. See for example, MA II 1-228.
100. MA II 2-181; KSA 2: 629-630. This passage represents one of the first portraits of the man of negative power, about whom more will be said in the next chapter.

demands. Positive power seeks an autonomous overcoming of the self, while revenge evades self-responsibility and only attempts to augment one's power (*"Machtzuwachs"*) by exploiting and mistreating external objects. The actual exploitation of others — or even the presence of a disposition to do so[101] — signifies the absence of both autarky and authenticity attaching to a personal, positive power. It can only result in an anarchistic and counter-productive process of *bellum omnium in omnes* — a perpetual chain of vengeful acts.

A social contract which stuctures group relations in accordance with the principles of justice and equality is incompatible with the psychic "instinct for dominance" (*Trieb nach Übergewicht*).[102] Yet this drive differs essentially from the will to power which, it has been argued, is defined precisely in *contrast* to the desire to control and dominate others, being sublimatory and inwardly directed. It is noteworthy that Nietzsche does not object to social organization in principle, and regards it as a necessary condition — if at times a necessary evil. He describes the sublimatory processes as appearing only when the "state of nature" is transformed by the necessary establishment of a social order.[103] The instinct for dominance is sublimated in the process. Even so, this particular sublimatory act is not to be identified with the emergence of the will to power: the former follows from the coercions of an extrinsic social order, while the latter is spontaneously generated out of the dynamic interaction of the Apollonian-Dionysian components of the inner personality.

One must conclude that Nietzsche recognizes a distinction

---

101 Nietzsche's unequivocal rejection of human exploitation even causes him to qualify his known objection to socialism: "The *exploitation* of the worker was ... a piece of stupidity, and exhausting of the soil at the expense of the future, an imperilling of society." (MA II 2–286; and see *ibid*, 285).
102. MA II 2–31; KSA 2: 563.
103. *Loc. cit.*

between two types of sublimatory process: the autonomous (expressing the spontaneous self-overcoming of the will to power) and the heteronomous (deriving from external exigencies and operating on those instincts incompatible with social coexistence). The heteronomous processes of sublimation provide a kind of safety valve preserving culture and social organization.[104] Ultimately, however, they only work to displace certain drives (the Freudian *"Verschiebungen"*) rather than spontaneously and directly sublimating them. And it is only through sublimation, Nietzsche maintains, that culture will develop creatively and fruitfully. Nietzsche's conclusions at the historical level thus parallel the distinction drawn earlier at the level of the individual: just as the will to power provides the motivating force for the formation and determination of the individual, so too does it not merely preserve culture, but is continually creating and recreating it.

104. See, for example, MA II 2–226.

Part Three:

PHILOSOPHY AND MORALITY OF POWER

CHAPTER SIX

NEGATIVE VERSUS POSITIVE POWER

Introduction

The second part of this study traced the transition from Nietzsche's method of psychologization to his positive psychology of power. Having analyzed the different psychological connotations of the power concept, one must now ask whether these connotations allow Nietzsche to take a constructive attitude towards *morality*. Does power oppose morality? Does Nietzsche adopt any positive moral stance, or does power become a substitute for morality? Is morality entirely rejected through psychologization and treated as an illusory super-structure?

In attempting to demonstrate that Nietzsche endorses a morality of positive power, I shall first examine whether it is possible to base any kind of morality on the Nietzschean concept of power, and whether this concept is an adequate starting point for an ethical perspective, occupying a space beyond the nihilistic standpoint and the psychologistic perspective. Finally, I will discuss whether and how Nietzsche provides sound justifications for his moral preferences.

Much has been written about Nietzsche's critique of morality.[1]

---

1. Arthur C. Danto, *Nietzsche* (esp. Chapter Five); Philippa Foot, "Nietzsche: The Revaluation of Values", in *Nietzsche*, ed. Robert C. Solomon (New York, 1973), pp. 156–168; Karl Jaspers, *Nietzsche* (esp. Book Two, Chapter

I shall attempt to deal with this subject mainly from the perspective of his psychology, as discussed in earlier parts of this book. The previous chapter argued that power cannot be accurately translated into force and its external manifestations, since in essence it is an internal connection between an individual and his selfhood. A serious question emerges from this analysis concerning the status of morality: Does not this emphasis on the independence of power throw the individual into a quasi-monadic state, indifferent to socially meaningful interaction and devoid of any moral fabric? Does it follow that Nietzsche, for the sake of power, must become an ethical nihilist?

This has been the conclusion of several of Nietzsche's interpreters, depicting him as an antimoralist *par excellence*. Yet Nietzsche, as if anticipating this criticism, addresses the possibility that some tension might exist between what he describes as power and morality: It is not coincidental that the work written immediately after his exposition of power in *Human, All Too Human* was devoted chiefly to the treatment of moral issues. In the preface to *Daybreak: Thoughts on the Prejudices of Morality* Nietzsche confirms that at this stage his philosophy had begun "to undermine our *faith in morality*".[2] But this 'undermining' is not motivated by an attitude of nihilism, negating morality as such and aiming at complete social anarchy. It is only, according to Nietzsche's own testimony, a critique of a specific pattern of morality prevalent in his culture, a pattern which has no foundation in positive power. Indeed, he explicitly

One); Walter Kaufmann, *Nietzsche* (esp. Part III); Alexander Nehamas, *Nietzsche: Life as Literature* (Cambridge, Mass., 1985), pp. 170–234; Richard Schacht, "Nietzsche and Nihilism", in *Nietzsche*, pp. 58–82; *idem, Nietzsche* (London, 1983), pp. 341–475; Robert C. Solomon, "Nietzsche, Nihilism, and Morality", in *Nietzsche*, pp. 202–225; John T Wilcox, *Truth and Value in Nietzsche*; and many others.
2.   M-V2; KSA 3: 12.

states that "In this book faith in morality is withdrawn — but why? *Out of morality*".[3]

It follows that Nietzsche does not reject morality as such; he only rejects a specific pattern of morality in order to reinstate an authentic morality based upon positive power. For Nietzsche, the criterion of a truly powerful person endowed with a genuine and exceptional selfhood is his ability to overcome his given nature and basic drives — including the drive towards aggressive predominance and excellence. *Daybreak* is an attempt to expose the fact that our prevailing ethics *disguises* the drive towards domination and humiliation; *eo ipso* it points towards an alternative authentic morality. We have seen that violence expresses an inferior, feeble power, relying on external reinforcement by the manipulation of our fellow-men. This, then, is the morality of negative power; the authentic affirmative moral pattern will be called the morality of positive power. Nietzsche's positive tendencies (however critical) persisted in the work that followed *Daybreak*, namely, *The Gay Science*. He himself remarks of these two works:

> The *Daybeak* is a Yes-saying book, deep but bright and gracious. The same is true also and in the highest degree of the *gaya scienza*.[4]

Nietzsche posits two basic patterns of morality: one deriving from the existence of positive power and another from its absence (allied with the will to achieve it). He necessarily finds, then, two conflicting patterns in other fields of human creativity, and *The Gay Science* (as well as works that follow it) draws the distinction between positive and negative philosophy, religion and science. The will to attain power always lies under the

3. M-V4; KSA 3: 16.
4. EH-FW; KSA 6: 333.

surface of all of man's spiritual expressions. This is a clear psychological principle that Nietzsche applies to all mental patterns. It follows that the specific object of the psychologist's task is power and its manifestations in culture and history; we can say that Nietzsche-as-psychologist is actually a philosopher dealing with the morality of power and its manifestations. As he says himself, "What was at stake in all philosophizing hitherto was not at all 'truth' but something else — let us say, health, future, growth, power, life".[5] The specific identification of power with life and growth accords with our interpretation of the concept of power as it emerged in Nietzsche's earlier works. But now he makes an all-embracing generalization which posits monistic power underlying all the transfigurations and expressions of the human spirit. The transition from primary dualism in *The Birth of Tragedy* to unified psychological monism culminated in *The Gay Science*. As we shall see, however, this monism has two diametrically opposed anthropological-psychological manifestations: the negative and the positive.

I. Negative versus Positive Power

Negative power is symptomatic of a weak personality, lacking in power but incessantly attempting to obtain it. In Nietzsche's view this pattern was characteristic of the early Christians, who formed their religion out of a desperate need for power:

> There are recipes for the feeling of power, firstly for those who can control themselves and who are thereby accustomed to a feeling of power; then for those in whom precisely this is lacking. Brahminism has catered for the men of the former sort, Christianity for men of the latter.[6]

5. FW-V2; KSA 3: 349.
6. M 65; KSA 3: 63.

In a sense, Christianity reconstructed the concepts of sin, bad conscience and guilt, and used them as instruments of cruelty and vengeance; these concepts have often justified the abuse — even the torture — of others, thereby intensifying the Christian's own feeble powers:

> Oh, how much superfluous cruelty and vivisection have proceeded from those religions which invented sin! And from those people who desired by means of it to gain the highest enjoyment of their power![7]

Clearly, no positive power is exhibited in the satisfaction derived from abusing and dominating one's fellow beings. Disguised cruelty and its attendant (perverse) pleasure are called on only to reinforce an unstable character lacking the requisite inner power. Here we must distinguish between such pleasure as accompanies the direct and unforced expression of an already given positive power and the pleasure that is only instrumental in reinforcing a derived *sense* of power. Negative power does not express itself spontaneously, but derivatively: it is fundamentally deficient and defective, striving to encourage and fortify itself by pleasure derived from abuse and cruelty.

The tendency of certain individuals to excel at all costs, moved by the *"drive to distinction"*,[8] also belongs to this negative pattern. The ambitious, competitive personality lacks the "feeling" of positive power, and struggles to attain it by distinguishing itself and overpowering its rival. By contrast, a man who possesses genuine positive power needs neither the approbation of his surroundings, nor the medals and decorations that allegedly attest to this power; nor does he require the various pleasures stemming from abusive domination in order to

7. M 53; KSA 3: 57.
8. M 30; KSA 3: 39–40.

intensify his "feeling of power" — for it is already intrinsically a part of him.

To illustrate this distinction between negative and positive power, one may contrast the genius to the merely ambitious intellectual. The excellence of the former is natural and spontaneous, and all his activities carry its stamp. The ambitious intellectual, by contrast, aspires to achievements which are disproportionate to his talents: he is preoccupied with the passionate and hopeless pursuit of a grace that he lacks. His pretensions urge him to excel, to gain recognition from his social and professional environment. His actions become a means for acquiring a feeling of power, rather than directly expressing a power that is naturally his. The genuine genius is well aware of his exceptional, natural power and does not need external confirmation.

II. The Impotence of Negative Power

Nietzsche's criticism of the moral patterns prevalent in his culture and history could be constructive only if guided by a regulative idea of an alternative moral pattern. He does not posit power *against* morality, but proposes an active morality of positive power against the traditional passive pattern, opting for courageous creativity and autonomy based on the mature selfhood of the moral agent. He contrasts the characteristic features of these two moralities:

> All actions may be traced back to evaluations, all evaluations are either *original* or *adopted* — the latter being by far the most common.[9]

This passage again echoes Kant's distinction between

9. M 104; KSA 3: 92.

autonomous and heteronomous morality. Nietzsche maintains that the main reason for the latter is moral cowardice,[10] shunning the courageous expression of power and its morality. The mechanism for adopting traditional morality includes a passive internalization of external maxims, making them into a habit, an acquired "second nature" or a Super-Ego. This given, habitual morality, conditioned in childhood,[11] stands in contrast to the evaluations made by a mature "selfhood".

The transmitted morality of tradition, which mechanically and arbitrarily conditions our "highest selves" is in fact anti-individualistic, obscuring man's selfhood and repressing his authentic personality. Hence the traditional morality (generally conceived as altruistic) actually suppresses the Ego and directs excessive violence against the "individuum", making him into a "dividuum". Nietzsche proposes an egoistic morality which instead springs out of the Ego's power and expresses itself authentically. The violence (*"Gewalt"*) of the "highest self" against the Ego now explains the impoverishment, pessimism and depression of the individual. His vitality withers away, leaving a feeling of weakness, discontent and *"the profoundest misery"*.[12] This moral wretchedness, and other expressions of the traditionally accepted ethos, are all manifestations of the will to power, the essence of man as man. However, it is only the supreme expression of *negative* power, characterized by fear and weakness. The power impelling traditional morality is not sufficiently strong or independent and so the individual suffers from a perpetual anxiety that it may be underminded. This causes men to develop defence-mechanisms by means of which they

---

10. "To admit a belief merely because it is a custom — but that means to be dishonest, cowardly, lazy! — And so could dishonesty, cowardice and laziness be the preconditions of morality?" (M 101; KSA 3: 90).
11. M 104; KSA 3: 92.
12. M 106; KSA 3: 94.

seek to guard and intensify their doubtful and unstable negative power. Nietzsche therefore maintains that the supporters of authoritative morality are directed by "an obscure anxiety and awe"[13] of losing their influence and power. In consequence, their "moral commands" must be violent and oppressive, attempting to enhance and reinforce power by exploiting other fellow-beings. It follows that fear and anxiety are derivative of negative power, of a lack of self-confidence, and are not primary, independent, psychological phenomena.[14]

Nietzsche portrays in detail the cunning, devious, moral mechanisms with which people of negative power reinforce and affirm themselves. Their strategy is to establish the morality of duty, thus assuring their "self-regard".[15] They achieve this by shrewdly and insidiously assuming a sovereignty over individuals. Certain "rights" are granted which signify their recognition of others' powers, but in return for these rights others are required to comply with certain duties and to concede them their rights in return. Thus all are trapped within a network of duties and rights, which eventually reinforces and reaffirms the defective power of the moralists of duty.

But why do those who supposedly possess genuine positive power still fall into the circle of moral duty? Nietzsche says that persons who have "more than enough" power do not need to

13. M 107; KSA 3: 94 (my translation).
14. This view deviates from Kaufmann's interpretation to the effect that in *Daybreak* Nietzsche still attempts to explain psychological phenomena "in terms of two key concepts: fear and power" (*Nietzsche*, p. 188). However, my reading of this book suggests that fear and all the moral patterns founded upon it are to Nietzsche an epiphenomenon of negative power, occurring in all people who need morality as an efficient defensive system in overcoming the feeling of impotence that besets them in their lack of positive, autonomous and affirmative power. Moreover the concept of power had already become the exclusive monistic principle of Nietzsche's psychology in *Human, All Too Human* — as was seen in Chapter Five.
15. M 112; KSA 3: 100.

accept any rights — since rights would be an external and superfluous token of recognition of their power by their surroundings. Whoever accepts the concept of "rights" as *externally conferred* has only a "feeble sense of power".[16] The willingness to accept certain rights is an indication that one is not at the top of the power hierarchy. However this may be, by granting rights and demanding certain duties in exchange, the "sovereign" of negative power has succeeded in controlling others. It follows that all traditional morality, based upon a system of duties and rights is impelled by the *"striving for distinction"*, especially pronounced in people of negative power moved by "the psychical extravagance of the lust for power!"[17]

In contrast to this morality of duty, a man of positive power who has successfully overcome himself attains rights autonomously and freely, and generously confers them on others — out of an abundance of personal power and not as part of a manipulative negotiation.[18]

Nietzsche's morality of power closely resembles Kantian morality in its emphasis on the autonomous legislation of moral laws. Nietzsche draws an ideal picture of an entire culture conducted by men of positive power: independent, unprejudiced, creative, gentle and courageous, lacking any desire for expansion or domination.[19] At the end of *Daybreak* he describes (in an almost Platonic vein) the moral state of the future and expresses his wish for a sincere morality based on the virtues of positive power.[20] Nietzsche's table of values is not new, and he creates no new hierarchy. He repeatedly stresses the familiar and traditional values of Western culture. What is novel in his

---

16. *Ibid.*, 3: 101.
17. M 113; KSA 3: 104.
18. M 437 and M 449.
19. M 163; M 164; M 546.
20. M 551; M 556, and see M 199.

morality of positive power is not the specific *content* of its values but their *origin*. Not "what" but "how" is of importance here, and Nietzsche seeks to overcome the prevalent moral patterns not because of their content, but because they originate in (and serve to perpetuate) a negative, impotent and cowardly power.

III. The Unconscious and the Morality of Power

To this point, Nietzsche's criticism of current moral patterns has been based on the concepts of positive and negative power. He offers another critique, directed against Socratic-intellectualist morality which assumes that right knowledge is necessarily followed by right action. This critique does not originate directly from Nietzsche's concept of power, but from his original psychological interpretation of human consciousness — "a more or less fantastic commentary on an unknown, perhaps unknowable text".[21] In opposing Socratic ethics, then, it is not surprising that Nietzsche adverts to the idea of the unconscious.

The concept of the will to power assumes an unconscious mental agency which urges man to action, although he is unaware of the nature and content of its underlying drives. Will to power, especially negative power, drives the weak man to establish moral patterns that lend him support. But man is not typically aware that by pursuing power he is being driven to dominate others through a refined cruelty which is obscured in an authoritative morality of duty and guilt. Hence Nietzsche requires the notion of active, but unconscious, mental life, in order to present the idea of power while rejecting those moral patterns it has invented through ethical rationalizations.

Since the idea of the unconscious clashes with the whole tenor of Socratic teaching, it is especially appropriate to

21. M 119; KSA 3: 113.

234

emphasize its role in a critique of Socratic ethics. If motivations are conceived of as unconscious, man cannot know completely what moves him to action. The psychology underlying the Socratic-intellectualist ethics, by contrast, holds that man can know himself and that his knowledge of the good must impel him to act in accordance with it:

> Socrates and Plato ... were ... innocently credulous in regard to that most fateful of prejudices ... that 'right knowledge *must be followed* by right action' — in this principle they were still the heirs of the universal madness and presumption that there exists knowledge as to the essential nature of an action ... all actions are essentially unknown.[22]

Socratic ethics emphasizes the concrete content and the consequences of our acts (as they appear to our consciousness). Nietzsche transfers the main weight and the moral consideration from results to motives, from the deed to the incentive. In Socratic ethics the driving motives are assumed to be transparent and generally known, and only the consequences of actions are doubtful and unpredictable. A morality that allows serious consideration of the possibility of an unconscious mental life can acknowledge that actions are relatively more predictable and better understood than their motives. Only the latter remain obscure. Therefore, in order to establish and maintain morality the philosopher must uncover the unconscious mechanisms of the moral agent. Only this might diminish the conflict between our psychological constitution and the demands of morality. In this light the Socratic presuppositions of a voluntarist rational morality can be seen to be irrelevant. The Socratic dictum, 'to know the good is to do it' is inappropriate when directed to particular individuals, for the presupposition of any feasible

22. M 116; KSA 3: 108–109.

ethics must be that 'ought' implies 'can'.[23] Nietzsche holds that to legislate a morality that cannot be executed reduces ethics to empty speculation.

At this point it is profitable to briefly consider Kantian ethics, which stands midway between Platonic and Nietzschean moralities. Like Nietzsche, Kant emphasizes the moral value of the motive for action; like Plato, however, he still tends to ignore the difficulties encountered when the ethical maxims are directed from *above* — to human beings who act from *within*. Kant fails to deal adequately with the concept of the unconscious,[24] and this lacuna creates an unbreachable gulf between his 'pure ethic' and the psychological nature of the beings required to enact it. Human psychology is not naturally disposed to respond to the categorical demands of "pure reason".

In any case, there is no doubt that Nietzsche's call for a shift in emphasis in moral theorizing follows directly from the role his psychology ascribes to the unconscious dimensions of the human character.[25] In place of the naive Socratic demand to

23. Kant, for example, claims that there must be a correspondence between the anthropological-psychological dimension and the ideal of *a priori* moral prescription: "When we say that something ought to be, we mean that a possible action is capable of being good" (*Lectures on Ethics*, New York, 1963, p. 2).

24. This does not mean of course that Kant does not occasionally refer to the unconscious. He mentions *das Unbewusste* especially in "Anthropologie in pragmatischer Hinsicht" in *Kants gesammelte Schriften* (Berlin, 1900), Bd. 7, 135ff., 139ff., 143, 176, 177, 268ff., and in several passages of "Kants Handschriftlicher Nachlass", *KGS*, Reflexion 176, 177, etc. See also: "Consciousness of oneself ... would be a source of great joy, but of joy to which we cannot attain", *Lectures on Ethics*, p. 78 and *ibid.*, p. 75, and *Kant's Political Writings*, 1970, p. 69. The idea of the unconscious is also relevant to Kant's "Schematism", and is implicit in the context of the precognitive syntheses, expounded by him *qua* philosopher, but not consciously known to him *qua* common man.

25. See also: M 129, where Nietzsche speaks about "the actual 'conflict of motives': — something quite invisible to us of which we would be quite unconscious" (KSA 3: 119).

"know thyself", Nietzsche asks us to explore and come to terms with our unconscious realm of interests, wishes and motives. Thus an additional element is introduced into the essential process of self-overcoming: the overcoming of the unconscious by uncovering, mastering and creatively utilizing it within a free, conscious *moral* context.

The anti-moral origins of prevailing moral patterns can be revealed by exposing their unconscious motives. For example, Nietzsche opposes the morality of pity and compassion *("Mitleid")* not only because it is an expression of weakness, negating positive power,[26] but also because it is a subtle, unconscious and sophisticated way of "self-defence" and "revenge".[27] It is illuminating in this regard to contrast Nietzsche's approach with a quite similar move in Kantian moral theory. Kant rejects pity on the ground of the irrelevance of any pathological drives to an *a priori*, purely rational morality. Nietzsche, however, does not oppose the sensual motives as such, and does not regard them as contradicting moral praxis. The Christian virtue of pity is rejected instead because it unconsciously expresses anti-moral psychological drives, contrasting with authentic moral patterns. Pity is typically motivated by the all-too-human, petty and mean drives of *ressentiment* and revenge. Moreover, in "pitying" there is "something underlying" the altruistic morality of pity "elevating and productive of superiority".[28] Pity thus serves negative power motivated by fear and weakness.[29]

In sum, negative power is externalized in negative morality, driven by unconscious, anti-moral motives disguised in various pseudo moralistic rationalizations. The morality of guilt also

---

26. M 134.
27. M 133; KSA 3: 125.
28. M 138; KSA 3: 131.
29. M 142.

belongs to this category, for it originates in "a new excitation of the *feeling of power*".[30] A frustrated and impotent personality exploits the notion and emotion of guilt in order to avenge itself on others and intensify its own sense of superiority. Allegedly 'altruistic' patterns likewise may be manifestations of negative morality in so far as self-sacrifice can be a means of providing oneself with the sense of a "positive enhancement" and "the general feeling of human *power*".[31]

To replace altruistic morality, Nietzsche suggests the egoistic pattern which would eliminate the hypocritical self-deception implicit in any morality originating in anti-moral motives. Egoistic morality does not employ the concepts of guilt and the guilty, of sin and sinners, of revenge and the revengeful.[32] Nietzsche ironically suggests that an egoistic morality could actually realize Kant's categorical imperative, enabling us to regard our fellow beings as ends in themselves and never as a means only:

> If only those actions are moral which are performed for the sake of another and only for his sake, as one definition has it, then there are no moral actions![33]

It seems that Nietzsche is enticing us to embrace the morality of positive power in part by appeal to the Kantian maxim that is so widely accepted. He implies that even if the categorical imperative expresses morality *par excellence* it will only be attained by way of positive, rather than negative, power. Moreover, by exposing the unconscious motives that underlie the "altruistic" morality of pity and self-sacrifice he reveals that these moral patterns (originating in negative power) cannot generate an authentic altruism.

30. M 140; KSA 3: 132.
31. M 146; KSA 3: 138.
32. M 164; M 202.
33. M 148; KSA 3: 139.

The exclusive drive impelling the weak person is his self-interested desire to acquire power, and so he is necessarily obliged to regard others instrumentally as a means of promoting that end. Nietzsche proposes the egoistic morality of positive power in part because it is able to meet the categorical demands of Kant's morality.

This is by no means an absurd conclusion. It follows directly from Nietzsche's concept of power, for only a man possessing a full sense of positive power does not need to exploit others to confirm and enhance his own self. Hence, only such an individual can allow himself to regard others not as a means only, but also as ends in themselves. Only a person whose own abundant power enables him to be autarkic is not tempted to enter into instrumental social interactions whose main purpose is self-promotion. Thus, it might be contended that Nietzsche imparts to Kant's purely formal morality the kind of psychological foundation which could finally make it realizable in the practical human context.

So again, Nietzsche does not oppose morality as such. During the writing of *Daybreak* he remarked: "It is impossible to live without morality".[34] Life and the affirmation of life are the supreme values in Nietzsche's anti-nihilistic philosophy; he clearly cannot attempt to diminish them. Nietzsche regards morality as the necessary (though not sufficient) condition for the preservation and confirmation of life. Moreover, in perceiving man as a creative power comprised of drives, instincts and emotions, Nietzsche cannot demand the complete abrogation of these drives or the need to express them creatively in external moral patterns. If morality is the sublimatory expression of a drive, it could not be abolished without seriously undermining man's creative selfhood. It is not surprising, then, that Nietzsche

---

34. *Musarionausgabe*, Vol. 10 (München, 1924), p. 366 (my translation).

speaks of the "moral drives".[35] The human intellect is a tool which establishes morality, formed in the course of "combating the various drives, refining thereby their activity".[36] Thus considered, morality is an Apollonian consequence of sublimating the barbarian Dionysian drives. Still consistent with his attitude in *The Birth of Tragedy*, Nietzsche endorses it as such. Far from denying the importance of morality, he only attacks those 'moral' patterns which do not manifest the healthy, creative sublimation of drives but aim to repress them — for these patterns are *immoral!*

An interesting shift now occurs in Nietzsche's application of the method of psychologization. While this technique was initially intended to expose and freeze the unconscious and immoral motives of perverted morality, Nietzsche now seeks to use it in order to re-establish authentic moral patterns based upon positive power. If the task of psychologization was, in the first instance, "to determine the erroneousness of all these [moral] reasons and the whole nature of moral judgements to date", it now has the decisive and constructive task of furnishing genuine "goals of action".[37]

This positive psychologization must also deal with the unconscious, for much of the mind functions unconsciously. The perceptive depth psychologist must contend with these unconscious processes and subject them to an exhaustive genealogical analysis. The shift in Nietzsche's attitude faithfully reflects his altered approach to the purpose of psychologization:

35. *Loc. cit.*
36. *Ibid.*, pp. 365–366 (my translation).
37. FW 7; KSA 3: 379.

it is in fact derived from it. As long as the purpose of psychologization was basically negative — to expose unconscious motives — Nietzsche needed only the epistemology of the unconscious; he had only to commit himself to the position that we are unconscious of certain mental processes. But in entrusting to psychologization a positive role in explicating an authentic morality, he is obliged to commit himself to the ontology of the unconscious, that is, to the view that the unconscious constitutes not merely a functional but a *structural* substratum of the mental life. In order to activate his morality of power, Nietzsche has to affirm that such a power potentially exists and should be exploited, and that this potential has lain dormant within the realm of the unconscious mind. This entails a certain ontological position with regard to the unconscious:

> All of us harbor concealed gardens and plantings ... we are, all of us, growing volcanoes that approach the hour of their eruption ... whoever feels these powers in himself must nurse, defend, honor, and cutivate them against another world that resists them.[38]

But the change from negative to positive psychologization was not made instantaneously, and the parallel transition from the concept of negative power to that of positive power is achieved gradually. So too, the transition from a functional description of the unconscious to ontological structuralism is a developmental processs, beginning in Nietzsche's first works where he speaks of the "Dionysian-barbarian" forces of man's *Id*. The reference to Freud's concept may emphasize another striking resemblance to Freud's theoretical development. Freud too initially spoke of the unconscious merely from a functional, economical and epistemological point of view; but at a later stage he was forced

38. FW 9; KSA 3: 381.

to commit himself to an ontological structure, postulating the existence of the *Id* as a viable component of our mental lives.[39]

To sum up these points: the emergence of the notion of a positive morality of power required a deeper understanding of the ontological status of the unconscious. It demanded a knowledge of its formation, its sublimation, its rise to consciousness and its employment in reactivating the morality of power.

In *Daybreak* Nietzsche spoke of the need to turn the morality of power into second nature, into a fixed habit of man. In *The Gay Science* he speaks of the task "of *incorporating knowledge and making it instinctive*".[40] Knowledge must become one with the unconscious as a necessary stage in establishing the morality of positive power. "The transfiguration of nature" also requires the transfiguration of the nature of our unconscious, not only on the functional level of turning unconscious processes into conscious ones, but also on the structural level of harnessing the Dionysian forces of the *Id* to the constructive maintaining of patterns of life within an enduring culture. The uncovering of man's positive power and of the mental forces of his unconscious are thus parallel processes serving the same purpose.

39. The adjective *"unbewusst"* was initially used by Freud to describe mental elements outside the field of the conscious at any given moment. This usage was merely "descriptive" and not yet clearly topographical. In the ontological structural sense the concept *"das Unbewusste"* began to be used by Freud to describe one of the mental systems, that which contains all the repressed elements whose conscious reappearance is prevented. Freud arrived at this later concept as a consequence of his rich experience in psycho-analytical treatment, which showed him that the mind cannot be reduced to the area of the conscious alone, and that certain of its elements can only be uncovered and revealed when the patient's resistance has been overcome. This brought Freud to postulate the existence of an independent mental realm and to affirm that the unconscious belongs to a special place in the mind, which cannot be described as a secondary consciousness, but as a complete autonomous system containing its own elements, mechanisms and energy. See: S.E., *1*, 233; *2*, 262ff.; *14*, 148ff., 181ff.; and cf. Paul Laurent Assoun, *Freud et Nietzsche* (Paris 1980), pp. 169–186.

40. FW 11; KSA 3: 383.

IV. The Culture of Power

Nietzsche now possesses the basic concepts needed to construct a comprehensive philosophy of culture, and to draw both the negative criticisms and the positive ideas into a unified matrix. The complete cultural construction will turn around the axis of the concept of power. But at the outset, Nietzsche returns to his basic distinction between positive and negative power: We can, he says, acquire and intensify our power "in two ways", by "benefiting and hurting others".[41] There are individuals who are very dependent on others, and often enter into relationships which cause them pain or pleasure. This fact indicates that most of us do not yet have a positive and autarkic feeling of power, thereby relying on external relations as a substitute. The absence of power arouses our impulse to acquire it: "Certainly the state in which we hurt others ... is a sign that we are still lacking power, or it shows a sense of frustration in the face of this poverty".[42] These words accurately describe psychological predicaments of negative power. Time and again Nietzsche tells us of the misguided and perverse ways in which men have sought to attain power — leading to a whole catalogue of external cultural expressions of negative power. We are told, for example, how negative power causes one to wish to control and subdue another human by an act of love, in which the lover "desires unconditional and sole possession of the person for whom he longs ... He alone wants to be loved and desires to live and rule in the other soul".[43] Certain forms of morality derive from negative power, such as the instrumental morality of altruism: "The 'neighbor' praises selflessness *because it brings him advantages*". In this context Nietzsche observes that "the *motives* for this morality stand

---

41. FW 13; KSA 3: 384.
42. *Ibid.*, 3: 385.
43. FW 14; KSA 3: 387.

opposed to its *principle*",[44] and that it must be totally rejected. He broadens his criticism to include religion, which also exhibits an intricate network of *post factum* rationalization. He does the same with regard to aesthetic judgements, in which case, as in moral judgements, the weak "enforce it tyranically".[45]

Nietzsche stresses that his criticisms of the morality, religion and aesthetics of negative power are not sufficient to undermine them: he must counteract them with the positive and constructive alternatives.

How foolish it would be suppose that one only needs to point out this origin and this misty shroud of delusion in order *to destroy* the world that counts for real, so-called 'reality'. We can destroy only as creators.[46]

Later, when discussing Schopenhauer and Wagner, Nietzsche demands the autonomous self-expression of positive creative power. "*Everyone who wishes to become free must become free through his own endeavor* ... freedom does not fall into any man's lap as a miraculous gift".[47]

Nietzsche now presents us with positive counterparts deriving from the direct expression of positive power. He describes positive art, for example, which offers strength to the man of tragic awareness. In contrast to negative art, which flees from serious and "tragic truth", positive art serves "tragic insight" and does not repress it. Its purpose is not to escape the truth but to help man bear it. In this respect, art is an important means of preserving the right perspective, and through its light and ironical tone it introduces a spirit of "gay science" into the severe, exigent arena of moral judgement. Nietzsche is aware that the

44. FW 21; KSA 3: 393.
45. FW 39; KSA 3: 407.
46. FW 58; KSA 3: 422.
47. FW 99; KSA 3:157.

philosophical task he assumed (reconstructing the morality of power) is likely to turn him into a stern and inflexible moralist, like others before him. But he abjures the role of the "grave" moralist, observing that a vital element of the morality of power is the lightness and subtle mockery which prevents the powerful man from taking himself too seriously.

Nietzsche prefers the morality of the cheerful dance hall to that of the gloomy house of prayer. In his view, gaiety and lightness characterize true positive power, which performs the most difficult tasks happily, like a virtuoso dancer. Positive art offers such lightness to the man of positive power; this is its primary purpose. Art ceases here to function as a consolation (as it did in *The Birth of Tragedy*) and becomes a spontaneous expression of positive power. Equipped with "shining" and dancing art, Nietzsche can turn directly to the metaphysical core of the "gay science" and investigate the "serious truth" which expresses the philosophical consciousness of positive power.

V. "The Gay Science" of Power

The ontology of the world of positive power provides for the existence of power and its essential characteristics. These are: immanence, autonomy, self-creativity and spontaneous expression. Such a world would be free of projections and anthropomorphic patterns: "Nor does it have any instinct for self-preservation or any other instinct".[48] It is quite impervious to all our aesthetic and moral judgements. This dehumanization of nature is contrasted to the instinctive, creative human power which is actually a psychological and aesthetic principle, rather than ontological. Nietzsche's separation of nature from any anthropomorphic God effects a purification designed to make

---

48. FW 109; KSA 3: 468.

sense of the spontaneity and creativity of power, neither restrained nor organized by any heteronomous or transcendental principles and forces.[49] It is only possible to act independently and without limitations on assumption of a cosmic *tabula rasa*. In this aesthetic model the whole world is conceived as chaotic raw material which human creativity may organize and mould without any ontological constraints. The creative power is an instinct that manifests itself also in the spheres of theoretical knowledge and science. Philosophy too "became a *power*",[50] and Nietzsche's own doctrine of power is an example of "one organizing force within one human being".[51]

Nietzsche rejects the Kantian rationalistic *a priori* explication of consciousness by imposing on reason an energetic creative power, and by abolishing the idea of autonomy as an *a priori* structure fixed and shared by every subject. The introduction of the concept of power into Kant's categories (which is in effect the material of sections 108–113 of *The Gay Science*) results in a dynamic open activization of formal Kantian reason. Kant had seen the creative aspect of human consciousness, but he placed *a priori* constraints on this activity. Nietzsche of course preserves the creativity, but he removes the constraints altogether.

A morality of power demands the kind of philosophy presented in *The Gay Science*. Positive power is genuine only when it recognizes the truth of the "gay science" and makes use of this 'serious' consciousnesss in a healthy and creative way: by constructing positive spiritual patterns that are nourished by power itself. It uses the world as basic material to be moulded by the imprint of its forms and needs. Within unstructured nature,

49. Therefore Nietzsche declares that only in a world without God and his "shadows", when "we complete our de-deification of nature", will man again become "a pure, newly discovered, newly redeemed nature" (FW 109; KSA 3: 469).
50. FW 110; KSA 3: 471.
51. FW 113; KSA 3: 473–474.

power establishes its morality, its religion and its sciences. Positive power is characterized above all by a kind of ruthless insight about the nature of the world around it and the nature of the man within it. By contrast, negative power is distinguished as a flight from serious truth and tragic consciousness, using the cultural constructions as a shield against the recognition of the truth. Thus a dynamic paradox develops in which the product created as a means of defence turns against its creator and restrains and curbs him. Traditional morality and transcendental and ascetic religion all tend to inhibit and suppress the further expression of the very power which gave rise to them. The 'products' of positive power do not exhibit this dynamic: the philosophy and the morality of power, as well as its art and religion, directly help positive power to develop and enrich its cultural products and sublimations. The elimination of God from nature enables the positive power behind it to prepare the foundation for its uninterrupted and unrestrained activities. The purpose of joyful art and the morality of power is to reinforce manifestations of positive power in all areas of human spiritual culture. The relationship between positive power and its products is a relationship of sublimation and relevance, in the Latin sense of *relevare* — as giving help in the bearing of a heavy burden. In contrast, the relationship between negative power and its products is one of mutual repression, suppression, and interference.

VI. From Negative to Positive Religion

Wherever there is a need for faith, Nietzsche says, the will is weak and the personality is frail. Paraphrasing Tertullian (*Credo quia absurdum est*: "I believe because it is absurd") one can formulate Nietzsche's position as, "I believe because I do not will". Active volition gives way to passive faith only out of weakness. This approach suggests a criterion of positive power:

How much one needs a faith (*einer Glauben*) in order to flourish ... that is a measure of the degree of one's strength (or, to put the point more clearly, of one's weakness) ... The demand that one *wants* by all means that something should be firm .. that *instinct of weakness* ... which, to be sure, does not create religious metaphysical systems, and convictions of all kinds, but — conserves them.[52]

This provides a specific description of negative religion which stems from the absence of strong and positive will and power. (Nietzsche mentions both Buddhism and Christianity in this context.) The psychological need for faith as "a support, a prop" is considered a symptom of weakness of will, or in Aristotle's terms, of *akrasia*. This analysis anticipates William James's discussion of religious experience and its psychological function.[53] But while James advocates religion as an existential metaphysical crutch essential to survival, Nietzsche rejects this negative function. In his view, it perpetuates weakness, endowing it with a "holy" transcendental legitimacy, denying man the incentive to reinforce his feeling of power by means of his own positive efforts and resources. Where crutches are provided for the cripple (in will and spirit) there is no incentive for him to overcome his handicap and walk independently. This only leads man into a condition of psychological slavery.

Faith is always coveted most and needed most urgently where will is lacking ... the less one knows how to command, the more urgently one covets someone who commands, who commands severely — a god, prince,

---

52. FW 347; KSA 3: 581–582.
53. See: William James, *The Will to Believe and Other Essays in Popular Philosophy* (New York, 1897); *The Varieties of Religious Experience: A Study in Human Nature* (New York, 1902).

class, physician, father confessor, dogma or party conscience.[54]

The consequences are not restricted to the arena of religion but permeate most of our social and cultural activities. Man may flee from his freedom, for example, towards totalitarian regimes and extreme forms of heteronomous rule, such as the dictatorship of an individual or a party. Negative religion is a *"disease of the will"*[55] and as an illness it must be combatted and cured. This is the intention of Nietzsche's anti-religious criticism. A healthy man — a man of positive power — does not need the therapy; a symptom of psychic health is that "a freedom of the will .. [will] take leave of all faith". The man who does not require religion or faith is "the *free spirit par excellence*".[56]

But Nietzsche is not opposed to negative religion merely because it handicaps the free development of positive power; he regards it as inimical to life itself. Religion, and specifically ascetic religion, not only annihilates the will but represses the instinct to live at all, glorifying death and abstinence. Wherever vital life is repressed, (as Nietzsche noted earlier in *The Birth of Tragedy*) a culture and a spontaneous creativity are condemned to die. Religion is not only a passive symptom of a sickness of will and of power; it actively aggravates the disease and kills the patient. It is not merely one nihilistic symptom among others, but leads to complete nihilism, the negation of life itself. From this point of view it is Nietzsche's primary enemy.[57]

Nietzsche's opposition to (negative) religion is also importantly related to his morality of positive power: "I myself have now slain

---

54. FW 347; KSA 3: 582.
55. *Loc. cit.*
56. *Ibid.*; KSA 3: 583.
57. Nietzsche deals with this nihilism of negative religion in an aphorism entitled "Christianity and Suicide" (FW 131) and elsewhere.

all gods .. for the sake of morality".[58] As has been noted, Nietzsche sought to freeze our psychological need for religious faith in order to prepare the human consciousness for a morality of genuine power. He recognized that behind the moral patterns of negative power loom the negative religions that justify them.

Many of Nietzsche's commentators often overlook an interesting aspect pertaining to this point of his philosophy: Nietzsche does not reject religion as such altogether. Indeed, he finds some of its characteristics most appropriate to the central aim of his philosophizing, viz., arousal to positive power. One could subsume such characteristics under the label "positive religion", thereby indicating that they help to reactivate humanity's positive resources. This feature is especially emphasized in one of Nietzsche's comments on the origins of science:

> Do you really believe that the sciences would ever have originated and grown if the way had not been prepared by magicians, alchemists, astrologers, and witches whose promises and pretensions first had to create a thirst, a hunger, a taste for *hidden* and *forbidden* powers? ... Even as these preludes and preliminary exercises of science were *not* by any means practiced and experienced as such, the whole of *religion* might yet appear as a prelude and exercise to some distant age. Perhaps religion could have been the strange means to make it possible for a few single individuals to enjoy the whole self-sufficiency of a god and his whole power of self-redemption ... would man ever have learned without the benefit of such a religious training and pre-history to experience a hunger and thirst for himself and to find satisfaction and fullness in *himself?*[59]

58. FW 153; KSA 3: 496.
59. FW 300; KSA 3: 538–39.

A religion need not be nihilistic. Some of its values and ideas may have served as the vital conceptual and emotional stimulation for the emergence of the morality of positive power. Some of the properties predicated of God (e.g., autonomy, power, capacity for infinite creativity) formed a model for Kant's doctrine of autonomous morality, and constitute to this day the heuristic model of a being graced with creative and intrinsic power: "this would surely have to result in a happiness that humanity has not known so far: the happiness of a god full of power and love".[60] This comment implies that Nietzsche himself borrowed his concept of power — among other things — from a divine model, the divine power of an ideal being. Would it have been possible to conceive the idea of the *Übermensch*, for example, possessing most of the God-like attributes, had there not already been available the idea of a free, omniscient God, the universal creator, the infinitely powerful being? Nietzsche admits these basic elements of religion and divinity as a positive introduction to his morality of power and the *Übermensch*. Negative religion suffocates both will and life and obstructs the development of positive human power, but positive religion (or the positive components within religions) prepares the path to the Nietzschean morality.

> Even we seekers after knowledge today, we godless anti-metaphysicians still take our fire, too, from the flame lit by a faith that is thousands of years old, that Christian faith.[61]

The transition that Nietzsche makes from the creative and positive power of the redeeming Christian God to the creative and autonomous power of the *Übermensch* is itself made possible by Christianity. To be more precise, it is inherent in the prevailing positive aspects of the Christian faith. The concept of

60. FW 337; KSA 3: 565.
61. FW 344; KSA 3: 577.

power, for example, is taken not only from psychology but also from Christian theology, and from the philosophical tradition that preceded it.[62]

We cannot enter into a full discussion here of Nietzsche's ambivalent attitude to religion.[63] It will be of interest, however, to address a few remarks to the relation between the philosophy of power and the positive elements within religion.

Nietzsche's conscious approval of certain expressions of positive power in religion is shown in his attitude towards the "Old Testament, the book of divine justice". Here he finds that "there are human beings, things, and speeches in so grand a style that Greek and Indian literature have nothing to compare with it".[64] Generally speaking, wherever Nietzsche finds expression of positive power in Judaism, he praises it. This element of his thought is characterised by passages in *The Antichrist* and elsewhere, which speak approvingly of ancient Judaism and its rituals. For example, he says that the ancient Jewish god and his followers were "the expression of a consciousness of power (*des Macht-Bewusstseins*), of joy in oneself, of hopes for oneself".[65] Clearly it is not religion as such that concerns Nietzsche, but its connection with the key concept of his thought *(Macht)* which he derives in part from religious contexts.

62. FW 377. And compare Nietzsche's demand, quoted by Jaspers, that we would "overcome everything Christian by what is more than Christian and not merely rid ourselves of it" (*Nietzsche*, Chicago, 1969, p. 392). See also Nietzsche's letter to Gast (July 21, 1881), where he confesses his personal and intellectual proximity to Christianity.
63. Comprehensively discussed by Karl Jaspers, *Nietzsche and Christianity* (Chicago, 1961). See also Eugen Biser, "Nietzsche's Relation to Jesus", in *Concilium: Nietzsche and Christianity* (Edinburgh, 1981), pp. 58–64, who describes Nietzsche's shift from criticism of Christianity to admitted affinity with it.
64. JGB 52; KSA 5: 72.
65. A 25; KSA 6: 193, and see my "Nietzsche on Jews and Judaism", *Archiv für Geschichte der Philosophie*, 67 (1985): 139–161.

Nietzsche is not, then, indiscriminately opposed to religion but only to specific improper uses to which it may be put. As with the different types of historical consciousness, which were only good or evil with respect to the particular uses made of them by powerful or weak types, the moral value of religion varies with its applications. Like other expressions of culture, religion possesses "influence, always destructive, as well as creative and form-giving". This "selective and cultivating influence" is "always multiple and different according to the sort of human beings who are placed under its spell and protection".[66]

The strong and independent philosopher, the free spirit, "will make use of religion for his project of cultivation, and education".[67] Indeed, this is sometimes Nietzsche's practice: to collect the positive elements in religions for the purpose of educating and enticing others towards positive power. It is reasonable to assume that he believed this 'enticement' could succeed precisely because its object, the phenomenon of power, is deeply rooted in the religious history of mankind.

Nietzsche explains positive religion as a temporary means rather than an ultimate end. As soon as religion turns into an end in itself, it becomes negative:

> One always pays dearly and terribly when religions do not want to be a means of education and cultivation in the philosopher's hand but insist on having their own *sovereign* way, when they themselves want to be ultimate ends and not means among other means.[68]

The religious category of creative power figures prominently in Nietzsche's atheistic transformation, but he also incorporates two supplementary sacred features: *amor fati* and redemption

---

66. JGB 61; KSA 5: 79.
67. *Loc. cit.*
68. JGB 62; KSA 5: 81.

from metaphysical salvation and consolation. The first is well expressed in the following remark: "Resignation and modest demands elevated to godhead — that is the best and most vital thing that still remains of Christianity".[69] Faith in this immanent world is, certainly, no less daring than faith in another. The second, central idea of 'redemption' clearly originates in religious thought, and it seems that Nietzsche is trying to overcome belief in God by means of an idea basic to and deriving from religious faith. Redemption by God or redemption from the need for God — these assume very similar roles.

The phenomenon of suffering is another category of religious pathos which is preserved in Nietzsche's thought. Suffering is considered existentially significant because, as a necessary condition of the process of self-overcoming, it is characteristic of the powerful individual who prefers the pain of a sober and tragic view of life to delusive comfort and consoling faith. The glorification of suffering which is common to both Nietzsche and the Christian tradition appears in certain autobiographical passages (e.g., in *Ecce Homo*) and is also interwoven in passages describing the *Übermensch*:

> The spiritual haughtiness and nausea of every man who has suffered profoundly .. determines the order of rank *how* profoundly human beings can suffer ... Profound suffering makes noble, it separates.[70]

Nietzsche's final goal cannot be suffering, of course, as this would run counter to his emphasis on the spontaneous vitality and gaiety of healthy life. Moreover, if he were to choose suffering over health, he would begin to resemble the ascetic whom he attacks for preferring to "will *nothingness* than *not* to

69. M 92; KSA 3: 85.
70. JGB 270; KSA 5: 225, and cf. NW 11–3.

will".[71] It is more plausible to assume that for Nietzsche suffering constitutes only an intermediate psychological and existential stage on the path to positive power, which too must be overcome.

VII. From Negative to Positive Science

Nietzsche also distinguishes between the positive and the negative manifestations of power in the sphere of science. He identifies a "scientific-positivistic" tradition which, like negative religion, is derived from a widespread *"instinct of weakness"*.[72] It is a tradition issuing from a *"demand for certainty"*, and is an expression of weakness of will, of negative power, seeking to attach itself to a world of positivistic 'truths', in much the same manner as religions may express a flight to a transcendental God. This escape to 'another world' — a world of static, sempiternal scientific truth — stems from the fear of facing our own world in which the only "serious truth" is that there are no eternal truths *per se*. This position of course raises the problem of self-reference, as well as the issue of epistemological status of "serious truth" within the context of Nietzsche's scepticism.[73] However, these matters cannot be pursued here.

Negative science, which like religion and metaphysics 'negates' this immanent world, also expresses a "concealed will to death".[74] The positivist's devotion to eternal truth at any price is seen by Nietzsche as an expression of the desire to achieve absolute certainty by contriving a world devoid of all spontaneity and creativity. The instincts and dynamic vitality are suppressed no less by this than by asceticism. Nietzsche declares that

---

71. GM III-28; KSA 5: 412.
72. FW 347; KSA 3: 581–582.
73. See, e.g., B. Magnus, "Nietzsche's Mitigated Skepticism", *Nietzsche-Studien* 9 (1980), pp. 260–267; A. Parush, "Nietzsche on the Skeptic's Life", *Review of Metaphysics* 29 (1975–76), pp. 523–542.
74. FW 344; KSA 3: 576.

"science also rests on a faith; there is simply no science without presuppositions".[75] Previously, in his discussion of negative religion, he had maintained that faith precluded positive power. He therefore rejects now the whole array of faiths, both religious and scientific, which express the weakness of the will and its flight from volition. The "unconditional will" of the scientist "to truth" at any cost is described as a determination never to "allow oneself to be deceived".[76] Positivistic science is thus a direct derivative of negative morality.[77]

Yet there is a more specific aspect to this criticism. Positivistic — but negative — science in fact depends on a complex of dogmatic presuppositions, such as the notion that truth is a supreme value of human consciousness and activity, corresponding precisely to the world as it is. This dogmatism limits the creative freedom of the will and even freezes the very speculative activity it is intended to support.[78] The restriction of the space of human consciousness, and expression of our fear of its infinitude (much like Pascal's fear of real space), is ultimately unjust to both ontology and epistemology with regard to "the perspective character of existence".[79] Nietzsche's doctrine of perspectivism should be regarded as the extreme antithesis of positivistic dogmatic science; its purpose is, among other things, to pave the way to a limitless expression of man's positive power in scientific-cognitive pursuits. The world is "infinite" in its nature: "it *may include infinite interpretations*".[80] To adhere to a single

75. FW 344; KSA 3: 575.
76. *Loc. cit.*
77. "I will not deceive, not even myself; *and with that we stand on moral ground*", *loc. cit.*
78. Here Nietzsche's analysis resembles Kuhn's descriptions of normal conservative science which revolves around one accepted paradigm seeking to defend and strengthen it; cf. T.S. Kuhn, *The Structure of Scientific Revolutions.*
79. FW 374; KSA 3: 626.
80. *Ibid.*, 3: 627.

interpretation when presented with such a fine array of possibilities is symptomatic of "a crudity and naiveté",[81] of a flight from such a fully creative life. Although the adepts of the creative life, led by positive power, may be "more endangered" they are also "more fruitful human beings, happier beings!"[82]

Negative science must be rejected by Nietzsche if he is to open up the infinite horizons to positive science — a science aware of the perspectival nature of existence. This science would investigate nature without any dogmatic preconceptions, and with a deep appreciation of the fact that "the secret for harvesting from existence the greatest fruitfulness and the greatest enjoyment is — to *live dangerously!*"[83] and to dance "even near abysses"[84] to the music of the "gay science". The Niezschean scientist therefore abandons the positivistic attitude and adopts a perspectival approach fostering creativity and fruitful exploration.[85]

Nietzsche's criticisms of negative science conclude with a description that anticipated Kuhn's psycho-social analyses of scientists' motives by almost a century:

> Without this new passion ... to know — science would still be promoted ... The good faith in science, the prejudice in its favor that dominates the modern state and is actually based on the fact ... that science is considered not a passion but a mere condition or an 'ethos' ... for many people ... their 'scientific impulse' is their boredom.[86]

This passage remarkably parallels Kuhn's suggestion that "normal science" often 'diddles' at intellectual 'crossword

---

81. FW 373; KSA 3: 625.
82. FW 283; KSA 3: 526.
83. *Loc. cit.*
84. FW 347; KSA 3: 583.
85. FW 373 and 374.
86. FW 123; KSA 3: 479.

puzzles' in pursuit of social recognition or in flight from boredom, or as a mere means of securing a livelihood. Nietzsche likewise rejects those negative expressions of science that stem from negative power and suppress creativity and innovation.

Yet Nietzsche somewhat modifies his fierce criticism of science, much as he did in the case of religion, acknowledging certain of its positive aspects. He emphasizes, for example, the scientist's self-discipline, and approvingly describes the "severity of science" and the "virile air"[87] in which self-control and creative power may find expression. These positive elements are precisely those required by the courageous man of science who uses positive and creative power and is undaunted by the potential infinitude of human cognition.

VIII. From Will to Pathos of Power

It has been argued that most of Niezsche's ideas may be interpreted in terms of his basic distinction between positive and negative power. This revelation of the 'power phenomenon' constitutes the most original foundation of his philosophical psychology — giving new definition to familiar patterns. This is in fact how Nietzsche himself describes the originality of his contributions: "What is originality?", he asks, "To see something that has no name as yet and hence cannot be mentioned although it stares us all in the face".[88]

It is important to stress that the central concept of Nietzsche's philosophy is not the 'will', but the psychological phenomenon of the *feeling* of power. Indeed, Nietzsche denies the existence of the will as such, opposing what he considers an invalid transition from "the feeling of *will*" to the concept of "the will

87. FW 293; KSA 3: 533–534, and cf. FW 300.
88. FW 261; KSA 3: 517.

itself".[89] The intensification of power is reflected in a consciousness that tends to see it in ontological terms, but the will is a fictitious entity. Nietzsche rejects any reification of will, and conceives of volition only in terms of functions and activities: there is no will but only "willing".[90]

He also rejects Schopenhauer's cosmic will, emphasizing that his own central concept is not the will to power but power itself — its feelings, experiences and effect: "True pathos of every period of life",[91] containing, among others, "the pathos of nobility and distance"[92] and "the Yes-saying pathos".[93] Hence it would be a mistake to accept Nietzsche's (unauthorized) *The Will to Power* as representative of his mature philosophy; even the title is quite misleading.

Nietzsche occasionally identifies the 'will to power' with pathos: "The will to power not a being, not a becoming, but a *pathos*";[94] the phrase 'will to power' does not express an ontological principle referring to some entity underlying the phenomenon of pathos. The very concept "phenomenon" assumes an ontologically distinct "thing in itself", suggesting a Kantian dichotomy between the world as it appears and the world as it is in itself. But Nietzsche repeatedly criticizes such traditional dualistic metaphysics, and it has no place in his conception of pathos. As an experience, a feeling or a sentiment of a particular individual, pathos requires no definite ontological status or metaphysical commitment. If Nietzsche identifies pathos with power, it follows that the latter is not ontologically or metaphysically hypostasized.

The word 'will' carries the connotation of conscious and

---

89. FW 127; KSA 3: 482.
90. See GM I-13.
91. FW 317; KSA 3: 549.
92. GM I-2, and JGB 257; EH-UB 3.
93. EH-Z 1.
94. WM 635 and 692.

rational intention. But as we have seen, most of the expressions of power occur spontaneously and non-rationally, and often even unconsciously. Nietzsche might have seemed more consistent, then, if he had used the expression 'the pathos of power' instead of 'the will to power'. Here, as elsewhere, his language is not altogether compatible with the central direction of his thought. (We should also recall that the term 'the will to power' occurs most frequently in the text so titled, a text which Nietzsche did not officially authorize for publication.)

'Power' does not refer to a metaphysical principle, but to various sentiments, temperaments, varied emotional states and types of pathos of the personality. Nietzsche's use of this notion, then, does not require justification for calling power either an epiphenomenon or a phenomenon, behind which is the ontologically 'real':

> Suppose nothing else were 'given' as real except our world of desires and passions, and we could not get down, or up, to any other 'reality' besides the reality of our drives.[95]

This immanent human reality excites the various types of pathos in any transitory period or given occasion of our life. Nietzsche identifies "the reality of our drives" with "the development and ramification of one basic form of the will — namely, the *will to power*".[96] The concept of the 'will' is superfluous here, or is at least emptied of its rational and purposive meaning, and the identity between pathos and power is again emphasized. On this point of interpretation, we should heed Heidegger's warning not to be led astray by Nietzsche's language — the 'will' is "only a word"[97] to which we succumb "owing to the seduction of language", as Nietzsche himself cautions us.[98]

95. JGB 36; KSA 5: 54.
96. *Ibid.*; KSA 5: 55.
97. Heidegger, *Nietzsche* (Pfullingen, 1961), Bd. 1, 650.
98. GM I-13.

I propose that Nietzsche's concept of 'power' is the psychological or, more correctly, *patho*logical function that externalizes the various transitory types of pathos; power transforms moments of pathos into interpretations through which they become enduring creations. Creativity (as a synthesis of the Apollonian and Dionysian) also becomes a projection of the various types of pathos within every individual. No one perspective is more correct than another, just as there is no one pathos that is truer than others. It is impossible to assign a truth-value to emotional and psychological states and their various moods. Each pathos has equal epistemological legitimacy; the whole complex of possible moments of pathos and their correlative perspectives is collectively subsumed under the title 'power'. Nietzsche does not reject the 'negative' types of power/pathos because they are incorrect; they are rejected as *detrimental* for various psychological reasons discussed above.

Nietzsche might have had yet another reason for refusing to reify power. If power had been treated as a kind of ontological substratum supporting a moral structure, he would have been in danger of committing a naturalistic fallacy in consequence of attempting to derive an 'ought' from an 'is'. But because he carefully refrains from locating the concept of power in an ontological foundation, stressing solely the acts of power, Nietzsche tries to avoid such a naturalization of morality.

IX. The Matrix of Power

All of Nietzsche's basic concepts and ideas were derived from his fundamental distinction between positive and negative power. We will now explore how the notions of the *Übermensch*, the eternal recurrence and *amor fati* are interwoven into a comprehensive whole in which the concept of power is centrally located.

Positive power has no purpose external to itself: it is relatively autonomous and autarkic. From this Nietzsche draws his last important idea about the "eternal recurrence of the same". The immanence of positive power inevitably brings Nietzsche to "eternal recurrence". Positive power has no purpose, for every purpose requires a means to attain it; the climactic expression of positive power is characterized precisely by not needing an instrumentalist approach. Power has no point but to express itself spontaneously, and true spontaneity has no purpose towards which it is directed and which it aspires to achieve. Genuine power — much like the omnipotent God — has no purpose; the existence of an aim or target suggests a *privatio* and implies that a complete power is not yet realized. The ideal of a fully positive power contains within it affirmation alone. It is not an aggregate of finite units — of intelligence, creative skill, self-sufficiency, etc. Such an aggregate model would interpret power in terms of finality, limitation and lack — in short, *privatio*. Nietzsche's concept of positive power is analogous to the absolutely positive concept of Spinoza's infinite being in the *Ethics*. Here we can note a further influence of philosophical theology — apart from the concept of power itself — on Nietzsche's philosophy.

Moreover, Nietzsche made a shift, as we have seen, from the concept of force to the concept of power, thereby emphasizing the continuous creativity and dynamism of the latter and avoiding the suggestion of anything akin to the physical laws of inertia and conservation of force and energy. To allow for indefinite creativity, he opposes any fixed or static habits and perspectives, saying that positive power demands change and looks with "mistrust to everything that wishes to become firm in us".[99] As an

99. FW 296. Permanence obstructs spontaneous creativity and one must therefore conquer such fixations by psychologizations and self-overcomings. This is very similar to the Freudian psycho-analytic doctrine, where the purpose of the treatment is, among other things, to overcome the existence of unconscious fixations that obstruct development and cause

alternative Nietzsche proposes "the eternal recurrence of the same". This idea allows for both continuous change and enduring stability, such that all change occurs within a determinate circle of indeterminate possibilities. It incorporates both change and permanence, where perpetuity of change guarantees creativity, while everlasting cyclical recurrence preserves it without purpose, without progress, and without immanent reason. There is no transcendental obstacle to the self-creative expression of positive power. The only barrier it may encounter is contained *within* its universe and is expressed in "the eternal recurrence of the same".

This idea also becomes an important moral formula. A man who wills and affirms himself without any reservations, who truly wants to be what he is, will embrace the idea of eternal recurrence. The formula of *amor fati* is then transmuted into the formula of eternal recurrence. For Nietzsche, the Kantian criterion of rational universalization leads to a morality of negative power. In its place he proposes the eternal recurrence as a yardstick for the morality of positive power that affirms itself endlessly:

> If this thought gained possession of you, it would change you as you are or perhaps crush you. The question in each and every thing, 'Do you desire this once more and innumerable times more'? would lie upon your actions as the greatest weight. Or how well disposed would you have to become to yourself and to live *to crave nothing more fervently* than this ultimate eternal confirmation and seal?[100]

The concept of the *Übermensch* is also derived directly from his

---

regressions and self-deceptions. On "Fixierung" (fixation) in Freud, see S.E., *14*: 148 and 348; *11*: 17; *12*: 67; *17*: 115.
100. FW 341; KSA 3: 570.

fundamental distinction between negative and positive power. It is an idea intended to capture a detailed concretization of a psychological personality endowed with full positive power. Nietzsche is aware that such a personality is impossible to realize completely; the *Übermensch* provides only a regulative idea, a model to which one can at best approximate. And indeed he does not offer concrete historical examples of this type of positive power, being careful not to attach to the *Übermensch* any historical name:

> To be a human being with one elevated feeling — to be a single great mood incarnate — that has hitherto been a mere dream and a delightful possibility; as yet history does not offer us any certain examples. Nevertheless history might one day give birth to such people too — once a great many favorable preconditions have been created and determined.[101]

The necessary 'precondition' is the re-activation of the values of the morality of positive power. We have seen that this morality required Nietzsche to discard conventional patterns of morality. These patterns expressed negative power which constitutes the main obstacle to the growth of a morality of positive power and the emergence of the *Übermensch*. But Nietzsche, despite his harsh criticisms of negative power, had no inclination to impose a "true morality" in an evangelical fashion. He was satisfied with an explication and description of the morality of positive power and did not intend to assume a missionary role.[102] It is perhaps fair to say that Nietzsche wanted to *entice* us towards his type of morality simply by depicting it vividly and impressively.

An exceptionally enticing description of the morality of

101. FW 288; KSA 3: 529.
102. FW 292.

positive power is offered by *Thus Spoke Zarathustra*. This text should be viewed as a work of epic poetry[103] in which the hero, the prophet Zarathustra, has overcome the patterns of negative morality and has passed through self-transformation on the way to attaining the moral patterns of positive power. The figure of Zarathustra appears for the first time in the concluding passages of *The Gay Science* in the original 1882 edition.[104] The image of Zarathustra as a concrete hero occurred to Nietzsche only after he had finished sketching the essential features of the morality of positive power. It is an image fully expressing the supreme personality of man as one who has achieved positive power and has lived it without any compromises. In the absence of a historical example that could provide an appropriate model, Nietzsche relied on his literary imagination. Zarathustra becomes a literary paradigm of how positive art can lead towards the morality of positive power. Nietzsche himself acknowledges the special role of this 'enticing' heuristic technique:

> Consider how every individual is affected by an overall philosophical justification of his way of living and thinking: he experiences it as a sun that shines especially for him and bestows warmth, blessings, and fertility on him; it makes him independent of praise and blame, self-sufficient, rich, liberal with happiness and good will ... How I wish that many such new suns were yet to be created ... the exceptional human being ... The moral earth, too, is round ... has its antipodes. The antipodes, too, have the right to exist.[105]

---

103. Some, out of the many poetic aspects, of *Thus Spoke Zarathustra* are dealt with *et passim* by Philip Grundlehner, *The Poetry of Friedrich Nietzsche*, (New York, Oxford, Oxford University Press, 1986).
104. FW 342.
105. FW 289; KSA 3: 529.

These moral antipodes, which Nietzsche repeatedly describes, are the morality of negative versus positive power. *Descriptions* — not authoritative prescriptions — are offered to awaken us from our moral slumber and to guide us towards the world of the morality of power: "There is yet another world to be discovered — and more than one. Embark, philosophers!"[106]

Nietzsche seeks to describe rather to than prescribe and legislate an alternative morality. We shall see in the concluding chapter that the doctrine of morality he offers is more explicative than justificatory. Moral prescription is contrary to the spirit of the morality of positive power, which consists in self-creation and self-overcoming. Nietzsche, therefore, can only educate and entice the reader towards his authentic self. Once a man has created himself — has become himself through the self-overcoming — the supreme personality of power will emerge within him. But he cannot be aided in this creative endeavour by any artist other than himself:

> To 'give style' to one's character — a great and rare art! It is practiced by those who survey all the strengths and weaknesses of their nature and then fit them into an artistic plan until every one of them appears as art and reason ... through long practice and daily work at it.[107]

This is the fundamental *raison d'être* of Nietzsche's philosophical psychology — to be influential in the work of enticement to positive power. "To become who you are" can only be done by oneself, through one's own positive power. Nonetheless, it is possible to arouse, to educate and to entice one to do just this without constraining one's free self-achievement.

---

106. *Ibid.*; KSA 3: 530.
107. FW 290; KSA 3: 530.

CHAPTER SEVEN

CONCLUSION: NIETZSCHE'S ENTICEMENT TOWARDS POWER[1]

Introduction

Gradually it has become clear to me what every great philosophy so far has been: namely, the personal confession of its author ... also that the moral (or immoral) intentions in every philosophy constituted the real germ of life from which the whole plant had grown. Indeed, if one would explain how the abstrusest metaphysical claims of a philosopher really come about, it is always well (and wise) to ask first: at what morality does all this (does he) aim?[2]

Nietzsche's "moral intentions" and the practical objective of his philosophizing are both concerned with the recognition and creative use of our power in authentic patterns of life. His moral theory of power ultimately is revealed as the hub around which all his earlier and later views "become ... more and more firmly attached to one another ... entwined and interlaced with one another."[3]

---

1. The first and concise version of this chapter was presented before the Fifth Jerusalem Philosophical Encounter, held in 1983 and subsequently published as "Nietzsche's Enticing Psychology of Power" in Y. Yovel (ed.), *Nietzsche as Affirmative Thinker* (Dordrecht, 1986), pp. 160–182.
2. JGB 6; KSA 5: 19–20.
3. GM V-2; KSA 5: 248.

This logical and ideational interrelation of central Nietzschean concepts and motives transforms what initially seems to be a loosely connected and aphoristic work into a positive and comprehensive philosophy and psychology of power — one which can be discussed coherently.

Nietzsche's new psychology, unlike others, "dared to descend into the depths,"[4] and became what he called *"the doctrine of the development of the will to power".*[5] In so doing, it unmasks the basic instinct of the human-all-too-human soul: its power.

In his early work, *The Birth of Tragedy*, Nietzsche had already sketched the cardinal objective of his philosophy: attaining a mental state which would allow us to "gaze" courageously into the horrors of the *"tragic insight".*[6] The same fundamental motif recurs later in the distinction between a weak, "gentle, fair ... skepticism"[7] that paralyzes the will and results in a nihilistic denial, and "another and stronger type of skepticism" that "does not believe but does not lose itself in the process".[8] Nietzsche's philosophy, and the psychological means he employs, purports to lead us to this positive skepticism, moving us closer to the "great spirits"[9] who — like Zarathustra — are sceptics out of an abundance of power, and sustain their skepticism in all vitality and creativity.

To dance "even near abysses" is the only alternative left after the "Death of God"; it is the ability to embrace this alternative that is the "proof of strength", and an indication of the "free spirit par excellence" with its positive power. Nietzsche's objective is thus to provide modern man with an intellectual therapy by preparing him for a creative life in a world without dogmatic

---

4.   JGB 23; KSA 5: 38.
5.   *Loc. cit.*
6.   GT 15; KSA 1: 101.
7.   JGB 208; KSA 5: 137.
8.   JGB 209; KSA 5: 141.
9.   A 54; KSA 6: 236.

beliefs. The death of dogma will not lead to the end of man and his culture, but will rather liberate the creative resources that have heretofore been constrained by repressive morality. It will open new horizons to new beliefs, but these will function now solely as life-enhancing "perspectives". Once they lose their usefulness, such beliefs will be discarded and painlessly exchanged for other perspectives.

Nietzsche's own psychology is to be regarded as just such a belief — a temporary perspective, to be left behind once it has fulfilled its therapeutic aim. This in part explains why so many of the psychological passages in Nietzsche's writings read as the self-diagnosis of a desperate physician who proposes a pattern of mental health, while suffering himself from a serious malady.

Hence, Nietzschean psychology is to be a means: "a mere instrument"[10] to entice us to reach and freely employ our positive powers. In view of this, Nietzsche unquestionably belongs to "these philosophers of the future" who may have a right to be called *"Versucher"*[11]: "This name is in the end a mere attempt and, if you will, an enticement".[12]

Nietzsche describes the essence of this *"Versuchung"*, this enticement: "One has to test oneself to see that one is destined for independence and command — and do it at the right time".[13] *Versuchung* is an "experiment", an "enticement" and a "hypothesis" directing man's efforts toward positive power, and

10. JGB 6; KSA 5: 20.
11. JGB 42; KSA 5: 59.
12. *Loc. cit.* (my slightly revised translation). See also the statement that "the genuine philosopher ... feels the burden and the duty of a hundred attempts (*Versuchen*) and enticements of life" (*Versuchungen*), JGB 205; KSA 5: 133 (my translation). Nietzsche's play on the words "Versuch" (hypothesis or experiment) and "Versuchung" (seduction or enticement) is far from unintentional; it clearly points to one of the most significant features of Nietzsche's philosophy, namely that it is a sophisticated mode of enticement.
13. JGB 41; KSA 5: 58.

testing his ability to reach and activate it in his life's endeavours. These "experiments", "tests" or "enticements" are the psychology of power, which becomes Nietzsche's principal "instrument" for attaining his philosophical and existential goals.

The method of enticement is indeed a valuable means, since it seeks to draw us into embracing positive patterns of life. Indeed, the word "enticement" in itself has no negative connotations but signifies a neutral process. Its positive or negative value depends solely on its purpose. Nietzsche is consistent in carefully distinguishing between the positive enticement to pathos — or the pattern of positive power which he calls *Versuchung* — and the negative seduction used by Christianity to suppress positive expressions of power, which he calls *Verführung*:

> This Jesus of Nazareth, the incarnate gospel of love ... was he not this seduction (*die Verführung*) in its most uncanny and irresistible form ...?[14]

Hence we understand why Nietzsche calls himself the "Anti-Christ". He is like Christ insofar as he uses the same method (of enticement) that Christ used to divert mankind toward negative ideals. But Nietzsche is also Christ's opponent, since he uses enticement to re-activate and intensify the positive powers of man and his culture. Nietzsche posits the antithesis of the Christian gospel of salvation (which is the seduction towards negative power — *die Verführung*) by offering a salvation from this negative salvation in the form of psychological enticement to power (*die Versuchung*).

I have said that this psychology of power becomes, in Nietzsche's hands, the principal instrument of enticement. It is not, however, the only one. From this psychological perspective we can now view some of his other so-called metaphysical ideas

14. GM I-8; KSA 5: 268.

— especially the eternal recurrence of the same — as additional devices for the positive enticement and transformation of the reader.

The metaphysical hypothesis of the eternal recurrence appears frequently in Nietzsche's writings, not as an absolute dogma but more as an "experiment", (*Versuch*), which is also a test and an enticement. The acceptance or rejection of this hypothesis becomes an important indication of man's mental resources and powers.[15] Thus, a quasi-metaphysical doctrine becomes a sort of Darwinian-psychological test, designed to distinguish between different patterns of power. It is important to emphasize that in the passage where this thesis is first introduced (in the "as-if" version, by the testing "demon") Nietzsche leaves room for only two possible responses:

> Would you not throw yourself down and gnash your teeth and curse the demon who spoke thus? Or have you once experienced a tremendous moment when you would have answered him: 'You are a god and never have I heard anything more divine!'[16]

Nietzsche does not allow for an indifferent or objective reaction, which would be appropriate to a scientific or metaphysical hypothesis. The strongly emotional reaction which he expects corroborates the contention that the "eternal recurrence" was not really meant to be a metaphysical thesis, but rather a sort of

15. See, for example, MusA, 14: 187. Thus I am here proposing a reconciliation between what Bernd Magnus aptly calls the "normative interpretation of recurrence" (*Nietzsche's Existential Imperative*, Bloomington, 1978, p. 142), which stresses the psychological consequences of this doctrine, and Magnus' own interpretation emphasizing the existential-heuristic role of this teaching. The introduction of the concept of "enticement" in this context is therefore an attempt to capture the psychological importance of this doctrine without attaching it too narrowly to its truth value — as does, for example, the normative interpretation.
16. FW 341; KSA 3: 570.

gedanken Experiment. Its strong existential and psychological impact is manifested in either succumbing to it or in escaping from its consequences. This impact spells a significant change in the life of the man who encounters it:

> If this thought gained possession of you, it would change you as you are or perhaps crush you.[17]

The motif of temptation and transformation explains why Nietzsche does not trouble to provide (in his published writings) any rational basis for the "eternal recurrence". What really matters to him is not the validity or truth of his thesis, but whether one possesses enough positive power to believe in it and to change oneself accordingly. Since there is no logical connection between the truth of any idea and a willingness to accept it, Nietzsche is not required to provide rational substantiation for his thesis. Its primary aim is to entice the reader to reach and activate his positive power. This is why Nietzsche regards Zarathustra, who personifies the educational project of his psychological philosophy, as "the teacher of the eternal recurrence".

Nietzsche is aware of the fact that his therapeutic enticement is not appropriate for everyone. In fact, he considers our reaction to his therapy as an additional criterion of distinction between different patterns of power. He suggests that if we fail to respond to his enticement, this is not because of any inner flaws in the therapy or because it lacks a moving appeal. Such failure will be a consequence of our own inability to raise ourselves to the level of its demands:

> What serves the higher type of men as nourishment or delectation must almost be poison for a very different and inferior type ... There are books that have opposite values

17. *Loc. cit.*

for soul and health, depending on whether the lower soul, the lower vitality, or the higher and more vigorous ones turn to them: in the former case, these books are dangerous and lead to crumbling and disintegration; in the latter, heralds' cries that call the bravest to their courage.[18]

This passage suggests three kinds of responses to enticement. The challenges stand in direct correspondence to the psychological type at whom they are directed: the "inferior type" of negative power rejects the enticement, is confused by it and escapes from its consequences; the "higher type" of adequate positive power accepts it and becomes more powerful, independent and authentic; the *"Übermensch"* of optimal power does not respond to this enticement since he does not require it. He is already endowed with the highest capacity for self-creation, and overcomes even this Nietzschean enticement by creating his own perspective and values. Here the rejection of Nietzsche's challenge does not stem from cowardliness or weakness (as in the first case), but out of a *surplus* of power and an abundance of self that requires no psychologistic crutches.

By viewing Nietzsche's philosophical psychology as an educational enticement of the reader, we can explain the poetic style, the powerful pathos, and the provocativeness which he deliberately introduces in his writings. Not only the specific content but also the stylistic form of Nietzsche's psychology aims at softening and reducing our resistance to its therapy. It is no accident that in several places Nietzsche insists on the close interrelation between his goal as a psychologist of morality and his peculiar personal style.[19] "Whatever is profound loves

---

18. JGB 30; KSA 5: 48–49.
19. For example, GM III-19; KSA 5: 385, and also EH III-5. See also Alexander Nehamas' illuminating discussion of the philosophical significance of Nietzsche's literary styles in his *Nietzsche: Life as Literature* (Cambridge, Mass., Harvard University Press, 1985).

masks", declares Nietzsche, and whatever educates loves the enticing mask behind which lies "so much graciousness in cunning".[20]

Nietzsche clarifies his task as the enticing psychologist in a retrospective passage:

> To give an idea of me as a psychologist, I choose a curious bit of psychology from *Beyond Good and Evil.*[21]

This passage runs as follows:

> The genius of the heart, as that great concealed one possesses it, the tempter god (*der Versucher Gott*) and born pied piper of consciences whose voice knows how to descend into the netherworld of every soul; who does not say a word or cast a glance in which there is no consideration and ulterior enticement; whose mastery includes the knowledge of how to seem — not what he is but what is to those who follow him one more constraint to press ever closer to him in order to follow him ... the god *Dionysus*, that great ambiguous one and tempter god ... this type of deity and philosopher ... often reflects how he might yet advance man and make him stronger, more evil, and more profound than he is.[22]

In brief, the enticing "philosopher" is endowed here with a more powerful pathos of the positive power, what is called elsewhere the "Yes-saying pathos par excellence"[23] or "The pathos of nobility and distance".[24]

The main strategy of the figure of Nietzsche-"Dionysus" is his

---

20.   JGB 40; KSA 5: 57–58.
21.   EH III-6; KSA 6: 307.
22.   JGB 295; KSA 5: 237.
23.   EH-Z 1; KSA 6: 336.
24.   GM I-2; KSA 5: 259.

psychology. Psychology is "the path to the fundamental problems" or the path to the fundamental patterns of positive power. However, being only a path, it is naturally abandoned once it has come to an end. Nietzschean psychology will then have become a sort of temporary scaffolding, a provisional hypothesis or a metaphoric structure (in the original meaning of the term *meta-phora*), to be abandoned once it has served its purpose.

An analogy that may illuminate this unique function of Nietzsche's psychology is the concept of the ladder at the end of Wittgenstein's *Tractatus Logico-Philosophicus*. Wittgenstein asks his reader to "throw [it] away ... after he has climbed it".[25]

Nietzsche's enticing ladder is composed of four distinct steps: psychologization, positive psychology, explication of power, and genealogy of power.

All the components of Nietzsche's psychology confront us with tragic insight and Dionysian scepticism. The process of psychologization unmasks illusions and peels off intellectual defence-mechanisms such as religion, science, philosophy, etc. Beneath these Nietzsche exposed the positive power of man. The finer the quality of the power the better it will work, vitally and creatively until it reaches the optimal point at which it will no longer need the psychological ladder and can dispense with it. One may think of Nietzschean psychology as being simultaneously an instrument for freezing repressive ideologies and a means for enticing and intensifying the will. In the preliminary stages of maturation, power still needs therapeutic and psychological crutches. But with the full ripening of power — with the attainment of Nietzsche's "self-creation" — man's

---

25. "6.54". Trans. D.F. Pears &. B.F. McGuiness (London, 1961). Another analogy between Wittgenstein and Nietzsche may be found in Erich Heller, "Wittgenstein and Nietzsche", in *The Artist's Journey into the Interior* (New York, 1959), pp. 201–226, which discusses several similarities between Nietzsche and the later Wittgenstein of the *Philosophical Investigations*.

authentic power must shed its supports and prove its authenticity by being able to thrive without them. So the way leading to power must already include this very power; it carries this power as a potential for full actualization through a painful and gradual process of reactivation. The psychological ladder does not create the power or its positive patterns and pathos *ex nihilo*. It merely explicates and activates this power. This is the central meaning of the Nietzschean conception of the philosopher's "thinking" which is, in fact, far less a discovery than a recognition, "a remembering, a return and a homecoming to a remote, primordial, and inclusive household of the soul". Therefore, "philosophizing is to this extent a kind of atavism of the highest order".[26]

This explicative-descriptive dimension of the ladder also includes a personal meaning clearly indicated by Nietzsche's mention of "the personal confession" and "mémoire".[27] Here we have not only a theoretical explication and analysis of *Macht*. He is also offering an existential explication of a man who, by his philosophizing, strives to express his positive power; Nietzsche attempts to lead us toward this power while exposing and intensifying it within his own "household of the soul". This instrumental psychology is intended to fulfil Nietzsche's needs as well as our own; his explication of power becomes at the same time a kind of self-psychoanalysis. Freud was probably well aware of this.[28] Nietzsche's analysis of power and self-analysis

26. JGB 20; KSA 5: 34.
27. JGB 6.
28. Witness his biographer Ernst Jones, who in describing the meeting of the Vienna Psychoanalytic Society of 28 October 1908, devoted to the analysis of *Ecce Homo*, remarks that Freud

> Several times referred to Nietzsche as to the man who 'had a more penetrating knowledge of himself than any other man who ever lived or was likely to live'.
>
> E. Jones, *Sigmund Freud: Life and Work*
> (London, 1955), Vol. 2, p. 385.

are parallel and complementary processes, but they are not derived from one another. For while it is true that in his enticing psychologizations Nietzsche himself is enticed, and that in giving directives for our maturation Nietzsche himself matures and becomes powerful, these two processes are nonetheless clearly distinct. Both of them are separate manifestations of Nietzsche's one "common root", of his *"fundamental will"*.[29] The "common root" is always power, whether used for self-overcoming or for the overcoming of one's epoch. More precisely, this power is used to overcome all these patterns of life and their cultural rationalization that hinder the spontaneous and creative employment of positive powers hidden in Nietzsche and his contemporaries.

This self-psychoanalytic, subjective component of Nietzsche's thought in part explains why he did not elaborate a philosophical, impersonal system — why he resisted the ideal of philosophy as science, and objected to the notion of the autonomy of reflexion. The subjective component also accounts for Nietzsche's

Coming from the founder of psychoanalysis this is no small compliment. Moreover, Freud and his followers believe that man is able to reach deep self-knowledge only by following a long and intensive psychoanalysis. Freud therefore implies in this passage that Nietzsche, who possessed self-knowledge "more than any other man who ever lived" (including Freud himself, who, as is well known, performed self-psychoanalysis while writing *Die Traumdeutung*), had acquired such knowledge as a result of a painful process of introspection, similar to Freud's. That this is so appears from some comments made by Freud at the same meeting:

> He makes a number of brilliant discoveries in himself ... The degree of introspection achieved by Nietzsche had never been achieved by anyone, nor is it likely to be reached again.
> *Minutes of the Vienna Psychoanalytic Society*
> (New York, 1967), Vol. 2, p. 32.

See also Freud's other observation on Nietzsche in his 1934 letter: "In my *youth* he signified a nobility to which I could not attain" (my italics). Quoted in Jones, III: 460 (New York, 1953–57).

29. GM V-2; KSA 5: 248.

personal manner of writing and for its partially aphoristic and associative form. This form closely resembles the psychoanalytic treatment which employs a spontaneous outburst of "primary associative processes", as well as more objective interpretations and theoretical reflections upon these processes. Both evoke and nourish these processes and are in turn elicited by them again and again.[30]

Consideration of Nietzsche's psychology from a therapeutic perspective clarifies the problem of the (apparent) vicious circle between his positive doctrine and his sceptic-perspectivist epistemology. The emphasis on enticement in Nietzsche's thought shows that there is no logical reason for rejecting his enticing psychology, since it does not contradict any criteria of objective truth. If scepticism is regarded as one of the vital components in the therapeutic attempt to expose and to activate the positive powers of man and his culture, the problem of the circularity between Nietzsche's anthropology and epistemology becomes less acute than is generally considered. In other words: the issue about the epistemological status and truth of Nietzsche's views is beside the point *vis à vis* their enticing, existential effect for human life.

I. The Explication of Power

Nietzsche's psychology of power is not an inductive theory or an empirical hypothesis, as Kaufmann claims.[31] Apart from the

---

30. The interlocking of Nietzsche's self-analysis with the wider, theoretical context of his thought is manifested also in the sporadic nature of his writing. His is not an ordered and established style, but rather one resulting from thoughts composed while walking, in various notebooks, on scraps of paper, in sudden eruptions and in fragmented flashes of intensive creativity. And see Hollingdale's description of Nietzsche's characteristic solitary monologues in *Nietzsche: The Man and His Philosophy* (London, 1965), Ch. 8.

31. Walter Kaufmann, *Nietzsche*, pp. 92 and 183.

speculative method of psychologization it also contains a conspicuous explicative and typological dimension — in contrast to the constructive and explanatory aspect of the empirical sciences. This dimension is vividly expressed in Nietzsche's analyses of the different patterns of power and his distinction between its two central manifestations: the positive and the negative. The explication, careful description and analysis of a given phenomenon do not include its rational justification and foundation, but the former may surely function as a necessary preparatory introduction for the latter. This is what Nietzsche has in mind when he says that all previous philosophers have "wanted to supply a rational foundation" for the prevalent morality, but have completely ignored its vast variety and immense richness. Thus they were involved in providing a justifying philosophy, a "science of morals" (namely, a rational ethics) and did not deal with the preliminary "typology of morals".[32] Because of this exclusive preoccupation, the philosophers "left in dust ... the task of description", and were not at all concerned "to collect material, to conceptualize and arrange a vast realm of subtle feelings of value and differences of value which are alive, grow, beget, and perish". They completely neglected "attempts to present vividly some of the more frequent and recurring forms of such living crystallizations", forgetting thereby that "the real problems of morality ... emerge only when we compare many moralities".[33] Nietzsche dealt extensively with such comparisons, and with descriptive typology and the "subtle" distinctions between different moralities in his main writings.

This explicative dimension is an indication of the important fact that Nietzsche is not searching for new, esoteric values. Nor does he intend to establish a new ethics. His objective is to

32. JGB 186; KSA 5: 105.
33. JGB 186; KSA 5: 105–106

crystallize, to intensify, to re-activate a number of values that are regarded by most of us as good and useful, securing the social order and fostering our mental health.

This is revealed by examination of the characteristics of positive power. The long list of positive predicates of the man endowed with power includes no original or novel values but rather notions such as self-suffiency, heroism, creative sublimation of instincts, intellectual tolerance, generosity, nobility, dynamic vitality, courage, the will to life, self-control, faith in oneself, the ablity to accept contradiction, the lack of bad conscience, etc.

Most of these values appear in traditional philosophical ethics, such as the theories of Plato, Spinoza and Kant, to whom Nietzsche frequently refers. The term "ethics" typically refers to the rational foundation and justification of moral norms. Nietzsche, however, does not believe that reason is capable of providing any such rational foundation. This, of course, raises the questions: why should we prefer the morality of positive power and reject the various expressions of the morality of negative power, if neither can be transcendentally justified? Why should we prefer the *Übermensch* to the ordinary man? Why should we choose creativity and sublimation and reject repression, which in two millennia has brought about Christian-moral culture with its glorious tradition? Or, to put it very directly: why be a moral agent at all?

Nietzsche was well aware of this meta-ethical question, which in the above-cited aphorism he calls: "The problem of morality itself". It is implicitly answered in his explicative treatment of morality as such. He emphasizes psychology just because he does not believe in the possibility of a philosophical justification of morality. However, even psychology at its best can do no more than offer us good reasons for the adoption of this or that pattern of life; it is unable to provide the ultimate justification for the adoption of such a pattern. Nevertheless, providing reasons for adopting the morality of positive power is not the only function of Nietzsche's psychology. Its other important role, as I have indicated above, is to be an enticing, persuasive tool, a heuristic and therapeutic means for helping us to discover and actualize our power. In Nietzschean terms, it can be said to be a monumental psychology, functioning in a way similar to his heuristic "monumental history".

Now, it is impossible to entice someone and persuade him to act in some specific manner unless he already possesses the inherent ability to meet the challenge or yield to it. Positive power must already be hidden in mankind (and its expression in everyday life and culture must be possible).

As in Freudian psychoanalysis, Nietzsche does not assume that we could be injected with patterns of positive power from the outside, so to speak. These must lie within us and it is the task of psychology to activate them creatively. There is no contradiction, then, between the fact that Nietzsche has no esoteric, ideal prescriptions, and his insistence in calling on us to live creatively, to widen our intellectual horizons and to lead original lives. Originality, Nietzsche believes, springs from the inherent sources of power. Nietzsche's psychology is intended to assist us in overcoming the impediments that have inhibited the spontaneous manifestation of that power. Enticement will help us to uncover the origins of creation. Nietzsche supposes that these origins of power are rooted deeply within ourselves, but because of various psychological handicaps (cowardice, for example), we have repressed them and have prohibited their free operation. These handicaps have been projected as an ideological network with patterns of negative power, and Nietzsche uses his psychological "hammering" method to shatter the prohibiting "idols" while freezing our faith in them.

The very process of freezing our belief in most of the prevalent values of negative power is founded on the assumption that the "frozen" personality will reject certain values and accept other norms, which already exist both in his social surroundings and within himself. An illuminating example of this sort of "freezing", explicative and psychologistic process can be found in Nietzche's critical analysis of the negative power expressed by the ascetic ideal:

> It is my purpose here to bring to light, not what this ideal has done, but simply what it means; what it indicates; what lies hidden behind it, beneath it, in it … And it is only in pursuit of this end that I could not spare my readers a glance at its monstrous and calamitous effects, to prepare them for the ultimate and most terrifying aspect of the question concerning the meaning of this ideal.[34]

There is a striking similarity between the procedure of "coolly placing on ice"[35] and the aphoristic tactics employed by Socrates, whom Nietzsche ambivalently admired. Socrates "froze" by logical means whereas Nietzsche does this solely by means of genetic psychologizations. In his dialogues, Socrates is seeking to freeze the listener's belief in X, for example, by showing him that this logically entails a belief in Y. The listener is not ready to endorse belief in Y because of his belief in the set of values: p, s, t … which he shares with Socrates.

Nietzsche employs almost the same method. He shows his readers that their most "sacred" values are rooted in negative power and the psychological "effects" of their endorsement are stagnation, repression, inhibition of creativity, depression, regression and so forth. Most of us typically consider these effects to be undesirable, and wish to eliminate them.

The enticing psychological arguments for the morality of positive power, therefore, are not presented directly and prescriptively. Instead, the process of freezing is employed

34. GM III-23; KSA 5: 395.
35. EH-MA I; KSA 6: 323.

indirectly by means of a genealogy, revealing the negative origins of prevalent norms and arguing that the effects of our accepting these norms are psychologically and existentially destructive.

All this is closely connected to Nietzsche's explicative attitudes, for in order to evoke positive power he must first overcome the inhibiting forces. Both the positive enticement and the negative freezing assume that men possess an implicit set of values that drive them to reject negative patterns. Therefore, along with his enticing psychology, Nietzsche must explicate these implicit norms and elaborate them using careful descriptive analysis.

These explications portraying a sublime pattern of life contain a strong heuristic element. The explication of an impressive ideal evokes our reverence (the Kantian *Achtung*), and indicates that the power in question is attainable, since it hides at the base of our mental and cultural life. It has already manifested itself frequently in history — in the noble moral patterns of the "masters".[36]

By focusing on a phenomenon latently implicit in our culture and its patterns, Nietzsche's explication of power functions like a sort of lighthouse, enticing us towards it. Hence these explications are (like most of his psychology) a monumental means that has its beginning in *"Schopenhauer as Educator"*, which portrayed several models of ideal human beings. The heroic presentation in itself, Nietzsche assumes, may tempt us to aspire to the sublime level of the heroes.

---

36. This tactic was already used by Nietzsche in his lectures on Greek Philosophy given in Basel in 1875–76. In these supra-historical surveys of the Pre-Socratic philosophers, Nietzsche wanted to place before the youthful generation, instead of the ideal of Nationalism, the enticing paradigm of Greek culture for the constitution of an authentic and humanistic society: "So this has existed — once, at least — and is therefore a possibility, this way of life, this way of looking at the human scene", Nietzsche, *Philosophy in the Tragic Age of the Greeks*, trans. M. Cowan (Chicago, 1962), pp. 23–24.

Another crucial passage stresses this explicatory feature of Nietzsche's discussion of the phenomenon of power:

> Wandering through the many subtler and coarser moralities which have so far been prevalent on earth, or still are prevalent, I found that certain features recurred regularly together and were closely associated — until I finally discovered two basic types and one basic difference.
>
> There are *master morality* and *slave morality* — I add immediately that in all the higher and more mixed cultures there also appear attempts at mediation between these two moralities, and yet more often the interpenetration and mutual misunderstanding of both, and at times they occur directly alongside each other — even in the same human being, within a *single* soul.[37]

Several central and thematic ideas are expressed in this passage, and may also be found in other related aphorisms.[38] Nietzsche describes his investigations of different moral patterns as a search for "certain features [that] recurred regularly together". This is obviously a description of the explicative method, which seeks to expose the definitive and essential features of certain phenomena. The two moral phenomena presented are actual cultural patterns, and are far from being *a priori* constructions of our minds. "Master morality" and the pattern of the *Übermensch* are historical phenomena which Nietzsche defines more closely in order to avoid confusion with the "slave morality".

This contention is confirmed not only by the explicative dimensions of Nietzsche's thought, but also by his thesis of the "eternal recurrence of the same". If we accept this idea literally — what has been will be again — the historical types of *Übermenschen* are of course included. The *Übermensch,*

---

37.   JGB 260; KSA 5: 208.
38.   For example in GM I-16; KSA 5: 285–286; and JGB 200.

therefore, is not a new additional element but an already existing person, who will reappear in the future. Indeed, Nietzsche maintains that in the figure of Napoleon: "... the problem of the noble ideal as such made flesh".[39] We must again emphasize here that in Nietzsche's own view his originality and innovative nature are not expressed by the establishment of a new and unique moral set, but rather by elucidating already existing moralities, and by giving them new names, throwing new light on their essential features.[40] Unless the moral phenomenon undergoes the most sustained explication, analysis and classification, it cannot influence or move us. In other words: it cannot become an operative and significant ideal.

This is how we should grasp Nietzsche's statement that "Never yet has there been an overman".[41] There has been no complete theoretical or concrete picture of the moral pattern of positive power. Such a pattern is given in the fictitious figure of Zarathustra, who consolidates the positive values scattered in the various patterns of negative power. An explicit moral ideal of positive power has been wanting. If we want such an ideal to move us, to inspire us, we must bring it to a full and conscious explication. However, once the explication of power has provided the necessary description of this implicit ideal, it will be transformed from an historical phenomenon into an influential regulative idea.

Nietzsche, observing the cultural history of morality, discovers "the interpenetration and mutual misunderstanding of both".[42] Moreover, history discloses the slow, gradual progression from the "morality of the herd" to a morality that increasingly stresses the value of the individual. The gradual emergence of the morality

---

39. GM I-16; KSA 5: 288.
40. FW 261; KSA 3: 517.
41. Z 2, "On Priests"; KSA 4: 119.
42. JGB 260; KSA 5: 208.

of positive power is already taking place in the history of mankind, Nietzsche claims.[43] Thus the main goal of his careful explications is to speed up this process of emergence and provide it with an operative and effective power.

It follows that we must understand Nietzsche's "transfiguration of all values", not as an abolition but as a gradual transfiguration of the morality of negative power into the morality of positive power. Of course, this is not a radical change, *ex nihilo*; in order for a significant change to take place, the changing element must already contain, at least implicitly, the seeds of this change. The process of "transfiguration", therefore, is well established both in our cultural history and also "within a *single* soul"[44] — fluctuating between the opposing vectors of positive and negative powers.

The explication of power thus reflects upon the "single soul" of the individual. Nietzsche, like Freud, occasionally delineates parallels between phylogenesis and ontogenesis — between the development of cultural patterns and their evolution in individual members of that culture. Thus, after claiming the interpenetration of the two moralities on the wider, historical level, Nietzsche goes on to make an ontogenetic statement, namely that such processes "occur directly alongside each other — even in the same human being".[45] It is difficult to speak about morality, which requires a social context, with reference to the "*single* soul". Hence Nietzsche is describing here a more transitory, fluctuating emotional and mental state of the individual: "the true pathos of every period of our life".[46] Such an individual "pathos of life" crystallizes into a social formation of moral patterns and positive/negative ways of life.

43. FW 117–120.
44. JGB 260; KSA 5: 208.
45. *Loc. cit.*
46. FW 317; KSA 3: 549.

It is very likely that Nietzsche, in speaking of the "*single* soul", also had his own personality in mind and was referring to the negative and positive sentiments it contained. Here is added to the explication of power another aspect — that of Nietzsche's self-psychoanalysis. This process of self-analysis reveals the conflict within himself between the powerful, healthy, vital and spontaneous life pathos, and the weak, sick, repressed, destructive and passive pathos. Such rapid and acute transitions from one type of pathos to another characterize, in psychoanalytic literature, the neurotic personality. In his writings, letters and the autobiographical essay, *Ecce Homo*, Nietzsche frequently describes such "neurotic" swings between ecstatic creative periods and prolonged repression, dejection and malady. According to his own testimony, his neurosis (to which Freud frequently referred) facilitated his psychological insights, and illuminated for him *contrasting* categories such as good and evil versus good/bad. Nietzsche identifies very intimate connections between sickness and philosophy, and claims that someone who has not experienced the pathos of negative power, the "disgust ... gloominess and loneliness" is not "predestined for knowledge".[47] Only a person who experiences such neurosis and overcomes it is able to "go inside" and to possess an "inborn fastidiousness of taste with respect to psychological questions".[48]

This ability to "go inside" and overcome the states of negative pathos is regarded by Nietzsche as the primary indication of an individual's positive power — his ability to make perspicuous the darkest recesses of his soul and explicate them for the sake of health and vitality.

It is easy, then, to see how Nietzsche's power philosophy contains the component of self-analysis, by means of which the

47. JGB 26; KSA 5: 44.
48. GM V-3; KSA 5: 249.

thinker seeks to overcome his own negative power. His philosophy, as he testifies on several occasions, is "written with his blood" — with the blood of his distress and struggle against his neurosis and negative power. However, what is first required for such a self-overcoming, is a "confession", a self-explication of the patterns of negative power, and in delineating it Nietzsche means not only to entice and direct us toward healthy morality, but also to guide himself in the same direction. This "psychoanalytic" confession requires, of course, that the acknowledged phenomena should actually exist. Indeed, Nietzsche is mostly preoccupied with the pathos of negative power and its numerous cultural expressions, but the confession and the will to overcome the negative pathos are themselves clear indications of the existence of positive power in the confessing man. At the time of his confession, this man already stands within the boundaries of positive pathos, firmly rejecting the negative accretions. This resembles the situation of the man who decides to undergo psychoanalytic treatment, for this very decision constitutes a recognition of positive power and a will to reject the elements that inhibit it.

Nietzsche's explicative "confession" then, is not only an operative recognition of positive power in a person able to confront "serious truth". It is *ipso facto* an implicit acknowledgement of the existence of a set of values enabling the philosopher to distinguish between positive and negative powers and prefer the former. Once again there is an analogy with psychoanalysis. The wish of the neurotic personality to suffer such laborious treatment and be cured, implies an implicit set of powerful values, choosing mental health rather than sickness — creative vitality rather than repressive *akrasia*.

Thus Nietzsche's psychology is directed at all those people in whom (as in the neurotic) the opposite vectors of positive and negative powers are in constant fluctuation and "interpenetration". The goal of this psychology is always the same: to assist these people to creatively actualize and exhibit their vital resources.

II. Nietzsche versus Husserl

We must now deal more critically with the validity and epistemological status of Nietzschean explication — especially against the background of his perspectivism and its sceptical connotations. This status might be best elucidated by comparing Nietzsche's method to Husserlian phenomenology.

Some similarity exists between Nietzsche and Husserl. Husserl's early "descriptive phenomenology" adopts a form of Nietzschean perspectivism and his rejection of the positivistic tendencies in science reminds one of Nietzsche's critique of the "negative" science. Still another parallel might be found between Husserl's noetic-intentional acts, which bestow meaning upon the stream of consciousness, and the similar function of Nietzsche's power, which by its interpretations and Apollonian projections forms meaningful structures in the chaos that confronts it.[49] From this narrow point of view Nietzschean power has the same constitutive status as Husserlian consciousness.[50]

Despite these similarities between Nietzsche and Husserl there remains one crucial difference between them that highlights the issue of the validity of Nietzschean explications of the phenomenon of power. This marked difference stems from the different objectives of each thinker. Whereas Husserl, by means of his phenomenological analyses, strives to attain the scientific ideal of the apodictic and "pure" consciousness, Nietzsche regards the scientific ideal as just another, and redundant,

---

49. See, e.g., WM 604–605.
50. On other comparisons between Nietzsche and Husserl, see R. Boehm: "Husserl und Nietzsche", in *Vom Gesichtspunkt der Phänomenologie* (The Hague, 1968), pp. 217–236.

"shadow" of the dead God. Philosophy, he holds, must assist us in attaining a specific pattern of life by revealing our personal power and helping us to overcome the obstacles in its way. Nietzsche's ideal is not rational but existential. He does not wish to achieve "pure knowledge", for he does not even believe in its existence, but rather to attain a way of positively powerful moral life.

Nietzsche's sceptical attitude towards the validity of intuitive knowledge, whether discursive or phenomenological, stems directly from his doctrine of perspectives. If a perception is the product of an interpretation and of a perspectival mould, it includes the immediate perception as well. Hence it is nonsense to speak about "immediate certainties; for example, 'I think' ... as well as 'absolute knowledge'". This is "the seduction (*Verführung*) of words!"[51] Nietzsche thus wishes to undermine the Cartesian foundation of the phenomenological attitude and the validity of its introspective reflection, which nonetheless is also manifest in Nietzsche's own explication of power. From this point of view it can be said that for Nietzsche even the explication is merely another interpretation.

Moreover, Nietzsche repeatedly rejects the main assumption of Husserlian phenomenology — the autonomy of reflexion — largely because of his suspicion "of all thinking", which is solely a matter of "perspective estimates and appearances".[52] In Husserlian terms, Nietzsche rejects the very possibility of the "phenomenological reduction", since it is impossible for reason to achieve "the unselfing and depersonalization".[53] Hence it is nonsense to speak about "disinterested knowledge" and the "objective person".[54] The very impossibility of the Husserlian

51. JGB 16; KSA 5: 29.
52. JGB 34; KSA 5: 53.
53. JGB 207; KSA 5: 134.
54. *Loc. cit.*

phenomenological-psychological reduction brings about the impossibility of the Husserlian *epoche* — of putting "the eternal world" within the phenomenological brackets.

All this brings Nietzsche to a certain methodological contradiction. The descriptive means for the explication of power is invalid, since this same power, which also operates the "perspectival" method, is not purely rational, and therefore it introduces an opaque, non-cognitive element into the explicative method. The object and the methodology of the investigation stand in basic contradiction to each other. Hence, Nietzsche is unable to validate power rationally and he must posit it dogmatically — as a subjective and arbitrary expression of his own will-to-power, accepting the resulting circularity: "Supposing that this also is only interpretation — and you will be eager to make this objection? — well, so much the better".[55]

Why then does Nietzsche use this explicative method at all, notwithstanding his belief that it is no more valid than other possible methods? Perhaps it can be said that he adopts it because it is efficient as an enticement towards positive power. This pragmatic, psychological, reason for the employment of any theory or research method is relevant to the theoretical distinction between the act of accepting X, which is an immediate act of the will (or in Nietzschean terms — of personal power), and the act of rationally judging whether this X is true or false (which in Nietzschean terminology is also an expression of power, but this time of a negative, "Socratic", and discursive power). Because of Nietzsche's will to express his positive power and to entice us to follow in his steps — he employs the explicative attitude, although he recognizes that it lacks real validity in the classical sense. In any case this explication is only a provisional tool employed on the way toward attaining power,

55.   JGB 22; KSA 5: 37.

and after it has served its purpose, it may be discarded together with all the other means used along the way.

But why should we employ the descriptive or any other method on this way to power, if none of these are any more "true" or valid than any other? Life of a certain moral pathos, although it lacks objective validity, may express a person's positive power. In the same manner the acceptance of the psychological scaffolding, in spite of the fact that it is devoid of any rational foundation, expresses "the ability to accept criticism and contradiction". For Nietzsche, this ability is always the sign of the positive power of "the liberated spirit"[56] and the sign of a powerful, vital sceptic who is not crushed under the weight of his own burden. Further, even if we are not enticed to climb the explicative ladder, we must still distinguish clearly between different possible causes of this unwillingness. If the enticement is defeated by rational argument or the prevalent morality, the failure is symptomatic of a personality motivated solely be negative power, in whom the positive elements are irretrievable: the enticement then lacks an object. Since in this case there is no possibility of, or condition for, the achievement of the "transfiguration of our nature," it would be nonsensical to attempt it. However, if we reject Nietzsche's enticement because we have our own original way (in the double meaning of autonomous origin and unique content), then he would say to us that we have already employed our autonomous positive powers, characteristic of such a unique individual who overcomes both social-cum-moral predicaments and the teachers of his age. We would then not need Nietzsche's enticement, for we would already be taking the path which he has cleared. I shall discuss this issue in more detail in section IV of this chapter.

Other objections, not stemming from Perspectivism, may be

56. FW 297; KSA 3: 537.

made to the explicative aspect of Nietzsche's psychology. First, there is the general contention that the absence of any explicit methodology (although compatible with Nietzsche's sceptical perspectivism), leads to a confusion among his various methodological means — the several psychological steps that should lead to the attainment of his philosophical objective: the pathos of positive power. The grounds for this objection are well illustrated here. Nietzsche has not explicitly clarified the nature of the relation between his psychology and his explicative-descriptive typology. Thus, in contrast to Husserl's phenomenological method, which aspired to be presuppositionless,[57] Nietzsche's psychologizations and explications apply various psychological presuppositions. I have in mind especially the presupposition of the unconscious, which explains why we are not always conscious of our positive power, of our will for maturity and of a whole set of values that motivate us and shape our judgements and way of life. The absence of such consciousness justifies the descriptive explications of the phenomena of power, since it is possible to uncover something, and sometimes desirable to do so, if and only if this 'something' is implicit and concealed from our eyes. Apart from the idea of the unconscious, there are several theoretical psychological concepts, such as sublimation, repression, internalization, self-overcoming, etc., that obviously have importance beyond the limits of explication alone.

Not only is there a confusion among the different methodological steps in the Nietzschean psychology of power, there is also confusion between the provisional means and the moral philosophical objective of that psychology. This can be regarded

---

57. See E. Husserl, *Logische Untersuchungen*, Bd. 2, V Para. 7. On Husserl's quest for a presuppositionless epistemology, see: M Farber, "The Ideal of a Presuppositionless Philosophy", in *Philosophical Essays in Memory of Edmund Husserl*, ed. M. Farber (Cambridge, Mass., 1940).

as a severe defect, especially by commentators who distrust the psychologisms of which Nietzsche may be accused.

Husserl is committed to the neutral attitude of the *epoche*, which purports to be independent of any personal attitude toward the explicated content of the phenomenological analysis. In contrast, Nietzsche expresses throughout his work a definite acceptance of some valuable patterns of positive power and their moral pathos, and an unequivocal rejection of the many expressions of the negative power. Nietzsche's writings are saturated with value judgements and criticisms that presuppose a complete set of values. His compositions are full of sharp polemics and adopt definite attitudes toward significant cultural issues. The title itself of the work in which his typological explications reach their pinnacle — *Beyond Good and Evil* — indicates that Nietzsche has moral commitments and preferences.[58]

Nietzsche not only refuses to abstain from holding a definite system of values during the performance of his explications, but he actually argues for the theoretical impossibility of such an abstention. We cannot close ourselves up within some neutral attitude towards phenomena, because our cognitive relations themselves are driven by the actions of our power. Indeed, it is impossible to conceive of a cognition which is completely severed from any perspective formation, and the perspectival interpretation itself is controlled by the will-to-power. Where we speak about man's will, it is possible in principle to evaluate and judge the effects of this will, including Nietzsche's perspectival

---

58. See also a later composition, where Nietzsche presents clearly his moral code: "What is good? Everything that heightens the feeling of power in man, the will to power, power itself. What is bad? Everything that is born of weakness." (A 2; KSA 6: 170).

effects. Nietzsche, therefore, does not believe in "the ideal scholar", who "places himself too far apart to have any reason to take sides for good or evil".[59] Such an ideal is implausible because behind any philosopher and behind any cognition and explication there hides "power, self-reliance", the will "to be master".[60] Hence, Nietzsche intentionally mobilizes his explicative typology for the sake of the moral ideal which is the *raison d'être* of all of his descriptions and analyses. As a result, the tenuous border between the "is" and the "ought" becomes ill-defined, even indistinct.

III. Beyond Psychologism and Crude Naturalism

Does Nietzsche's moral commitment on the explicative level suffice to meet the accusation of moral psychologism that may be levelled against him?

According to Husserl in the *Logical Investigations*, psychologism is an attitude that strives to derive normative rules in logic and ethics from empirical psychological laws. To derive moral norms in this way means to justify and ground them rationally on natural psychological laws. In *Philosophy as Rigorous Science*, Husserl describes such psychologistic procedure as "the naturalizing of ideas and consequently of all absolute ideals and norms".[61] Nietzsche (in one sentence) links both these aspects of psychologism — the rational justification of morality by psychological norms and the naturalization of its values:

59. JGB 207; KSA 5: 134.
60. JGB 207; KSA 5: 136.
61. Husserl, "Philosophy as Rigorous Science", in *Phenomenology and the Crisis of Philosophy*, trans. Quentin Lauer (New York, 1965), p. 85; and see my "Psychology from the Phenomenological Standpoint of Husserl", *Philosophy and Phenomenological Research*, 36 (1976): 451–471.

> Every morality is ... a bit of tyranny against 'nature'; also
> against 'reason'; but this in itself is no objection ...[62]

It seems that here Nietzsche would have rejected the criticism of
moral psychologism had any such charge been brought against
him. But is this rejection justified?

He is clearly opposed to naturalization of morality. Morality to
him is not something given and delivered but something created
and constructed. He opposes the tendency of most philosophers
to anchor and justify ethics on so called 'objective' and 'rational'
grounds. This opposition stems not only from his sceptical
perspectivism, which rejects absolute truth — according to which
it would be possible to justify morality metaphysically — but also
from several psychological reasons:

> What the philosophers called 'a rational foundation for
> morality' and tried to supply was, seen in the right light,
> merely a scholarly variation of the common *faith* in the
> prevalent morality; a new means of *expression* for this
> faith.[63]

If we do not find "psychologism" in the strong sense of the word,
as a rational derivation of values from natural laws of the *psyche*,
it is because Nietzsche's psychology does not function as a
theoretical basis for the constitution and justification of an
ethos or ethics. It does not seek to establish empirically any
'natural' laws in the manner of contemporary scientific
psychology. Rather, it explicates, and assists us by enticement
and persuasion to achieve powers and values that have already
partially emerged. This psychology is a therapeutic and heuristic
means and not a project of discovering or constituting. This is so

62. JGB 188; KSA 5: 108.
63. JGB 186; KSA 5: 106.

also because Nietzsche, out of his Perspectivism, rejects the independent validity of psychological laws and certainty of introspection. He has no psychological rules or norms from which to derive moral ideals. It follows that if there is a psychologism in Nietzsche, it exists only in a weakened form as a reasoning and enticement, not in the strong form of a justification and constitution. Can such an approach still be called a psychologism?

Left only with persuasive explication, we may still ask whether Nietzsche is not himself open to the accusation that he brought against the philosophers who expressed "the common *faith* in the prevalent morality" in their ethical discussions. Surely Nietzsche cannot be so accused, since he decidedly does not justify the prevalent morality. But it is perhaps still possible to contend that on the level of psychologistic reasoning and enticement, in explicating what actually exist, some belief in the prevalent is nonetheless retained.

However, Nietzsche affirms psychological power not as it is actually given in nature, but only after it has passed through the sublimative and rational process of transfiguration and self-overcoming. In short: the "is" properly becomes "ought" only if it undergoes an intensive elaboration and transformation.

We shall return to this crucial issue of Naturalism later. For the moment we must ask whether a certain inconsistency does obtain between Nietzsche's explications and his ideal of positive power, which is essentially an incessant overcoming of the given. What *is* — including prevalent or implicit values — becomes an obstruction to the activity of power; yet, the explicative method assumes the existence of values or the wish to materialize these values.

If positive power is a process of dynamic, continual becoming in a Heraclitean chaos without *logos*, then no eternal value is capable of expressing it. Indeed this power does not attach itself to fixed values. Rather, it is determined by impermanency, which is its positive pathos.[64] It seems, however, that an explication may be possible only for static and permanent elements of *logos* and ethos. Must we claim, paradoxically, that we are actually providing an explication of the dynamic pathos and the incessant overcoming? Here, however, we are reaching the limits of our capacity to speak rationally in a world of chaos and pathos without *logos*. And perhaps Nietzsche intended to bring us to this ultimate border in order to help us transcend his own thought as well, and thus enable us to reach the real maturity of positive power: standing ultimately on our own feet and throwing away all the external crutches, including Nietzsche's. Thus he says to us through his hero — Zarathustra:

"This is my way; where is yours?" — thus I answered those who asked me 'the way'. For *the* way — that does not exist.[65]

In this context it is appropriate to cite another passage, where Nietzsche speaks about the philosophers of the future, the "free spirits", amongst whom he wishes to be counted. These philosophers "will certainly not be dogmatists. It must offend their pride, also their taste, if their truth is supposed to be a truth for everyman ..."[66]

Finally, does not this hypothesis — that Nietzsche wants us to overcome even his own thought — stand in clear contradiction to my contention that he actually means to entice us toward the way of positive power? Not necessarily, since we are speaking

---

64. See JGB 41, where Nietzsche draws a model of a man with positive power (of the really free spirit), who does not adhere to any permanent value, since such a fixation hinders the dynamics of power. Therefore only a conditioned, detached life is possible for the one who "tests oneself" but does not adhere to the results of these tests.
65. Z 3 "On the Spirit of Gravity"; KSA 4: 245.
66. JGB 43; KSA 5: 60.

here about one of the final steps on the road of this enticing psychology. A vital part of the work of a good psychologist is to check, at any stage of therapy, whether his patient can continue on his own; whether enough power has been released to enable the patient to function without psychologistic assistance. Likewise, Nietzsche, at every stage of his psychology, tries to entice us to overcome even his own thought and influence. As he tells the reader:

It is a humanistic virtue of the teacher, to warn his student also against himself.[67]

Even if Nietzsche is not guilty of psychologism in the strong sense of psychological justification, it may be possible to insist that he is not altogether free from Naturalism in the sense of attempting to base his morality on certain natural phenomena.

Nietzsche affirms that power is the basic drive of human nature. As such and "in itself it has, *like every drive*, neither this moral character nor any moral character at all".[68] Therefore, if we keep in mind Nietzsche's statement that man is a will to power (a universal psychological principle) then any moral doctrine based upon it would necessarily be a naturalistic ethic, with the well-known attendant fallacies.[69] In my opinion, interpreting Nietzsche's moral attitude as purely naturalistic is grossly inaccurate.

It is difficult to render this naturalistic interpretation compatible with the extensive normative and prescriptive passages of Nietzsche's writings, which unequivocally reject the negative "slave" morality and prefer the positive "master"

67. M 477; KSA 3: 271.
68. M 38; KSA 3: 45.
69. See, for example, David Hume, *A Treatise of Human Nature* (Oxford, 1888, 1896), Book III, Part 2, section 1; G.E. Moore, *Principia Ethica* (Cambridge, 1903), Chs. 1–4; W.K. Frankena, "The Naturalistic Fallacy", *Mind* 48 (1939): 464–477.

morality. If Christianity is the 'slave revolt' aiming at seizing power from the masters, and if this rebellion has scored a decisive historical victory, it is hard to understand, on a naturalistic interpretation, why Nietzsche rejects this "natural" victory and strives to counteract it by reactivating, in a clearly normative manner, the defeated positive power morality. One of the basic tenets of naturalistic ethics is that whatever exists in nature (be it individual or historical and sociological) is also desirable from the moral point of view. It is not clear how Nietzsche, the so-called 'Naturalist', could reject Christian ethics and the historical revolt of the slaves in his attempt to "revaluate all values". This rejection of the historical "is" is viable if and only if some other set of norms is at work, invalidating the given moral patterns.

It might be argued that Naturalism does not imply that everything that actually happens is justified, but that whatever is considered "natural" or "essential" ought to dominate, even if this is not so in reality. This, however, assumes universal agreement as to what is "natural" and "essential", and a general consent that this should be manifested in actual cultural "praxis".[70] The essential gap between Nietzsche's moral attitude and that of the naturalistic argument appears precisely at this point. Nietzsche acknowledges that most persons do not wish to uncover their positive power and are afraid of reactivating it. On the contrary, they seek to repress it, to flee from it or to rationalize it away by a network of opposing moral norms which inhibit its spontaneous expressions. It follows that most men do not participate in any general consent, and thus it is unreasonable to accuse Nietzsche (as one may do Epicurus) of a naturalistic fallacy. Moreover, if the patterns of positive power were generally

---

70. At this point we may turn to Frankena's article, where the naturalistic fallacy of Epicurean ethics is illuminated in the following argument: "(a) Pleasure is sought by all men; (b) What is sought by all men is good (by definition); (c) Therefore, pleasure is good".

accepted values — Nietzsche would not need his enticing psychology to attract us to them.

Furthermore, Nietzsche consistently resists turning the preservation of life into a supreme value, as most people commonly regard it. The very fact that Nietzsche is not interested in life as such, but in a certain type of life, places him far apart from the simple and crude naturalistic attitude.

The normative network determining Nietzsche's rejection of traditionally accepted morality contains the key concept of *power*. Though this concept refers to certain psychological patterns, there is no power which is absolutely powerful, and the notions of the *Übermensch* or an entirely autonomous power represent rather a kind of a regulative ideals. Yet once we deal in regulative ideals it clearly makes no sense to speak about naturalistic ethics, which are anchored in the given and the natural.

Further, the naturalistic interpretation of Nietzsche's morality is unjust to those aspects of his thought that emphasize art as the model of all moral patterns. Nietzsche stresses spontaneous creativity and a synthesis between the formal Apollonian principle and the Dionysian drives as the vital aspects of human existence. He applies the model of art to moral considerations and pronounces the idea of creative formation — the "transfiguration of nature". A philosopher who talks about the improvement of human nature, the elevation of culture and the transformation of man into *"an aesthetic phenomenon"*,[71] is hardly — if at all — a moral naturalist. The ideal of a creative, unlimited and spontaneous activity would be seriously obstructed by grounding it in any natural phenomenon or principle, which by its very nature is limited and bounded.

The principle component of Nietzsche's morality is the element

---

71. GT 5.

of selfhood and genuine freedom. This selfhood and authenticity would be greatly restricted had Nietzsche attempted to base the moral conduct on empirical, natural fact. The essence of Naturalism allows very little room for spontaneous, creative and autonomous freedom which for Nietzsche is the *alpha* and *omega* of the possibility of morality.

Nietzsche's persistent attempt, by means of his psychologizations, to attain a "de-deification of nature", and vanquish the remnants of God's "shadows", stands in opposition to the notion of rewrapping this "pure ... newly redeemed nature"[72] in another web of values and concepts. To turn nature into a cradle of human and social morality is an illegitimate personification. Thus Nietzsche would reject any naturalistic morality that endows a certain fragment of the entire universe with an ethical significance:

> Wise and noble men still believe in the 'moral significance of existence'. But one day this music of the spheres too will no longer be audible to them! They will awaken and perceive that their ears had been dreaming.[73]

This remark also helps us to understand why Nietzsche consistently rejects *"The delusion of a moral world-order"*[74] and claims that in morality *"There is absolutely no eternal necessity"*.[75] While Nietzsche reached a psychology of power from a methodological basis of psychologization, this does not imply that in the moral sphere he regressed to psychologization and was trapped in the naturalistic fallacy.

It may be true that the concept of power around which Nietzsche designs his moral doctrine is composed of distinct

72. FW 109.
73. M 100; KSA 3: 90.
74. M 563.
75. *Ibid.*

psychological elements, but this does not justify the conclusion that the morality of power is simply a psychologistic ethics:

> Those moralists who perceive and exhibit the laws and habits of mankind ... differ altogether from those who explain what has been observed. The latter have to be above all *inventive* and possess an imagination *unchained* by acuteness and knowledge.[76]

Here we must distinguish between two separate meanings of the term "naturalistic". We may speak about a Naturalism that bases itself upon raw natural data. Man confronts these data within himself or in his surroundings, and uses them in establishing his moral norms, without shaping or changing them. Such an ethics directly transfers the empirical and natural data into the basis of the moral network. "Naturalism", however, also has a different connotation. Here too the raw material for morality is given and found in nature — but this in itself is *not enough*. Nature here is only the necessary but not sufficient condition of morality. The natural givenness is only the raw material which, so to speak, stores up in itself the potential for moral realization. But the realization will occur if and only if the potential psychological factors are thoroughly elaborated, refined and sublimated in a process of creative "invention" of natural morality. Thus we cannot speak here of a direct displacement from nature to morality, for Nietzsche offers a much more intricate and complex process of the "transfiguration" and "overcoming" of nature, within the context of an aesthetic morality. The natural "is" becomes the "ought" of positive power morality, not by a mechanistic, direct and passive displacement but by intentional and sublimatory acts of transformation and a prolonged period of education and creation of "a new nature" in us:

76.   M 428; KSA 3: 264; and cf. M 248.

So let us take care not to exchange the state of morality to which we are accustomed for a new evaluation of things head over heels and amid acts of violence — no, let us continue to live in it for a long, long time yet — until ... *the new evaluation* has acquired predominance within us and the little doses of it to *which we must from now on accustom ourselves* have laid down a new nature in us.[77]

Nietzsche certainly declares that he wished to construct "anew the laws of life and action" by creatively using "the foundation-stones" of the sciences, but "for this task our sciences of physiology, medicine, sociology [and, one might add, psychology] are not yet sufficiently sure of themselves".[78]

The transfiguration of nature and the sublimation of our natural character and psychological make-up, which together provide the necessary and sufficient conditions of the morality of positive power, distance Nietzsche from any crude naturalistic morality based on an ontology of the cosmic order, identifying it with the moral order.

'According to nature' you want to *live*? What deceptive words these are! ... Living — is that not precisely wanting to be other than this nature? Is not living — estimating, preferring, being unjust, being limited, wanting to be different?[79]

IV. The Genealogy of Power

Nietzsche now sets aside the explicative approach because it has fulfilled its function, and returns to psychologization,

---

77. M 534.
78. M 453; KSA 3: 274.
79. JGB 9; KSA 5: 81.

widening its range to the cultural and historical level, beyond individual psychological patterns.

This historical expansion of psychologization — which parallels Freud's shift from the neurotic conflicts of the individual to the entire generalized concept of "Civilization and Its Discontents" — was necessary because of the appalling gap between the results of Nietzsche's explication and the cultural predicaments surrounding him.

After explicating the positive and negative patterns of power, Nietzsche must now explain why the latter have become the dominant factor in history. The empirical supremacy of negative power challenges the results of Nietzsche's descriptive analyses, from which it would follow that the positive power is power *par excellence*, carrying the really authentic moral capacity. Thus it might be reasonable to expect that it should dominate our culture. Nietzsche himself declares that he wrote *On the Genealogy of Morals* just to deal with this issue. The third essay of this work answers "the question whence the ascetic ideal, the priests' ideal, derives its tremendous *power* although it is the *harmful* ideal *par excellence*, a will to the end, an ideal of decadence".[80]

I shall briefly survey Nietzsche's main reasons for passing from the descriptive explicative analysis of power to its historical genealogy.

The first reason springs from Nietzsche's general attitude towards philosophy. In his eyes philosophy, like all other cultural creations, is a manifestation of man's power.[81] As there are two patterns of power, there are, correspondingly, two kinds of philosophy — the negative and the positive. The former, deriving from negative power, imparts *post-hoc* rationalizations to the prevalent patterns of negative morality. Positive philosophy

---

80. EH-GM; KSA 6: 353; and see GM III-13.
81. See JGB 6.

(adopted by Nietzsche) originating in positive power and striving to evoke the creative pathos, is not interested in justification or description as such. It attempts to reactivate the positive power in historical praxis by encouraging and enticing us to revise our values; to initiate the historical process through which the transformation from negative to positive moral patterns might take place. In other words, positive philosophy's primary concern is to assist mankind in effecting the "transfiguration" of culture and thus facilitate the reappearance of the "higher types".

Nietzsche's descriptive analyses have shown that "*Morality in Europe today is herd animal morality ... beside which*, and after which many other types, above all *higher* moralities, are, or ought to be, possible".[82] His positive philosophy now attempts to uncover "The conditions that one would have partly to create and partly to exploit for their genesis".[83] That is, Nietzsche's moral philosophy is not especially interested in providing a theoretical meta-ethics, on the basis of which we may revaluate the nature and status of our moral judgements — it has an even more radical aspiration: revolution in the realm of human activity and conduct.

Thus Nietzsche abandons the explicative path and adopts the genealogical method, since he does not merely wish to freeze prevalent moral patterns, but also to find suitable conditions for activating positive power.

In Nietzsche's hands the genealogical method becomes an archaeological instrument for analysing why the positive moral patterns, once prevalent, yielded to the inferior "slave morality". Nietzsche is convinced that understanding the historical-psychological circumstances that abetted negative morality will help us to grasp the conditions required for reinstating the positive patterns:

82.   JGB 202; KSA 5: 124.
83.   JGB 203; KSA 5: 126.

we need a *critique* of moral values ... and for that there is
needed a knowledge of the conditions and circumstances
in which they grew, under which they evolved and changed
... So that precisely morality would be to blame if the *highest
power* and *splendor* actually possible to the type of man
was never in fact attained.[84]

Moreover, the usefulness of genealogy is not restricted to
pragmatic needs. Another, no less important, impetus for this
direction derives from the theoretical, immanent results of
Nietzsche's previous analyses. These investigations, as we have
seen, brought about the revelation of the impressive ideal and
figure of the *"Übermensch"*. One cannot avoid asking then: if the
morality of positive power is so sublime and good, how is it that
our contemporary social predicaments are so very remote from
manifesting it and its high qualities? In Nietzsche's terms, how is
it possible to explain the "very remarkable" historical fact that
"Rome has been defeated beyond all doubt"?[85] The question
revolves around the causes of the historical failure of an ideal
human type and its social relations, which are unrivalled in their
superior morality. Nietzsche's questioning, which propels him
towards genealogy, is similar, though not identical, to the general
question of why "Utopia" is *Utopia* (nowhere)?

Nietzsche's intention, however, differs from the Utopian
striving to impose something alien to cultural history; he aspires
to bring about an operative intensification and re-enactment of
life patterns which have already been manifested in some manner
in history. How did it happen that despite the qualitative
supremacy of positive power and its occasional appearances in
history, it has never lastingly reigned in man's lives and has
always been pushed aside by an inferior social and moral ethos?

84. GM Preface 6; KSA 5: 253.
85. GM I-16; KSA 5: 286.

Nietzsche's rather extensive response to this question may be summed up as follows: it was not some inherent flaw in the ideal of positive power that prevented its enduring predominance, but rather the relative strength of the opposite patterns, arising from negative power, and ensuring their historical victory.

Thus, the exalted and morally supreme ideal of positive power on the one hand, and its failure to materialize itself fully in our culture on the other — the tremendous gap between the "ought" and the "is" — is the acute issue which requires a philosophical explanation and a genealogical discussion.

Nietzsche's genealogy also examines whether the emphasis upon the immanency, autarchy and extreme individuality of positive power is incompatible with morality within a social context. The genealogical account shows that the moral patterns of positive power were occasionally manifested within this or that social and historical context, though not always in their most distinct form. It also shows that factors external to these patterns were responsible for their disappearance. Historical testimony is thus provided for the absence of any essential contradiction between Nietzsche's ideal morality and social reality, and the way towards their mutual reconciliation remains, in principle, open.

Nietzsche's affirmation of society, as the necessary condition for the materialization of possible power, attenuates the apparent radical and revolutionary stance of his extreme individualism. And since Nietzsche affirms "a community"[86] and does not seek to destroy it, he must explain how the morality of positive power is at all possible within the social context, and analyse the nature of the interaction among the members of a society. This is exactly what he does in his genealogical inquiry. There he maintains that genuine justice is possible only within a social fabric composed of equally powerful members:

86. See, for example, GM II-9.

> Justice ... is the good will among parties of approximately equal power to come to terms with one another, to reach an 'understanding' by means of a settlement — and to *compel* parties of lesser power to reach a settlement among themselves.[87]

Nietzsche proposes that the powerful individual is characterized by egoism. His avoidance of any altruistic activity and ideology would seemingly contradict any possible moral system. This emphasis on the egoism of power does not prevent Nietzsche, however, from continuing to describe the moral and social network of the powerful individuals who would willingly and freely enter the restrictive social fabric:

> The noble soul accepts this fact of its egoism without any question mark ... it admits under certain circumstances ... that there are some who have rights equal to its own ... it moves among these equals with their equal privileges, showing the same sureness of modesty and delicate reverence that characterize its relation with itself ... every star is such an egoist — it honors *itself* in them and in the rights it cedes to them; it does not doubt that the exchange of honors and rights is of the nature of all social relations and thus also belongs to the natural condition of things.[88]

Nietzsche declares here that recognition of the value and freedom of others originates in egoism. Only an individual who possesses an abundance of positive power and a firm selfhood is able to grant similar rights and freedoms to all those whom he recognizes as his equals. He is not afraid that this might diminish or destroy his own power. It is a self-affirmation and confidence in one's power and virtues that psychologically enable the

87. GM II-8; KSA 5: 306–307.
88. JGB 264; KSA 5: 219–220.

affirmation of the other and his specific power. Human egoism and emphasis on selfhood do not contradict the social and moral order; they actually create the ideal conditions for its proper functioning.

Yet, Nietzsche is not solely occupied with characterizing the ideal features of the *"übermenschlich"* society. His descriptive explication does not require the genealogical discussion. He also seeks to show that the morality of positive power has already existed in one form or another in history, so that it is empirically feasible and does not stand in any *a priori* contradiction to society. He therefore uses the genealogical approach, speaking about "The essential characteristic of a good and healthy aristocracy",[89] and urging us to "look for once at an aristocratic commonwealth ... an ancient Greek *polis*, or Venice",[90] which in his view are the typical social and political examples "of the morality of the powerful".[91] He also refers several times to the historical patterns of "Rome", "the Renaissance" and "Napoleon", in whom "the problem of the *noble ideal as such* made flesh".[92]

At this point an important question arises: do the powerful need a society at all? Is it not the case that the need of others indicates a feebleness and insufficiency of positive power? In answer, one may point out that the powerful man is not identical with an omnipotent and absolutely perfect God. There is no upper limit to power and there is no optimum for absolute autarchy and self-sufficiency. Moreover, cultural enterprises necessarily require the association and collaboration of various creative powers, each contributing its distinct capacities to the common enterprise. Close cooperation and interaction of the different distinct powers is required. Moreover, to make the

89. JGB 258; KSA 5: 206.
90. JGB 262; KSA 5: 214.
91. JGB 260.
92. GM I-16; KSA 5: 288.

social manifestation of power possible, any creation, even the most individual, has as its necessary condition the social fabric and the mutual exchange of ideas and concepts. There is no power without creation and form giving, and there is no creation without some social order. Hence there is no power without society, and its essential manifestations are impossible in a complete severance from social context.

Further, since absolute power never actually exists, and since there is no creation *ex nihilo*, powerful men need each other, and need society and culture as the vital working framework within which they create. Society itself obviously also requires moral patterns that organize and consolidate it. Nietzsche, then, is not a negating "nihilist" and does not wish to overthrow society and go beyond its limits. The "antichrist" within him does not make him into an anarchist. And this is especially due to his positive psychology and its pivotal concept of *"Macht"*.

While Nietzsche was engaged in explicating from an immanent point of view the various patterns of the power phenomena, the problem of justifying these explications did not become acute. Nietzsche placed these explications within a subjective context of Perspectivism, maintaining that everything he said with reference to the concept of power expressed his own creative power. Despite its obvious circularity, it was perhaps possible to accept this attitude as long as Nietzsche's discourse remained within the immanent limits. Most of the criticism that might have been levelled against him would then have been of the immanent type — for instance, demonstrating possible internal contradictions between various predicates of power. However, as soon as Nietzsche breaks out of the internal framework of the explicative attitude and begins tracing the genealogy of morality, the problem of the validity of his genealogy becomes unavoidable. It is always possible to argue against the genetic psychological explanations from an external point of view and to go beyond the testing of the internal coherencey of the immanent set of predicates and concepts. Nietzsche was apparently quite aware of this problem and, having no alternative, he simply stressed the highly speculative status of his genealogical attitude towards morality:

> This is offered only as a conjecture; for the depths of such subterranean things are difficult to fathom.[93]

In any event, the validity of the genealogical interpretation is open to question, because of the logical possibility that is greatly facilitated by Nietzsche's own theory of perspectives; it may thus be challenged by different genealogical interpretation (e.g., Freud's) or by any other competing explanation or perspective. Would Nietzsche still maintain in such a case that his historical genealogy is nothing but an expression of his own subjective interpretative power? For if this is so, why should we accept it?

Here I may suggest that the theory of perspectives and its sceptical ramifications is yet another pedagogical means for enticing the reader to attain and activate his positive power. The various psychological reasonings that Nietzsche uses in order to convince us to adopt certain patterns of life (those of positive power) are not valid at all in the classical logical sense if we seriously admit his sceptical perspectivism. Such scepticism highlights the peculiar status of Nietzsche's psychology: it stands or falls neither because of its rational validity or invalidity, nor because of its truth or falsehood, but because of its therapeutic, enticing, function. It is supposed to help us in living fully and positively in a sceptical and purposeless world that *"may include*

---

93. GM II-6; KSA 5: 301; and see GM II-4.

infinite interpretations".[94] (Once again I must stress the point
that the *truth value of Nietzschean psychology is irrelevant to
Nietzsche vis-à-vis its enticing effect for human life.*) Hence
Nietzsche's enticing psychologistic discussions, deliberately
abjuring any cognitive foundation, are exclusively directed
towards raising the emotional pathos and evoking the instinctual
affects that express and stimulate our power. We should not
forget that for Nietzsche a life lived according to a certain moral
pathos (and not ethos) manifests the person's positive power.
His genealogical psychology attempts to lead and entice us into
such a pathos.

This enticement includes the sceptical component which is
intended to help us to ultimately overcome even Nietzsche's own
allure. But what sense can one make of an enticement which also
includes deterrent elements? It seems that Nietzsche believes
that when we have reached the advanced explicative and
genealogical stages, and have overcome the intellectual and
emotional barriers of the preceding scaffoldings, we will have
discovered and built up enough power and immunity to enable
us to withstand this scepticism. Moreover, any process of
enticement also tests our ability to be enticed. Thus Nietzsche,
by means of his Perspectivism, introduces the self-checking
mechanism designed to test the power of the enticed person. He
introduced Perspectivism explicitly only around 1887[95] — the
year in which he started to write his *"Genealogie"*, the fourth and
final stage of his ladder towards power. The whole process is
actually a dialectical one: the more efficiently power is uncovered
and reactivated the greater the likelihood that the person will
persevere through the more advanced stages—being able to

94. FW 374; KSA 3: 627.
95. Mainly in the fifth book of FW, which was added only in the second edition
of 1887 (FW 373, 374, etc.) and in the *"Nachgelassene Fragmente"* from this
period.

313

withstand both the sceptical test and the reality looming behind every step on the road towards intensified selfhood. If we have already reached this point our power will have been most favourably revealed. Only then would Nietzsche be able to disavow the psychologistic crutches he has given us and send us away to our own selfhood and its various creative expressions: "And if you now lack all ladders, then you must know how to climb on your own head".[96]

In the same way, the psychoanalyst seeks to attach us to himself and entice us by means of transference — so that we may finally free ourselves from his treatment and continue our development undisturbed. Likewise Nietzsche strives to set us firmly on his path in order to finally produce in us the epistemological-sceptical shock (by introducing his perspectivism). This will provoke us to find our own way — the ultimate objective.

At the beginning of his genealogical stage Nietzsche temporarily suspends his sceptical, perspectival attitude and invites us to seek the genealogical "truth", "even plain, harsh, ugly, repellant, unchristian, immoral truth".[97] Only after we have followed Nietzsche's call and have accompanied him in his revelations can he (in the third essay of the *"Genealogie"*) reject this ideal of "the martyr; to *suffer* for truth",[98] and present before us, as a final challenge, his idea of the "perspective knowing".[99]

The ideal of "absolute" truth is provisionally exploited in the course of the enticing process at the end of which "perspective" truth alone is revealed. In this way Nietzsche in fact is applying his 'Antichristian' principle, methodically transforming the 'negative' Christian *"Verführung"*[100] into a 'positive' *"Versuchung"*.

96. Z III 1; KSA 4: 195.
97. GM I-1; KSA 5: 258.
98. GM III-8; KSA 5: 355.
99. GM III-13.
100. GM V-6, aptly translated by Kaufmann as "a seduction".

He begins to entice us into adopting values and ideals already prevalent in our culture and reverently accepted by most of us (such as the ideal of objective "knowledge in itself"[101]). Thus he will find it easier to entice us by using such negative seductive means for what are, in his eyes, positive aims. The attainment of these aims will also presuppose our courageous realization of the negative dimensions behind the associated "sacred ideals". Only at the end of Nietzsche's genealogy, then, does it become clear to us that behind this "intangible form of seduction" (*Verführungsform*), behind "this unconditional will to truth, is faith in the ascetic ideal itself".[102]

This reading of Nietzsche is also based on several passages referring to the "will to truth" as something which "seduces" (*verführen*) us "to many a bold venture".[103] Nietzsche employs this negative seduction, and derives his philosophical "flame from the fire ignited by a faith millennia old, the Christian faith, which was also Plato's, that God is truth, that truth is divine";[104] this exposes its ascetic dimensions. Nietzsche's process of counter-seduction enables an overcoming and freezing the "will to truth" and incites our will to reactivate authentic personal power — the attainable *"Wahrhaftigkeit"* (truthfulness) instead of the inaccessible *"Wahrheit"* (truth).

Nietzsche nerver wearies of emphasizing this "revaluation of all values", or, in my terms, the process of transforming negative seduction into positive encitement:

> All great things bring about their own destruction through an act of self-overcoming (*Selbstaufhebung*) ... In this way Christianity *as a dogma* was destroyed by its own morality; in the same way Christianity *as morality* must now perish,

101. GM III-12; KSA 5: 364.
102. GM III-24; KSA 5: 400; and see also GM III-23.
103. JGB 1; KSA 5: 15 (my translation).
104. GM III-24; KSA 5: 400–401.

too ... Christian truthfulness (*Wahrhaftigkeit*) ... must end
by drawing its inference *against* itself; this will happen,
however, when it poses the question *"what is the meaning
of all will to truth?"* [105]

At the beginning of his genealogy Nietzsche needs a certain
criterion of truth, not only in order to attract us to his conception,
but also as a basis for rejecting other competing genealogical
attempts that fall outside his enticing framework. Thus he
suggests three criteria for the validity of his genealogy (which in
his view other investigations of the genesis of morality have
failed to meet) implying that we ought to award our rational
preference to his attitude and enter on his enticing road towards
power. These criteria are: external historical criticism,
psychological reliability and internal logical coherence. [106]
Obviously we can apply those criteria to Nietzsche's genealogy
itself, checking whether it meets his own standards.

The second essay of the *"Genealogie"*, concerned with the
genesis of "Guilt, Bad Conscience and the Like", can be criticized
both for question-begging, and for exhibiting "an inherent
psychological absurdity". [107] He refers to the double meaning of
the German word *"Schuld"* in an attempt to discover the origin of
"conscience", "responsibility" and "guilt". *"Schuld"* is both guilt
and a debt in the non-figurative sense, indicating that "the feeling
of guilt, of personal obligation, had its origin ... in the oldest and
most primitive personal relationship, that between buyer and
seller, creditor and debtor". [108] This explanation is doomed to
circularity, since the commercial interrelationship and the
consciousness of responsibility and "obligation" assumed the
pre-existence of a certain organized social context (namely of

105. GM III-27; KSA 5: 410.
106. GM I-2 and 3.
107. GM I-3; KSA 5: 260.
108. GM II-8.

morality and personal conscience) without which the terms "debt" and "responsibility" can have no meaning.

Logical circularity and "psychological absurdity" also threaten the complementary explanation in the second essay, which purports to give the basic cause of "bad conscience" and guilt-feelings. Nietzsche maintains that their true origin is to be sought in the phenomenon of *"internalization"*,[109] in which most of man's instincts were turned "inward" against "man himself" to protect "the political organization". But who is responsible for the constitution of the "State", this "oppressive and remorseless machine"? Nietzsche answers that these are the powerful men:

> Some pack of blond beasts of prey, a conqueror and master race ... with the ability to organize ... It is not in *them* that the 'bad conscience' developed ... but it would not have developed *without them*.[110]

By projecting their creative, organizing powers onto the inferior masses they evoked among the latter the feeling of *"ressentiment"* which characterizes the first stage of the "slave morality", becoming "bad conscience" in the second stage, when the *"instinct for freedom* [was] pushed back and repressed ... [and is] finally able to discharge and vent itself only on itself".[111] The powerful ones, however, these "born organizers" and "artists" — "do not know what guilt, responsibility or consideration are". In this essay Nietzsche, unlike Freud,[112] seems to believe that a society had once existed of the powerful "masters", men lacking the moral conscience (The Freudian Super-Ego), who have become an organized team imposing its

---

109. *"Verinnerlichung"*, GM II-16; KSA 5: 322.
110. GM II-17; KSA 5: 324.
111. GM II-17; KSA 5: 325.
112. See especially "Totem and Taboo", S.E. *13*; and consult Jerry S. Clegg, "Freud and the Homeric Mind", *Inquiry* 17 (1975): 445–456.

rules and "forms" upon the psychologically inferior "slaves". However, these powerful men must have been already operating within a specific social context, even if it were only "some pack" (Reidel),[113] and so already living within the circles of duty and responsibility, the necessary basic conditions of any social framework. Moreover, by creating and living within some sort of society, the powerful individuals would have necessarily internalized and repressed some of their instincts. Such a *"Verinnerlichung"*, is the origin of "bad conscience" and guilt feelings, and so the individuals with positive power could not have been only externally responsible for the development of these phenomena within the negatively powerful agents. Nietzsche's genealogical search for the primary origins of prevalent morality thus involves him again and again in circular explanation which does not meet his own criterion.

A measure of reliability can be achieved, perhaps, if we ignore the historical dimensions of Nietzsche's genealogy and concentrate on its psychological ramifications. We recall that the distinction between the negative and the positive powers was a consolidated generalized ideal of the various power vectors within the single individual. Man does not possess a pattern of positive or negative power, as if it were a definite and relatively stable socio-economic status. The two vectors of power and their opposing manner of operation constitute *alternating* sentiments and different types of pathos in permanent conflict within the human character. Thus any morality and any society necessarily manifest both the negative aspects of repression and violence as well as the positive dimensions of sublimation and creativity.[114] Every individual living within the social and moral framework is necessarily a slave repressing part (or most) of his drives; he is also a master, creating his values and

---

113. GM II-17; KSA 5: 325.
114. JGB 188.

sublimating his power. This perpetual conflict between man's two power components, and the repressive aspect of his social nature, renders man "*the* sick animal".[115] However, this sickness is necessary for restoring man's creative health: "The bad conscience is an illness ... but an illness as pregnancy is an illness".[116] Without the partial repression and restraint of our drives sublimatory creative activity would be impossible. Similarly, without repressive morality, social conscience and imposition of Apollonian forms upon our chaotic instincts, a society manifesting its positive creative powers would not be possible. The route to the superior sublimatory culture leads through the repressive processes of its originators. Man, however, can stop at the stage of repressive negative power and halt his progress towards the more advanced stage of sublimatory positive power. He is then detained at the stage of self-aggression, hatred, resentment and guilt-feelings. Christianity, for example, is according to Nietzsche founded upon repressive asceticism, turning it into its object and ideology, and fixating man in the stage of "pregnancy" which becomes a permanent sickness. Nietzsche intends to use the enticing psychology to free man from this fixation, from the stage of the "camel" (as in "The Three Metamorphoses" of Zarathustra), and to help him uncover and reactivate his positive power; psychology will undo his repressions and bring him to the stage of the "lion", in which both negative power and its moral implications will be overcome. The final objective of Nietzsche's genealogical psychology is the stage of the "innocent" and newborn "child", free of the oppressive load of guilt feelings and destructive repressions. He therefore repeatedly emphasizes the motif of self-overcoming, of vanquishing the negative power in all of us. However, this self-overcoming requires as its

115. GM III-13; KSA 5: 367.
116. GM II-19; KSA 5: 327.

319

antecedent condition the very repressive social morality that extricated us from the barbarian animal state and helped us to redirect our drives and form our souls and spirits.[117] This morality has actually prepared the way towards the morality of positive power. In every individual there is a constant struggle between positive and negative power, rendering self-conquest possible.

The recognition of the existence of different qualities and patterns of power within each individual helps to resolve the basic difficulty that beset Nietzsche throughout his later writings. How was it that the dominating "masters" were defeated by the "slaves" and were seduced by negative *"Verführungen"* in the shape of ascetic religions and moral patterns of guilt and bad conscience? *"Why do the weak conquer?"*[118] This problem might perhaps be solved by reference to the psychological (not the historical) aspect of Nietzsche's genealogy. The "masters" were successfully provoked and seduced by "slavish" manipulations, for the latter were directed towards their mentally negative components. Powerful individuals, operating within a social context, necessarily underwent the process of internalization and repression of drives. Therefore, they possessed in some degree the potential for "guilt, bad conscience and the like", and the seductive efforts of the masses were directed towards the vulnerable part of their mental makeup. These seductive manipulations were cleverly intensified by means of various religions, moral systems and rationalizations. As with positive enticement (*Versuchung*), negative seduction may succeed only if it contrives to evoke our inherent negative elements. The man of positive power was betrayed by his internal "fifth column".

Nietzsche seeks to present his enticing psychology as an antidote, directing intensifying positive enticements towards our healthy but inhibited elements of positive power. This procedure,

117. GM II-16.
118. WM 864.

he believes, will help to restore the delicate creative balance between the Apollonian and Dionysian elements. Return to a healthy and balanced synthesis rather than regression to sick repression or stormy barbarism is the necessary condition for reactivation of positive power.

We have already seen this call for a positive synthesis in *The Birth of Tragedy*, in the formula of *"the Socrates who practices music"*. Even then, what was proposed was not a simple return to the original Greek synthesis of the Dionysian and the Apollonian. Acknowledging the historical persistence of the Socratic-rationalistic culture, Nietzsche sought a new synthesis of the Apollonian-Dionysian with the Socratic — the artistic with the scientific — without eradicating any of these elements. His pervasive aim from beginning to end remained the same: to weave out of man's basic instincts the sublimatory rehabilitating framework within which his positive power would act and create in entire freedom. The primary purpose of Nietzsche's philosophy is the freezing of extreme negative expressions by means of genealogical antidotes, designed to overcome the three crucial handicaps: the cognitive, spiritual and moral manifestations of asceticism. Each of these three obstructing manifestations nourishes and enhances the others, so that Nietzsche is obliged to fight them all in order to pave the way for the reactivation of positive power. He must entice the "camel" to overcome these three dimensions of negative power.

V.The Three Counter-Seductions

Intellect was developed in the "slaves" as a result of the external pressures exerted on them by the powerful individuals. The "slaves" could not express their drives directly and had to repress them because of fear; the spontaneous externalization of drives was replaced by the process of *"Verinnerlichung"*. The latter helped to develop the cleverness and shrewdness that the "slaves exploited to deviously and obliquely overcome their oppressors and regain power". In short: the weak developed intelligence and reasoning as substitutes for the vital spontaneous powers which characterized the genuinely powerful. Nietzsche maintains that over-developed intelligence creates evil,[119] and is thereby able to overcome the values of the powerful:

> the weak prevail over the strong again and again, for they are the great majority — and they are also more *intelligent* ... *the weak have more spirit.*[120]

Here we find Nietzsche's explicit answer to the question of why the powerful "masters" were defeated in history by the powerless "slaves". They were not overcome because they were weaker (as regards quantity of energy) or more sluggish, but, on the contrary, because their abundant power, expressed in outward drives, did not require the over-development of Apollonian-rational mechanisms. Here one may ask whether the massive development of the rational Apollonian functions is not after all a necessary condition for the kind of creative life so enthusiastically endorsed by Nietzsche? The answer is clearly no, if it is achieved at the expense of the instinctual elements. The result of the victory of Apollo over Dionysus is the *cognitive asceticism* endorsed by the powerless who combat the vitality of the powerful. Where instinct is deficient neither creation nor artistic sublimation will emerge. This was already argued in *The Birth of Tragedy*, where Nietzsche contrasts Socrates to the Greek Dionysus. In his later writings he continues to develop this notion:

> ... science rests on the same foundation as the ascetic ideal: a certain *impoverishment of life* is a presupposition

---

119. GM II-15.
120. GD: "Skirmishes of an Untimely Man" 14; KSA 6: 121.

of both of them — the affects grown cool, the tempo of life slowed down, dialectics in place of instinct ... [121]

If reason replaces drives, and repression takes the place of sublimation, creative vitality and power are weakened. In this respect, Socrates paved the way to cognitive asceticism and caused the demise of culture.[122]

Against this world-wide tendency to asceticism, Nietzsche fights on three closely related fronts:

First, he pronounces the "Death of God". In so doing, he actually heralds the death of the ideal of absolute truth.[123]

Secondly, as an antidote to the dogmatism of "truth", Nietzsche introduces the sceptical attitude of perspectives, which liberates man from his cognitive prison and from his efforts to realize an exclusive "truth". Perspectivism opens up infinite latitudes for spontaneous, intellectual creativity, free of the constraints of objectivism. Thus Nietzsche's atheism and critique of rationalism become a method of counter-seduction, entering "upon the *reverse* course".[124]

Thirdly, Nietzsche enlists his genealogical psychology, which is directed at exposing the negative "ascetic ideal" and the nihilistic will hidden behind the "will for truth".

Nietzsche attacks another manifestation of repression — the excessive "Christian" spiritualization (*Vergeistigung*)[125] of our culture, which leads to *spiritual asceticism*, itself another facet of cognitive asceticism. The repression of instincts, originating in the establishment of "the political organization",[126] hastened the spiritualization of mankind, particularly of the weak, who

---

121. GM III-25; KSA 5: 403.
122. GD II-11.
123. GD: "How the 'True World' Finally Became a Fable".
124. GM II-20; KSA 5: 330.
125. GM II-16.
126. GD V-5.

required "spirit" in their struggle with the powerful. "Whoever has strength dispenses with the spirit ... by 'spirit' I mean care, patience, cunning, simulation, great self-control, and everything that is mimicry".[127]

Spiritual asceticism as a terminus of internalization, produces personal characteristics essential to the survival of the weak. The psychologically vulnerable person, however, need not be weak with respect to energy and strength; on the contrary, from the quantitative viewpoint he may be far stronger than the powerful personality, for the weak function in accordance with the processes of repression. Repression may take the upper hand over processes of sublimation, since the powerful have externalized and exhausted the sublimative mechanism while creating culture and political organization. The powerful invest and lose part of their instinctual energy in their products and creations, while the "weak" solely repress and internalize their drives — leaving them with an immense reservoir for their fight against their powerful oppressors. This explains why Nietzsche firmly rejects any culture based upon excessive repression, regarding it as catastrophic in the long run.

Nietzsche maintains that the idealist philosophers who offered the ideological rationalization for the "disease" of spiritualizing and desensualizing were indeed poor seducers since "*ideas* are worse seduceressers (*schlimmere Verführerinnen*) than our senses".[128] Nietzsche offers as an alternative his own positive enticement to return to the vitality of the senses. He wishes to reverse the nihilistic process — the excessive desensualization of the Dionysian by the repressive Apollonian — by luring us into that full sensual life which is represented by the metaphor of "the splendid *blond beast*".[129]

127. GD IX-14, and see GM III-15.
128. FW 372; KSA 3: 624.
129. GM I-11; KSA 5: 275.

Nietzsche believes that the way leading back from repression to sublimation must inevitably pass through the rejection of the former. Thus, we must restore to mankind in the first place the reservoir of drives which culture has unduly and harshly repressed. The choice is never between culture or raw barbarian nature. The Birth of Tragedy has already opposed the "Dionysian-barbarian" (which is no less nihilistic than the excessively Apollonian desensualization). The dilemma is not culture versus nature, but culture versus civilization. Nietzsche prefers less civilization (less repression and spiritualization) in favour of more culture (more sublimation and vital creation). He cannot endorse the prospect of the chaotic turbulence and uncontrolled prowling of the "blond beast" of prey, for this would necessarily lead again to fear which, as we have seen, tends to produce the same internalization of drives and ascetic life patterns that Nietzsche wishes to eradicate. The "blond beast", then, that represents the "lion" of the second metamorphosis in *Zarathustra*, is the inevitable intermediate stage but not the final and ultimate goal of Nietzsche's thought.[130]

Another ramification of repression and the undermining of the balance between Apollo and Dionysus is *moral asceticism* and the formation of guilt feelings and "bad conscience". The internalization and repression of drives is the necessary condition for consolidation of moral authority in man. Apollonian reason, also a drive to Nietzsche, forms the repressive morality, and thereby ends up serving negative power. Yet this same reason may equally well serve positive power and essentially

---

130. This was not grasped by Thomas Mann who, in his "Nietzsche's Philosophy in the Light of Recent History" in *Last Essays* (New York, 1959), pp. 141–177, accuses Nietzsche of "heroization of instincts". Nietzsche does not call for the massive and anarchic release of repressed instincts, but for their artistic sublimation. So he does not subscribe to the "heroization of instincts", but perhaps only to the heroization of sublimation.

contribute to such creative morality as is based, not on repression, but on sublimation.

Nietzsche's psychology, enticing us to reactivate our positive power, is therefore obliged to lure us into overcoming our pervasive guilt feelings, exposed by his genealogy as cruel and tyrannical. But it does not follow that Nietzsche seeks to assist us in completely subduing our "higher self" (the Freudian 'Super-Ego'), which is the source of all our duties and conscience; for without this mental agency no society and morality, that is, no culture is possible. Being vital to sublimation,[131] he cannot ask us to forego completely the mechanism of repression, that "serious illness that man was bound to contract".[132] Culture is a legitimate and essential expression of our creative instinctual power, and to disqualify the mental agency which is responsible for its foundation amounts to replacing one kind of repression by another. Nietzsche, after all, affirms morality and maintains that without it man would remain merely bestial. In our time of prevailing negative morality, man is solely *"Übertier"* (*an over-animal*);[133] this, however, is only a provisional stage, necessary for the emergence of the *"Übermensch"*. The appearance or reappearance of the latter would be possible if mankind were able to transform culture founded upon repression into a culture based on sublimation.

Here, as elsewhere, we may turn to the psychoanalytic field for a useful analogy. The aim of psychoanalytic treatment is not to

---

131. "Man's growing inwardness ... in the artist there reappears the repressed power to dissimulate and lie" (WM 376); and see Eric Blondel's perceptive remark: "bad conscience is the mother, or the primal condition, of sublimation, in the same way that, for Freud, primal repression (as well as regression or fixation) first makes sublimation possible" ("Nietzsche: Life as Metaphor", in *The New Nietzsche*, New York, 1977, p. 153).

132. GM II-16; KSA 5: 321.

133. MA I-40.

transform a neurotic person (characterized by repression and self-aggression and possessing a rigid, punitive super-ego) into a psychopath who discharges his drives without inhibitions. The therapy proposes to help the patient overcome his acute guilt-feelings, liberating him from his self-inflicted aggression and excessive repressions. The mental energy thus released may then be redirected into productive creative channels of self-realization in work and love. Psychoanalysis does not aspire to turn rigid moralists into overt immoralists, but to re-establish the delicate balance between nature and culture, allowing them to become creatively functioning moral agents. This is also the ultimate objective of Nietzsche's psychological philosophy, which seeks to reactivate our positive power without completely uprooting the negative power, which has developed out of it. The repressive negative power pattern contains a number of positive elements which may again become available for creative utilization by positive power after the pathos of guilt, bad conscience and *ressentiment* has been overcome. If positive power also contributed to the emergence of negative moral patterns, then these patterns must have included some positive qualities, such as self-control, self-overcoming, responsibility, and so on.[134] With proper handling, they may again serve positive power. The dichotomy between the two patterns of power is not clear-cut and exclusive. As sublimation includes the element of repression, so negative power contains several elements of positive power. This makes feasible an ongoing transmutation between the two, and it must be possible to return to a more creative phase, when positive power reigned freely without guilt or other inhibitions.

Nietzsche wishes to entice us towards the rehabilitating synthesis by showing, through his genealogical argument, that

134. GM II-1, 2 and 16.

it had previously prevailed in the pre-Christian period of Greek Pagan culture.[135] It is with this in mind that Nietzsche concludes that "Atheism" (beyond Christianity, Platonism and various kinds of asceticism) "and a kind of *second innocence* belong together".[136] The three transformations of the spirit are demonstrated by his psychology. The "lion's" overcoming of the negative patterns — especially the "camel's" guilt morality — will turn him into a "child", and "a new beginning" and "innocence"[137] will lead him to the life patterns of the *"Übermensch"*. However, even an innocent "child" needs the social and moral context, and only within it will he be able to effect his creative sublimatory processes.

Here we may ask whether sublimation and creation have not triumphed also in the sphere of negative power. Christian culture, for example, has given us sublime masterpieces of man's spirit. If this is so, why should we prefer the sublimations and creations of positive power to those of ascetic culture? Before answering this question we should recall that Nietzsche always situated asceticism and creativity as opposites, as he did repression and sublimation. Ultimately it is only individuals endowed with positive power that are the true creators and value givers. Even the ascetic priest who created, say, the Christian *mores* and its ascetic ethos and values, is an exception in that he proves the rule: actually a man of positive power who, due to certain circumstances, had to turn it against himself. We should also recall that in fact there has never been a period when only one kind of power dominated. Intermingling, "interpenetration"[138] and struggle between both powers has always occurred in every period and within each "single soul". Thus, the different kinds of

135. GM II-23.
136. GM II-20; KSA 5: 330.
137. Z I "On the Three Metamorphoses".
138. JGB 260.

creativity were occasionally manifested in artists, philosophers, and creative people in whom the positive pathos had gained the upper hand, even during periods of mainly negative patterns. During the Renaissance, for example, or even in other Christian periods, the influence of the powerless individuals was sufficiently diminished to make possible the emergence of extensive artistic creativity. This is true in the wider cultural context as well as on the level of the single individual. Even a person whose negative power is dominant passes through certain "pathos of life", where his inherent positive power is reactivated and manifested. Even an ascetic priest or monk may sometimes be creative, and certainly is not completely or essentially prevented from attaining the creative sublimatory pathos.

This conclusion leads me to reject a possible criticism of Nietzsche's preference for the sublimation of drives over their repression. It may be maintained that because most of us are not gifted with special creative talents, Nietzsche's solution is an elitist one, and possible only for the spiritual aristocracy. If this is so, the slaves will always be bound to rebel against the masters. The aristocratic minority of individuals with positive power will not be able to withstand the masses and once again sublimation will be vanquished by repression. Once again will the "higher types" be overcome by the "inferior types".

In speaking about the mechanism of sublimation Freud referred to this problem of elitism:

> The task here is that of shifting the instinctual aims in such a way that they cannot come up against frustration from the external world. In this, sublimation of the instincts lends its assistance. One gains the most if one can sufficiently heighten the yield of pleasure from the sources of psychical and intellectual work ... And the weak point of this method is that it is not applicable generally: it is

329

accessible to only a few people. It presupposes the possession of special dispositions and gifts which are far from being common to any practical degree.[139]

Is sublimation, then, designed exclusively for the gifted minority? Is positive creative power the property of only the spiritual aristocracy? Not necessarily. Freud himself expresses his reservations concerning the above-quoted statement in a footnote, where he grants the capacity for sublimatory activity to any sort of creative work and to all individuals who are able to dedicate themselves to any work of any creative kind:

> the ordinary professional work that is open to everyone can play the part assigned to it by Voltaire's wise advice[140]... Professional activity is a source of special satisfaction if it is a freely chosen one — if, that is to say, by means of sublimation, it makes possible the use of existing inclinations, of persisting or constitutionally reinforced instinctual impulses.[141]

Voltaire's (and Freud's) advice to return to the "garden" of sublimation is also presented in great detail in Nietzsche's philosophical psychology, which was not exclusively designed, after all, for the intellectual elite. Every man is a creative power. Each of us possesses the Dionysian-Apollonian mechanism which is ready to be activated in any certain context of activity, and which impresses forms upon the chaotic elements within and around us. Every man is potentially capable of overcoming various inhibitions which restrain the spontaneous expressivity of his power. Nietzsche seeks to entice all of us to free ourselves from the chains that fetter growth, maturity, and creative intensification. He believes in a superior culture where the

139. Freud, "Civilization and Its Discontents", S.E., *21*: 79–80.
140. *Ibid.*, p. 75. The reference is, of course, to *Candide*.
141. S.E., *21*: 80 fn.

community of the "higher types" is preoccupied with sublimatory activity in different walks of life and varieties of creative activity. Writing, building, farming, — all kinds of sustained work — are evidence that we are capable of following Nietzsche's enticement to positive power.

BIBLIOGRAPHY

I. Editions of Nietzsche's and Freud's Works Cited

Friedrich Nietzsche Sämtliche Werke Kritische Studienausgabe, hrsg. Giorgio Colli and Mazzino Montinari, 15 Vols. (Berlin, Walter de Gruyter, 1980), cited as KSA. I have preferred to use this easily available paperback edition which contains a page-to-page concordance to the parallel, clothbound edition: *Kritische Gesamtausgabe* (Berlin, Walter de Gruyter, 1967 ff.).

Most of Nietzsche's texts are cited in English from Walter Kaufmann's translations: *The Birth of Tragedy* and *The Case of Wagner* (New York, Random House, 1967); *The Gay Science* (New York, Random House, 1974); *Beyond Good and Evil* (New York, Random House, 1966); *On the Genealogy of Morals; Ecce Homo* (New York, Random House, 1969); *The Portable Nietzsche* (New York, The Viking Press, 1968) — which includes: *Twilight of the Idols; The Antichrist; Nietzsche Contra Wagner; Thus Spoke Zarathustra* — cited as TPN.

Other English translations cited: *Philosophy in the Tragic Age of the Greeks*, trans. Marianne Cowan (Chicago, Henry Regnery, 1962); *Untimely Meditations*, trans. R.J. Hollingdale (Cambridge University Press, 1983); *Daybreak*, trans. R.J. Hollingdale (Cambridge University Press, 1982); *Human, All Too Human*, trans. R.J. Hollingdale (Cambridge University Press, 1986).

As to the problematic *Nachlass*, I made use primarily of Kaufmann's and Hollingdale's translation, *The Will to Power* (New York, Random House, 1967), because of its ease of access for English-speaking persons, and also because the materials cited exist in the *Kritische Gesamtausgabe*, and by using the *Nietzsche-Studien* "Konkordanz" (Bd. 9, 1980: 446–490) it is easy to locate them.

In several cases, when the English translations were not sufficiently exact, I modified them slightly, and occasionally even provided my own, more literal translations.

On rare occasions, when I could not locate the relevant passage in the KSA, I used the following German editions: *Friedrich Nietzsche Werke*, hrsg. Karl Schlechta (Frankfurt/M, Ullstein Materialien) 5 Vols., 1972–1980, cited as FNW; and *Gesammelte Werke* (München, 1923–1929), Musarionausgabe, cited as MusA.

Nietzsche's letters are cited from Vol. 4 of the Schlechta edition, and from: *Selected Letters of Friedrich Nietzsche*, ed. and trans. Christopher Middleton (Chicago, University of Chicago Press, 1969).

Quotations from Sigmund Freud's writings and letters are taken from: *The Standard Edition of the Complete Psychological Works*, ed. and trans. James Strachey (London, Hogarth Press, 1966–1974), 24 Vols., cited as S.E.; *The Complete Letters of Sigmund Freud to Wilhelm Fliess*, ed. and trans. Jeffrey Moussaieff Masson (Cambridge, Mass., Harvard University Press, 1985); and *The Origins of Psycho-Analysis*, ed. Maria Bonaparte, Anna Freud, and Ernst Kris; trans. Eric Mosbacher and James Strachey (New York, Doubleday, 1957).

II. Other Works Cited

Assoun, Paul-Laurent, *Freud et Nietzsche* (Paris, Presses Universitaires de France, 1980).

Avineri, Shlomo, *Hegel's Theory of the Modern State* (Cambridge, Cambridge University Press, 1972).

Barrack, Charles M., "Nietzsche's Dionysus and Apollo: Gods in Transition", *Nietzsche-Studien* 3 (1974), pp. 115–129.

Bäumler, Alfred, "Nachwort" zur *Kröner Taschenausgabe*, Vol. 78, 1930.

Bilz, R., "Der Verdrängungsschutz — Eine Untersuchung über das Paradigma der Verdrängung bei Nietzsche und bei Freud", *Der Nervenarzt* 29 (1958), pp. 145–148.

Biser, Eugen, "Nietzsche's Relation to Jesus: A Literary and Psychological Comparison", in *Nietzsche and Christianity*, ed. C. Geffre and J.P. Jossua (Edinburgh, T. Clark, 1981), pp. 58–64.

Blondel, Eric, "Ödipus bei Nietzsche", *Perspektiven der Philosophie* 1 (1975), pp. 179–191.

———, "Nietzsche: Life as Metaphor", in *The New Nietzsche*, ed. David B. Allison (New York, Delta, 1977), pp. 150–175.

Boehm, Rudolf, "Husserl und Nietzsche", in *Vom Gesichtspunkt der Phänomenologie: Husserl Studien* (The Hague, Martinus Nijhoff, 1968), pp. 217–236.

Borges, Jorge Luis, "Funes the Memorious", in *Labyrinths* (London, Penguin, 1970), pp. 87–95.

Brandt, Rudolf J., "Freud and Nietzsche: A Comparison", *Revue de l'Université d'Ottawa* 25 (1955), pp. 225–234.

Brown, Norman O., *Life Against Death* (Middletown, Wesleyan University Press, 1959).

Camus, Albert, *The Myth of Sisyphus*, trans. Justin O'Brien (London, Hamish Hamilton, 1955).

———, *The Rebel*, trans. Anthony Bower (New York, Knopf, 1954).

Clegg, Jerry S., "Nietzsche's Gods in *The Birth of Tragedy*", *Journal of the History of Philosophy* 10 (1972), pp. 431–438.

———, "Freud and the Homeric Mind", *Inquiry* 17 (1974), pp. 445–456.

Cooper, David E., "On Reading Nietzsche on Education", *Journal of Philosophy of Education* 17 (1983), pp. 119–126.

————, *Authenticity and Learning: Nietzsche's Educational Philosophy* (London, Routledge & Kegan Paul, 1983).

Dannhauser, Werner J., *Nietzsche's View of Socrates* (Ithaca, Cornell University Press, 1974).

Danto, Arthur C., *Nietzsche as Philosopher* (New York, Macmillan, 1965).

Darwin, Charles, *The Origin of the Species by Means of Natural Selection* (London, 1872).

Deri, Frances, "On Sublimation", *Psychoanalytic Quarterly* 8 (1939), pp. 325–334.

Descartes, René, *The Philosophical Writings* (Cambridge, Cambridge University Press, 1984), Vol. II.

Dimitrov, Christo and Jablenski, Assen, "Nietzsche und Freud", *Zeitschrift für Psychosomatische Medizin und Psychoanalyse* 13 (1967), pp. 282–298.

Ellenberger, Henri F., *The Discovery of the Unconscious: The History and Evolution of Dynamic Psychiatry* (New York, Basic Books, 1970).

Farber, Marvin, "The Ideal of a Presuppositionless Philosophy", in *Philosophical Essays in Memory of Edmund Husserl*, ed. M. Farber (Cambridge, Mass., Harvard University Press, 1940), pp. 44–64.

Fechner, Gustav Theodor, "Über das Lustprinzip des Handelns", *Zeitschrift für Philosophie und Philosophische Kritik* (Halle, 1848), pp. 1–30; 163–194.

Foot, Philippa, "Nietzsche: The Revaluation of Values", in *Nietzsche*, ed. R. Solomon (Garden City, N.Y., Doubleday, 1973), pp. 156–168.

Frankena, W.K., "The Naturalistic Fallacy", *Mind* 48 (1939), pp. 464–477.

Gaède, Edouard, "Nietzsche précurseur de Freud?", in *Nietzsche Aujourd'hui*, Vol. 2, (Paris, 1973), pp. 87–118.

Ginsberg, Mitchell, "Nietzschean Psychiatry", in *Nietzsche*, ed.

R. Solomon (Garden City, N.Y., Doubleday, 1973), pp. 293–315.

Glover, Edward, "Sublimation, Substitution and Social Anxiety", *The International Journal of Psycho-Analysis* 12 (1931), pp. 263–296.

Golomb, Jacob, "Psychology from the Phenomenological Standpoint of Husserl", *Philosophy and Phenomenological Research* 36 (1976), pp. 451–471.

——, "Freud's Spinoza: A Reconstruction", *The Israel Annals of Psychiatry* 16 (1978), pp. 275–288.

——, "Freudian Uses and Misuses of Nietzsche", *American Imago* 37 (1980), pp. 371–385.

——, "Jaspers, Mann and the Nazis on Nietzsche and Freud", *Israeli Journal of Psychiatry and Related Sciences* 18 (1981), pp. 311–326.

——, "Nietzsche's Early Educational Thought", *Journal of Philosophy of Education* 19 (1985), pp. 99–109.

——, "Nietzsche on Jews and Judaism", *Archiv für Geschichte der Philosophie* 67 (1985), pp. 139–161.

——, "Nietzsche's Enticing Psychology of Power", in Y. Yovel (ed.) *Nietzsche as Affirmative Thinker* (Dordrecht, 1986), pp. 160–182.

——, *Authenticity and Inauthenticity* (London, Unwin Hyman) forthcoming.

Gordon, Haim, "Nietzsche's Zarathustra as Educator", *Journal of Philosophy of Education* 14 (1980), pp. 181–192.

Granier, Jean, *Le Problème de la Vérité dans la Philosophie de Nietzsche* (Paris, Ed. du Seuil, 1966).

——, "Le statut de la philosophie selon Nietzsche et Freud", *Revue de Métaphysique et de Morale* 86 (1981), pp. 88–102.

Grimm, Rüdiger H., *Nietzsche's Theory of Knowledge* (Berlin, Walter de Gruyter, 1977).

Groddeck, Georg, *The Meaning of Illness* (New York, International University Press, 1977).

337

Groth, I.H., "Wilamowitz-Mollendorf on Nietzsche's *Birth of Tragedy*", *Journal of the History of Ideas* 11 (1950), pp. 179–190.

Gründer, Karlfried, ed., *Der Streit um Nietzsches "Geburt der Tragödie"* (Hildesheim, Olms, 1969).

Grundlehner, Philip, *The Poetry of Friedrich Nietzsche* (New York, Oxford, Oxford University Press, 1986).

Hegel, G.W.F., *Philosophy of Right*, trans. T.M. Knox (London, Oxford University Press, 1967).

Heidegger, Martin, *Holzwege* (Frankfurt a.M, Klostermann, 1950).

———, *Vorträge und Aufsätze* (Pfullingen, Neske, 1954).

———, *Nietzsche*, 2 Vols. (Pfullingen, Neske, 1961); the first part of which was edited and trans. by David Farrell Krell as *Nietzsche: The Will to Power as Art* (New York, Harper and Row, 1979).

Heller, Erich, "Wittgenstein and Nietzsche", in *The Artist's Journey into the Interior and Other Essays* (New York, Vintage, 1968).

Heller, Peter, *Studies on Nietzsche* (Bonn, Bouvier, 1980).

Hollingdale, R.J., *Nietzsche: The Man and His Philosophy* (London, Routledge & Kegan Paul, 1965).

Hollinrake, Roger, *Nietzsche, Wagner and the Philosophy of Pessimism* (London, George Allen & Unwin, 1982).

Hume, David, *A Treatise of Human Nature* (Oxford, 1888, 1896).

Husserl, Edmund, *Logische Untersuchungen* 2 Vols. (Halle, Max Niemeyer, 1921–1922).

———, "Philosophy as Rigorous Science", in *Phenomenology and the Crisis of Philosophy*, trans. O. Lauer (New York, Harper & Row, 1965.)

James, William, *The Will to Believe and Other Essays in Popular Philosophy* (New York, Longmans, 1897).

———, *The Varieties of Religious Experience: A Study in Human Nature* (New York, Longmans, 1902).

Jaspers, Karl, *Nietzsche: Einführung in das Verständnis seines Philosophierens* (Berlin, de Gruyter, 1950); trans. C.F. Wallraff and F.J. Schmitz as *Nietzsche: An Introduction to the Understanding of His Philosophical Activity* (Tucson, University of Arizona Press, 1965).

————, *Nietzsche and Christianity*, trans. E.B. Ashton (Chicago, Regnery-Gateway, 1961).

Jones, Ernest, "The Theory of Symbolism", in *Papers on Psycho-Analysis* 5th ed. (London, Bailliere, 1950), pp. 93–104.

————, *Sigmund Freud: Life and Work*, 3 Vols. (London, Hogarth Press, 1953–1957).

Jung, C.G., *Psychological Types*, trans. R.F.C. Hull (Princeton, Princeton University Press, 1971).

Kant, Immanuel, "Anthropologie in pragmatischer Hinsicht", in *Kants gesammelte Schriften*, Vol. 7 (Berlin, 1900).

————, *Kant's Political Writings*, ed. H. Reiss, trans. H.B. Nisbet (Cambridge, At the University Press, 1970).

————, *Lectures on Ethics*, trans. L. Infield (New York, Harper& Row, 1963).

Kaufmann, Walter, *Nietzsche: Philosopher, Psychologist, Antichrist* (Princeton, Princeton University Press, 1968).

————, "Nietzsche als der Erste Grosse Psychologe", *Nietzsche-Studien* 7 (1978), pp. 261–275.

Kierkegaard, Søren, *Attack upon Christendom*, trans. Walter Lowrie (Princeton, Princeton University Press, 1944).

Kirk G.S. and Raven, J.E., *The Presocratic Philosophers* (Cambridge, At the University Press, 1957).

Kuhn, Thomas S., *The Structure of Scientific Revolutions*, Second Ed. (Chicago, The University of Chicago Press, 1970).

La Rochefoucauld, Duc François de, *Réflexions, ou Sentences et Maximes morales*, ed. Jean Lafond (Paris, Gallimard, 1979).

Lauret, Bernard, *Schulderfahrung und Gottesfrage bei Nietzsche und Freud* (München, Chr. Kaiser, 1977).

Levey, Harry B., "A Critique of the Theory of Sublimation", *Psychiatry* 2 (1939), pp. 239–270.

Löwith, Karl, *Jacob Burckhardt: Der Mensch inmitten der Geschichte* (Lucern, Vita Nova, 1936).

———, *From Hegel to Nietzsche*, trans. D.E. Green (New York, Achor Books, 1967).

Madison, Peter, "Freud's Repression Concept", *The International Journal of Psycho-Analysis* 37 (1956), pp. 75–87.

Magnus, Bernd, *Nietzsche's Existential Imperative* (Bloomington, Indiana University Press, 1978).

———, "Eternal Recurrence", *Nietzsche-Studien* 8 (1979), pp. 362–377.

———, "Nietzsche's Mitigated Scepticism", *Nietzsche-Studien* 9 (1980) pp. 260–267.

Mann, Thomas, "Nietzsche's Philosophy in the Light of Recent History", in *Last Essays*, trans. R.E.C. Winston and T.E.J. Stern (New York, Alfred A. Knopf, 1959), pp. 141–177.

Maritain, Jacques, *Le Songe de Descartes: suivi de quelques essais* (Paris, R.A. Corrêa, 1932).

Marcuse, Herbert, *Eros and Civilization* (London, Sphere Books, 1969).

Mazlish, Bruce, "Freud and Nietzsche", *The Psychoanalytic Review* 55 (1968), pp. 360–375.

McGrath, William J., *Freud's Discovery of Psychoanalysis* (Ithaca and London, Cornell University Press, 1986).

Minutes of the Vienna Psychoanalytic Society, ed. H. Nunberg and E. Federn, trans. M. Nunberg, 2 Vols. (New York, International Universities Press, 1967).

Moore, G.E., *Principia Ethica* (Cambridge, Cambridge University Press, 1922).

Müller-Lauter, Wolfgang, *Nietzsche: Seine Philosophie der*

Gegensätze und die Gegensätze seiner Philosophie (Berlin, Walter de Gruyter, 1971).

Nehamas, Alexander, *Nietzsche: Life as Literature* (Cambridge, Mass., Harvard University Press, 1985).

Newmann, Ernest, *The Life of Richard Wagner*, Vol. 4 (New York, Knopf, 1946).

Parush, Adi, "Nietzsche on the Skeptic's Life", *Review of Metaphysics* 29 (1975–6), pp. 523–542.

Plato, *The Collected Dialogues*, ed. E. Hamilton and H. Cairns (Princeton, Princeton University Press, 1961).

Popper, Karl R., *The Logic of Scientific Discovery* (New York, Basic Books, 1959).

———, *Conjectures and Refutations: The Growth of Scientific Knowledge* (London, Routledge & Kegan Paul, 1963).

Ricoeur, Paul, *De l'interprétation; essai sur Freud* (Paris, Seuil, 1965).

———, "The Model of the Text: Meaningful Action Considered as a Text" *Social Research* 38 (1971), pp. 529–562.

Rieff, Philip, *Freud: The Mind of the Moralist* (Garden City, N.Y., Doubleday, 1961).

Roazen, Paul, *Freud: Political and Social Thought* (New York, Vintage, 1970).

Rohde, Erwin, *Psyche: the cult of souls and belief in immortality among the Greeks*, trans. W.B. Hillis (London, K. Paul, Trench, Trubner & Co., 1925).

Rosenstein, Leon, "Metaphysical Foundations of the Theories of Tragedy in Hegel and Nietzsche", *Journal of Aesthetics and Art Criticism* 28 (1970), pp. 521–533.

Salaquarda, Jörg, "Der Antichrist", *Nietzsche-Studien* 2 (1973), pp. 91–136.

Schacht, Richard, "Nietzsche and Nihilism", in *Nietzsche*, ed. R. Solomon (Garden City, N.Y., Doubleday, 1973).

———, "Nietzsche on Art in *The Birth of Tragedy*", in G. Dickie and R.J. Sclafani (eds.), *Aesthetics: A Critical Anthology* (New York, St Martin's Press, 1977).

———, *Nietzsche* (London, Routledge& Kegan Paul, 1983).

Schlechta, Karl, *Der Fall Nietzsche: Aufsätze und Vorträge* (München, Carl Hanser, 1958).

Schmitt, Richard, "Nietzsche's Psychological Theory", *Journal of Existential Psychiatry* 2 (1961), pp. 71–92.

Schopenhauer, Arthur, *Die Welt als Wille und Vorstellung*, 2 Vols., in *Sämtliche Werke* hrsg. von A. Hübscher (Wiesbaden³, 1966).

Sefler, George F., "The Existential vs. The Absurd: The Aesthetics of Nietzsche and Camus", *Journal of Aesthetics and Art Criticism* 32 (1974), pp. 415–421.

Silk, M.S., and Stern, J.P., *Nietzsche on Tragedy* (Cambridge, Cambridge University Press, 1981).

Solomon, Robert C., "Nietzsche, Nihilism and Morality", in *Nietzsche*, ed. R. Solomon (Garden City, N.Y., Doubleday, 1973), pp. 202–225.

Spinoza, Benedict de, *The Chief Works*, 2 Vols., trans. R.H.M. Elwes (New York, Dover, 1951).

Sterling, Marvin, "Recent Discussions of Eternal Recurrence: Some Critical Comments", *Nietzsche-Studien* 6 (1977), pp. 261–291.

Strong, Tracy, B., *Friedrich Nietzsche and the Politics of Transfiguration* (Berkeley, University of California Press, 1975).

Tramer, Friedrich, "Friedrich Nietzsche und Sigmund Freud", *Jahrbuch für Psychologie, Psychotherapie und Anthropologie* 7 (1960), pp. 325–350.

Waugman, Richard, "The Intellectual Relationship between Nietzsche and Freud", *Psychiatry* 36 (1973), pp. 458–467.

Wilcox, John, *Truth and Value in Nietzsche: A Study of his Metaethics and Epistemology* (Ann Arbor, University of Michigan Press, 1974).

Williams, Bernard, "Nietzsche's Centaur" *London Review of Books*, Vol. 3, No. 10 (1981), p. 17.

Wittgenstein, Ludwig, *Tractatus Logico-Philosophicus*, trans. D.F. Pears and B.F. McGuiness (London, Routledge & Kegan Paul, 1961).

INDEX